# Holiness: Divine and Human

# Holiness: Divine and Human

James M. Arcadi

LEXINGTON BOOKS/FORTRESS ACADEMIC
*Lanham • Boulder • New York • London*

Published by Lexington Books/Fortress Academic
Lexington Books is an imprint of The Rowman & Littlefield Publishing Group, Inc.

4501 Forbes Boulevard, Suite 200, Lanham, Maryland 20706
www.rowman.com

86-90 Paul Street, London EC2A 4NE, United Kingdom

Copyright © 2023 by The Rowman & Littlefield Publishing Group, Inc.

*All rights reserved.* No part of this book may be reproduced in any form or by any electronic or mechanical means, including information storage and retrieval systems, without written permission from the publisher, except by a reviewer who may quote passages in a review.

British Library Cataloguing in Publication Information Available

### Library of Congress Cataloging-in-Publication Data Available

ISBN 9781978701441 (cloth : alk. paper) | ISBN 9781978701458 (ebook)

♾️ The paper used in this publication meets the minimum requirements of American National Standard for Information Sciences—Permanence of Paper for Printed Library Materials, ANSI/NISO Z39.48-1992.

*In loving memory of my mother
Alison Ann Arcadi
1952–2019*

# Contents

| | |
|---|---|
| Acknowledgments | ix |
| Chapter 1: Prolegomena | 1 |
| Chapter 2: The Holiness of the Panentheistic God | 17 |
| Chapter 3: A Panpsychist Panentheistic Incarnational Model of the Holy Eucharist | 35 |
| Chapter 4: God the Holy Person | 53 |
| Chapter 5: *Homo adorans*: Giving Back to God What Is God's Own | 71 |
| Chapter 6: "You shall be holy, for I the Lord your God am holy" | 89 |
| Chapter 7: Redeeming Ownership: Transignification and Justification | 107 |
| Chapter 8: Unlimited Ownership: The Anglican Articles on the Means of God's Ownership of Humans | 121 |
| Chapter 9: Sanctification as Joint Ownership and the Indwelling of the Holy Spirit | 137 |
| Chapter 10: Pledging Allegiance to God and God's Holy Kingdom | 151 |
| Bibliography | 169 |
| Index | 177 |
| About the Author | 179 |

# Acknowledgments

I am first and foremost grateful to my wife and three children for their constant companionship on this scholarly journey, mostly for their providing non-scholarly respites along the way. This book has had a long gestation period. Because of this, there is a long list of scholars whose comments and conversations have been helpful in bringing this project to completion.

The first seeds of this study were sown around 2012–13 as I was engaging doctoral studies on the doctrine of the Eucharist. The fruit of this was born in my first publication, on consecration, in 2013. I applied this work to the Eucharist in my thesis, which concluded in 2015. As such, acknowledgment first goes to my *doktorvater* Oliver D. Crisp for his guidance during that period. My reasons for thanking Crisp only increased after my doctorate as I was privileged to be a postdoctoral research fellow from 2015–2018 on Crisp's Analytic Theology project at Fuller Theological Seminary. This afforded me further space and community in which to pursue many of the ideas that find themselves in this volume. I am very grateful also to Jesse Gentile, Steven Nemes, JT Turner, Jordan Wessling, Allison Wiltshire, and Christopher Woznicki for the years of theological reflection in the warm California sun. Also during this period, from 2015–2017, I was granted research funding and the opportunity to interact with scholars through the Herzl Institute's Jewish Philosophical Theology project. This was a great benefit to my study of holiness, and I immensely appreciated the two occasions I had to share my work and interact with others in Jerusalem for this project. I am specifically grateful to Craig Bartholomew, Lenn Goodman, Yoram Hazony, Berel Dov Lerner, Alan Mittleman, Jeramiah Unterman, Joshua Weinstein, and Jacob Wright.

Other support and feedback came from the following initiatives and individuals:

- *The Pantheism and Panentheism Project* at the John Hick Centre for Philosophy of Religion of the University of Birmingham, especially Andrei Buckareff and Yujin Nagasawa.
- The *¿Es Dios Persona?* project at the Universidad de Montevideo, especially Francisco O'Reilly, Juan Franck, and the participants in the 2021 workshop.
- *The Creation Project* at the Carl F.H. Henry Center for Theological Understanding, especially Geoffrey Fulkerson, Ian Prince, Matthew Wiley, Joel Chopp, Christina Bieber Lake, Jon Thompson, and Philip Woodward.
- Also, Richard Averbeck, Stephen Greggo, Te-Li Lau, David Luy, Douglas Sweeney, Eric Tully, Kevin Vanhoozer, Greg Forster, Matthew Kaemingk, Michelle Knight, Porter Taylor, Adonis Vidu, Ryan Chin, Scott Harrower, and Aaron Pendergrass.

My hope was to finish this book during the 2018–19 academic year, but three events prevented that hope from coming to fruition. First, I moved to take up a full-time teaching post, where the first year of teaching in a new environment coupled with moving my family across the country (again) sapped much of my research and writing time. Secondly, in the winter of 2019, my mother was diagnosed with an aggressive form of brain cancer that ultimately led to her demise at the beginning of the 2019–20 academic year. And then thirdly, March of 2020 brought on the global pandemic. I recall it being said that for some scholars, lockdown would prove to be a time of great productivity. It is likely these scholars were not pivoting to online teaching on the fly nor caring for school-age children at home. Finally, however, I received a year-long research leave for the academic year of 2021–22 during which I completed this project. For support during this time, I am especially grateful for Randall Price who served as my research assistant.

Given nearly a decade of gestation, many of the thoughts in this book have appeared in various forms in various places, which I list here with gratitude to the publishers and editors who first helped them see the light of publication:

"Unlimited Atonement: Anglican Articles and an Analytic Approach," in *Unlimited Atonement: Amyraldism and Reformed Theology*, eds. Scott Harrower & Michael Bird (Kregel Academic, 2023).

"Blessing God as Pledge of Allegiance: a Speech Act Theoretic Approach," in *Analyzing Prayer: Theological and Philosophical Essays*, eds. James M. Arcadi, Oliver D. Crisp, & Jordan Wessling (Oxford University Press, 2022).

"*Homo adorans: exitus et reditus* in Theological Anthropology," *Scottish Journal of Theology* 73.1 (2020)

"A Panpsychist Panentheistic Incarnational Model of the Eucharist," in *Panentheism and Panpsychism: Philosophy of Religion Meets Philosophy of Mind*, eds. Godehard Brüntrup, Benedikt Göecke, & Ludwig Jaskolla (Brill, 2020).

"'You Shall be Holy': a Speech Act Theoretic Theological Interpretation," *Journal of Theological Interpretation* 12.2 (2018).

"Redeeming the Eucharist: Transignification and Justification," in *Being Saved: Explorations in Soteriology and Human Ontology*, eds. Marc Cortez, Joshua R. Farris, & S. Mark Hamilton (SCM Press, 2018).

Finally, I am dedicating this book to the memory of my late mother as a minuscule acknowledgment of her contribution to my life—an act I promised to her on her deathbed. She was a constant and unfailing source of love and encouragement, believing in me and my prospects for life even when it seemed very irrational to do so.

*Chapter 1*

# Prolegomena

In St. John's apocalyptic vision of the heavenly throne room, he envisions the four living creatures continually speaking of God by saying:

> Holy, holy, holy,
> the Lord God the Almighty,
> who was and is and is to come.[1]

The implication of the vision is that God's holiness is so key, so central to God's very being that this term is the most apt to be repeated continually as a description of God. Highlighting God's holiness here at the end of the Scriptural canon is in keeping with a continual refrain throughout the Bible that among the attributes of God, holiness is a uniquely important feature of the divine.

However, holiness is not just a predicate of God, but rather is a term Scripture—and we—use for a variety of objects in the cosmos. Land, time, humans, the breast of a ram, temple accoutrements, bread, wine, books, moments, and a whole smattering of other entities are referred to as "holy." What makes them so? And how is one to understand the nature of this term when applied to such vastly—even infinitely—different entities such as God and a piece of bread? These are two puzzles that I think beset a philosophical-theological study of holiness: just what does this term mean when it is applied to God and how is it that this term can be applied to other entities besides God?

This monograph is an attempt to address these puzzles. I do so by offering a perspective on holiness that sees holiness as describing a unique relation between God and holy entities, a relation of ownership. Simply put, to be holy is to be owned by God. This definition applies to God as well as to non-divine entities. My argument progresses by means of testing the adequacy of this understanding of holiness in a variety of doctrinal areas in Christian systematic theology. Hence it is something of a cumulative case argument to show how this hypothesis can make good sense of a diverse set of data.

In what follows in this first chapter, I begin with an overview of what is to come in the rest of the book. Secondly, I offer an orientation for us to think about holiness including plumbing some of the biblical material that informs our initial conceptual impressions. Finally, I bring these discussions into conversation with some recent systematic theological discussions of holiness as a means of orienting my own constructive proposal.

## THE STRUCTURE OF THIS BOOK

This book follows a standard arc in Christian systematic theology. I move from discussion of prolegomena, to the doctrine of God, to various doctrines relating to humans such as theological anthropology, justification, atonement, and sanctification, before concluding with practical theology or—perhaps more aptly termed—theological reflection on practice. In this first section, I forecast these moves.

Prolegomena is that locus of systematic theology where we deal with first things. For this book, the prolegomenic material includes preliminary reflection on the definition of holiness, its place in Scriptural reflection, and a discussion of recent treatments in the systematic theological literature. The next major section deals with the doctrine of God; chapters 2, 3, and 4 all treat "theology proper." Chapters 2 and 3 focus on the God-world relation, as I take it that there are some specific puzzles emerging in this area when one attunes theology proper to the divine attribute of holiness. In this area, I engage with—what I call—deflationary panentheism as a way of conceiving of this relation. I note that chapter 3 includes a cameo by another standard systematic theological topic, Christology. One implication of any variety of panentheism might be to conceive of God as non-personal. Hence, the fourth chapter makes a case that not only ought we think of God as a person, but that the divine attribute of holiness actually motivates us to think this.

At chapter 5 we take a turn from theology proper to doctrines related to humans. The fifth and sixth chapters specifically deal with theological anthropology—humans in theological perspective. Chapter 5 focuses on the early pages of Genesis and engages debates regarding the *imago Dei*. My view is that perceiving this doctrine from the angle of holiness opens up a fresh manner for understanding how humans image God. Chapter 6 continues a meditation on the vocation of humans by interrogating a key passage related to divine and human holiness, Leviticus 19:2 ("You shall be holy, for I the Lord your God am holy"). Focus on the linguistic features of this passage opens up not only fresh ways for thinking about humans, but fresh ways for thinking about holiness.

With chapter 7 we come to another hinge in the text, turning towards doctrines relating to human salvation. Hence, to that point we will have moved from prolegomena, to the doctrine of God, to theological anthropology, to soteriology. There are three key sub-doctrines that fall under the heading of soteriology: justification, atonement, and sanctification. Those topics are studied in chapters 7, 8, and 9, respectively. As mentioned, and as will be specified further, I take holiness to be an instance of an ownership relation between God and the holy entity. In the realm of soteriology, we might say that sin and the fall is a transfer of the ownership of humas, or at least an attempt by humans to seize ownership of themselves from God. In justification, God redeems humans, taking them once more under God's own purview. Atonement theories often focus on the mechanism by which God achieves this redemption, but they also focus on the scope of the atonement in thinking about to whom the work of Christ applies. The latter is the subject of the eighth chapter of this book. Sanctification as a doctrinal locus encompasses a number of subsidiary areas of study, and a focus on holiness leads me to consider the human movement toward holiness that occurs by means of the indwelling of that Spirit we call "Holy."

Finally, to complete the systematic theological arc (knowing full well that there are standard doctrines that do not get a treatment in this text), the last chapter turns toward practical theology. Practical theology often encompasses reflection on the response of humans to God's act of reaching out to humans. Yet, the final chapter is less about *how* to respond and more about expositing what a human response means. Hence, I would categorize this chapter as practical theology that is a theological reflection on practice, in the vein of Nicholas Wolterstorff's recent work,[2] which serves as a dialog partner at various points in this monograph.

Before moving on to further preliminary material, I offer this caveat: the doctrine of the Eucharist serves as a recurring conceptual framework within which to think about issues pertaining to holiness. I do not treat this doctrine explicitly in this book—there is no one chapter on sacramental theology, for instance—but it is a backdrop in a number of the chapters. My constructive work on this doctrine can be found elsewhere.[3] As I indicated in the acknowledgments of this text, it was study of the Eucharist—what we sometimes call *Holy* Communion—that has led me to consider the topic of holiness. I do not think that the reflections on holiness in this text are dependent on conclusions in my previous book, but I simply offer this caveat as an explanation for why that doctrine shows up in the pages that follow. Having offered an orientation to what is to come in this text, I turn now to consider some biblical, conceptual, and recent systematic theological treatments of holiness.

## CONCEPTUALIZING HOLINESS

Despite the interest in the divine attributes within contemporary philosophy of religion, philosophical theology, and systematic theology, and despite the centrality of the attribute of holiness within Scriptural conceptions of God, holiness as a feature of the divine has not generated much interest in the last few decades. This tide, perhaps, is gradually turning. In the philosophical-theological literature, there have been three recent studies of holiness that are well worth the time. Alan Mittleman's 2018 *Does Judaism Condone Violence? Holiness and Ethics in the Jewish Tradition* is a rigorous philosophical study of holiness from a Jewish philosophical theology perspective.[4] From a similar angle, Lenn E. Goodman's 2019 *The Holy One of Israel* explores similar notions concerning God's holiness and how those ideas affect other areas of philosophical theology.[5] Moreover, Mark C. Murphy's 2021 *Divine Holiness and Divine Action* offers another sophisticated foray into this topic, both as it relates to holiness as an attribute of God and serves to explicate the notion of divine action in the world.[6] Although these authors are philosophers offering a philosophical explication of a divine attribute, they do not work from purely natural theological grounds. Each work is from within a particular faith tradition (Judaism for Mittleman and Goodman, Christianity—specifically Roman Catholic Christianity—for Murphy). With respect to contemporary systematic theology, John Webster's 2003 text, *Holiness*, stood alone in this domain until 2017 saw the publication of Bernie A. Van de Walle's *Rethinking Holiness: A Theological Introduction*. It seems to me that holiness is a feature of the divine that is ripe for further exploration in the contemporary theological and philosophical scene.

### That God Is Holy

The first instance in Scripture where the term holy (with the Hebrew root *qds*) is used is conspicuously not applied to God. Rather we find in Genesis 2:3 that God blessed the seventh day of the creation week and "made it holy."[7] Moreover, the next location we see this term is not until Exodus 3 when the ground around the Unburnt Bush is described as holy by God. Despite these two key passages not explicitly predicating holiness of God, I take it that one with even a passing familiarity with religion would understand the proposition *that God is holy* to be uncontroversial. Questioning whether God is holy seems to be questioning a tautology.

I have already mentioned the vision of the heavenly throne room from Revelation 4. This passage is clearly picking up a motif found in Isaiah 6; a passage that has long animated the theological imaginations of theorists of

God's attributes. During this vision, the prophet sees God seated on a throne in a high and exalted state. Around this visual manifestation of God are the seraphim who call to one another:

> Holy, holy, holy is the Lord Almighty;
> the whole earth is full of his glory.[8]

God is here described as not just holy, but thrice holy. Walter Moberly comments, "The first part of the seraphic cry, the threefold proclamation of YHWH's holiness is remarkable for its emphasis . . . it should probably be envisaged as a single 'holy' followed by an intensifying 'holy, holy' / 'utterly holy.'"[9] He goes on, "Such an emphatic formulation is tantamount to a definition of the *nature* of YHWH."[10] Holiness for Isaiah in his vision is at the very core of who and/or what God is.

Scriptural allusions to Isaiah 6 and Revelation 4 are also referenced weekly in the service of Holy Communion for those Christians that include the *Sanctus* as part of their liturgical tradition.

> Holy, holy, holy, Lord God of power and might,
> heaven and earth are full of your glory.
> Hosanna in the highest.
> Blessed is he who comes in the name of the Lord.
> Hosanna in the highest.

The emphatic affirmation of God's holiness emerges clearly from these thrice attributions of holiness to God.

We can continue to see in this brief biblical survey that the proposition *that God is holy* seems to jump off the pages of Scripture. I have already made mention of Isaiah's vision of the seraphim's call. One could also point to Moses' praises of God, which he made after the deliverance of the people of Israel from the hands of the Egyptians:

> Who is like you, O Lord, among the gods?
> Who is like you, majestic in holiness,
> awesome in splendor, doing wonders?[11]

The Psalms are full of the praises of God. A frequent reason given for praising or worshipping God is God's holiness. For instance, the psalmist writes in Psalm 99:

> Extol the Lord our God,
> and worship at his holy mountain;
> *for the Lord our God is holy.* [12]

God even attests to God's own holiness in calling God's people to share in this attribute with him, "You shall be holy, for I the Lord your God am holy."[13] Hence, it is clear that there is good warrant for holding that God possesses the attribute of holiness for those for whom Scripture serves as a valuable locus for descriptions of God.

## CHARACTERIZING HOLINESS

God is holy and so are many other things. What, then, does this predicate mean when applied both to God and non-divine entities? Part of the challenge with respect to characterizing holiness as a divine attribute centers on whether one thinks that this attribute is an essential feature of God or an accidental feature. Typically philosophical theologians hold that divine attributes like omnipotence, aseity, or omniscience are attributes that—at least in some respect—constitute the nature of God and are attributes that would be aptly predicated of God whether there were a creation or not. Once we get creation into our conceptual framework, other attributes of God follow along, for instance, *that God is the creator of heaven and earth, that God is the speaker to Moses from the Unburnt Bush*, or *that God loves human beings*. Attributes in this latter category are not apt of God outside of or independent of the created realm. Is holiness an attribute on the first list or the second? Is holiness an essential or an accidental feature of God?

### Essentially Relational?

The question of whether God's holiness is essential or accidental to God seems to me a helpful diagnostic question to probe the contours of proffered definitions of holiness. For example, Van de Walle defines holiness as follows, "the transcendence or absolute otherness that is basic to God's being."[14] This definition is rather typical of explications of holiness as a divine attribute. However, this definition and many like it are unfortunately confused and typify one of the main challenges with understanding holiness. Let me exposit Van de Walle's definition in order to draw out this definitional challenge.

I take it that "basic to God's being" connotes that holiness is, on Van de Walle's understanding, an essential attribute of God. He goes on to say that, aside from God, "nothing else is intrinsically holy."[15] God's holiness is an essential feature of God, intrinsic to God, basic to God's being. Seemingly, God would not be God without God's holiness. This essential feature of God is God's "transcendence or absolute otherness." Van de Walle reiterates, "holiness refers to God's absolute uniqueness, his lack of peer or rival, his wholly otherness, or what we might call his 'absolute categorical distinction.'"[16] However, part of the definition of such terms as "transcendence," "otherness," and "uniqueness" is that that they are relational terms. An entity cannot be "other" alone; it must be other than some other entity. An entity cannot be transcendent alone; it must transcend some other entity. An entity cannot be unique on its own; it must be distinguished from some other entity. X is only "other" when it is other than Y. For Van de Walle, holiness is a relational attribute of God, an attribute God possesses in virtue of standing in a particular kind of relation to another entity. However, traditional Christian theology holds that at some conceptual moment God was indeed alone, there was no creation and thus no entity which God could transcend, be other than, or be unique in comparison with. This seems puzzling.

Continuing in the systematic theological stream, Webster similarly embraces a relational understanding of holiness. Webster writes of God, "his holiness is a mode of relation to the creatures whom he sanctifies and calls to holiness."[17] Even explicitly does Webster define God's holiness in this relational manner. Webster likewise holds holiness to be an essential attribute of God when he writes, "All the attributes of God are identical with God's essence."[18] Seemingly, then, if holiness is an attribute of God, then for Webster it is an essential attribute. A Websterian conception of God's holiness requires that God possesses an essentially relational attribute.

Consequently, these definitional sketches offered by Van de Walle and Webster, when expressed within a traditional Christian theism, entail a contradiction. For, if holiness is a relational attribute of God ("transcendence or absolute otherness," "uniqueness," "mode of relation to the creatures . . .") and God is essentially holy ("basic to God's being," "intrinsically holy," "identical with God's essence"), then there must be some other entity that is both (a) co-eternal with God and (b) on which God is essentially dependent for God's being. This, however, does not comport with the traditional picture of a God who is *a se* and of a creation that was contingently created *ex nihilo*.[19] Any conception of an attribute of God that makes the attribute both essential and relational runs into an inconsistency. In sum, the conjunction of the following three propositions entails a contradiction:

1. Holiness is an essential attribute of God.
2. Holiness is a relational attribute of God.
3. Traditional Christian theism (including the propositions that God exists *a se* and that creation is from nothing).

When one is faced with a contradiction derived from a list of conjuncts, one can avoid the contradiction by revising one of the conjuncts.

Perhaps the easiest proposition to revise would be (1), the status of holiness as an essential feature of God. If, rather, this were a contingent feature of God, then there would be no trouble at all with it being a relative attribute, even within a traditional Christian theism. Like a proposition such as *being the creator of earth*, the proposition *that God is holy* would be stating an attribute of God that is dependent on God's act of creating (and, understood along the lines of (3), this would be a contingent act). From my vantage point, however, a revision of this nature would not seem to fit the Scriptural material the best. As our biblical survey above indicates, God's holiness is a repeated, central, and—I would say—an essential feature of God. So, for my part, I will agree with Van de Walle that God's holiness is basic to God's being as an essential attribute.

Proposition (3) refers to a cluster of attributes and features of God traditionally taken to be apt within Christian theology. If one held that holiness were essential to God and ought to be understood as a relational attribute ((1) & (2)), then perhaps one should give up on such traditional notions as divine aseity or *creatio ex nihilo* (3). For my part, my credence in (3) is much higher than my credence for (1) or (2), and so my tact would be to pursue adequate revisions of (1) or (2) first. It is unclear to me which of (1)–(3) Van de Walle or Webster would be most likely to revise, but I suspect that (3) would be lower on their list.

Revisions of (3), I take it, are a similar conceptual move with the divine attribute of love that has led some scholars like Thomas Oord to reject traditional Christian theism for, what are marketed, as open and relational theisms.[20] Within these discussions of love, "love" would be substituted for "holiness" in (1) & (2), and (3) would be rejected. There are some further similarities between discussions of holiness and love. For, is not love the sort of attribute the requires an "other" and is an essential feature of God, for "God is love" (1 Jn 4:8)? Typically, Christian theologians have rather wished to maintain the contingency of creation and so have tried to circumvent a view of God that requires the necessity of creation. The standard move in this domain is to show how the triune nature of God allows a sufficient "otherness" within the divine nature for there to be genuine, relational love while also not requiring there to be any non-God entities. That is, the Father, the Son, and the Holy Spirit are eternally existing, essentially divine persons who, by nature, love. Yet they do not need to love any non-divine entity in order to exercise the feature of being loving, they love each other. The distinction of persons but unity of nature shows the triune God to be such that there is sufficient otherness for love without positing any non-divine entities.

Could not this same move apply to holiness for someone like Van de Walle or Webster? I think not. Granted the divine persons are distinct from one another, they are indeed—in some sense—separated from one another (even as they are so united as to share one essence, one will). But mere separation is not what Van de Walle or others need, Van de Walle needs "transcendent" separation or "absolute otherness" for his definition. Minimally, I think, transcendence describes a hierarchical relationship, so to speak; the "trans-" connoting beyondness, aboveness, higherness. To introduce this kind of hierarchy into the nature of the triune God will just not do for traditional trinitarianism. It is no part of the trinitarian teaching of (3) to hold that, say, the Father is holy *because* the Father transcends the Son or vice versa. In fact, going down this path would inevitably lead to a contradiction (two or more members being transcendent from one another) or at least one member of the trinity being not holy. Hence, a relational attribute cannot be an essential attribute of God if that one side of the relata is a non-divine entity.

If holiness is taken to be (1) essential, (2) relational, and one embraces (3), then one is locked into a contradiction. For my part, I will offer a revision of (2) that saves some of the appeal of the relational nature of holiness while not categorizing it as a relational term for God—although it is such for non-divine entities.

## Owned by God

In offering a constructive account, I am not intending to offer an exhaustive characterization of holiness. Holiness is a multifaceted concept, which is reflected in the numerous linguistic and phenomenological presentations of the concept in Scripture and religion more generally. One might even go so far as to say that the facets of holiness do not even ultimately coalesce in anything like a unified definition. Mark Murphy, in his creative and helpful study of holiness, distinguishes what he calls, "primary and secondary holiness": the former referring to God's holiness, with the latter referring to the holiness of non-divine entities. Murphy asserts, "Characterizing holiness in terms of primary and secondary holiness requires us to give up the ambition of giving a unitary analysis of holiness, one that applies indifferently to all holy things."[21] I think this is a bit overstated and that a cohesive or unitary explication of holiness is possible. However, providing a unitary account does not entail an exhaustively singular account of holiness. Van de Walle and Webster are on to something, I think, in that aspects of separateness, transcendence, moral purity, distinction, power, and other conceptual ingredients all swirl around the conceptual holiness pool. Yet, I am looking for a single ingredient that can serve the purpose of both applying to God and non-divine entities and serve as a grounding to many of these other elements. The foundational conceptual principle I will be using to explicate the nature of holiness is divine ownership. To be holy is to be owned by God.

An ownership theme pervades biblical discussions of holiness. Take but for one example this utterance of God in Leviticus 20, "You shall be holy *to me*; for I the Lord am holy, and I have separated you from the other peoples *to be mine*."[22] Note that God says that God's people will be "holy to me . . . to be mine." This is possession language, ownership language. The people *of* God *belong* to God. As Philip Jenson comments, "Because holy refers to God's realm, it includes another idea that is often associated with holiness—ownership or belonging."[23] Yet, at the same time as the people here are denoted as the possession of God, God reminds that God Godself is holy. It would seem exceedingly odd if God intended there to be two distinct senses of holy in such close proximity. Rather, to be holy is to be owned by God, whether the owned entity is God or a non-God entity.

## God Owns God

Holiness is divine ownership. This can be stated more analytically,

$$X \text{ is holy } =^{\text{def}} X \text{ is owned by God.}$$

Observe that this definition applies to God and non-divine entities. It might seem a bit odd or even tautological to say that God owns Godself, but oddity does not entail falsity. In fact, to say that God is owned by God is no more and no less than what we tend to think intuitively about independent agents, which the doctrine of God's aseity conveys. Hence, this conception satisfies (1) above in holding holiness to be an essential attribute of God and (3) in being part of the package of traditional Christian theism that includes such an attribute as God's aseity. Etymologically speaking, to be *a se* is not to be independent, but to be *self*-dependent, to be from (*a*) one's self (*se*). That the *a se* one is also independent of any other entity save itself is a consequence of the attribute of aseity, but it is not constitutive of the attribute. To say that God is dependent upon God is not to introduce some sort of external dependence relation into the divine essence, but rather simply spells out in a longer fashion that God is from Godself. Moreover, this definition of the divine attribute of holiness gestures toward the relational character of holiness that (2) was intended to convey, for ownership is a relation. Yet, the relation in view here is not God's relation to creation, but God's relation to Godself. Hence, this definition of holiness as "ownership by God" secures the desiderata expressed by (1)–(3), even if (2) takes a slight modification toward thinking of the relational aspect of God to be an internal relation.

This definition is subtle because it also does not say that holiness amounts to self-ownership. This is an entailment of the conception when X is God, but this is only because the subject of the sentence and the direct object are identical. If holiness were identical to self-ownership, then the definition would be as such:

X is holy = X is owned by X.

If this were the case, then every self-owning entity would be holy. But if every entity were holy simply due to its own self-ownership, it would be hard to find how holiness could also connote transcendence or otherness or separation or indeed any relation to God—something also seemingly necessary for a proper understanding of holiness. In this, I agree with Van de Walle. Something is holy not because of self-ownership, but because of divine ownership.

## God Owns Holy Things

The subtlety of this distinction is especially important when we turn from thinking of holiness as divine ownership as a divine attribute to when we think of holiness as an attribute of non-divine entities. If one were to think that, for instance, creaturely entities could strive for an analogous aseity, this would be to reverse the definition of holiness I am proffering. Perhaps one thought, "look, God alone is holy because God alone has ultimate self-ownership. But humans can have an analogous self-ownership, perhaps the more self-focused or self-dependent the human is, the more like God in God's self-ownership the human can strive for, then the more holy the human can be." However, this conception is the near opposite of what I am offering here. It is not independence or self-ownership that is the mark of holiness, it is rather *God's* ownership that is the mark of holiness. For one and only one entity does God's ownership entail self-ownership, when that entity is God. For any and all other entities besides God, holiness entails the relative denial of self-ownership.

Rather, in its simplest form, holiness means divine ownership, and this applies to God and non-divine entities. However, we also see in Scripture and religion a prescriptive flavor to holiness, something on the order of the utterance by God to God's people to "be holy."[24] In this regard, we need to expand the sense of ownership in the definition slightly to include humans and non-human objects. For this, I offer:

X is holy = (a) God owns X, (b) X acts in a manner reflective of ownership by God, or (c) X is a means of producing, encouraging, catalyzing, facilitating, instantiating ownership by God.

To be holy is to be owned by God, act in a manner reflective of ownership by God (for agents like humans), or be a means of catalyzing ownership by

God (non-agential objects). Note that this sentence contains an inclusive disjunction, not exclusive. That is, an entity can both *be owned* by God and *act in a manner reflective of ownership* and *catalyze ownership* by God. This expansion allows us to see more naturally the mode of divine ownership in non-divine entities—appreciating Murphy's distinction between primary and secondary holiness—while not abandoning a unitary definition. For objects like land or the ground around the Unburnt Bush or various Temple accoutrements, the holiness of those objects is due to God's ownership of them and the role they play in facilitating God's ownership of humans. For humans, who are agents and thus act in the world, holiness includes acting in such a way as to display God's ownership of them.

## Two Poles

The point about agents acting in a manner reflective of ownership by God allows me to highlight a tension in explications of holiness. This tension is between more morality-focused conceptions of holiness and more, say, metaphysically focused conceptions of holiness. Van de Walle puts it this way:

> The association of holiness with morality and ethics has so captivated our minds that it can be difficult for us to imagine any other meaning of the word. Many of us simply assume the equation of holiness with moral perfection. Yet in Scripture holiness is not primarily about morality and ethics but about transcendence and otherness.[25]

My claim is to agree with Van de Walle—holiness is not primarily about morality and ethics—but I want to be sure to emphasize that holiness is at least in part about morality and ethics. Like Jenson says, "Holiness is not primarily a moral term, but neither is it inherently amoral."[26] There is a connotation of morality or ethics to holiness, but this connotation is not the sole feature of holiness. Rather, conceiving of holiness as ownership in the above definitions is offering us something like two conceptual poles of holiness: a metaphysical pole and an ethical pole. The metaphysical pole most closely captures (a) in the definition above, while also characterizing (c). The ethical pole more closely captures (b) in the definition while also characterizing an aspect of (c). I here expound this observation in conversation with some of Alan Mittleman's reflections on the nature of holiness.

Following Mittleman, let us continue to probe these two conceptual ranges that the term holy refers to, the ethical range and the metaphysical range.[27] The ethical conceptual range to which holy refers identifies—or nearly identifies—holiness with *ethical goodness*. Mittleman comments, "To impute the status of holiness is to recognize the quality of goodness. Pursuing justice or treating others with compassion is holy just insofar as it promotes the good."[28] Humans are holy when they are acting in accordance with the law as laid down in, for instance, the Torah. I here use the term "ethical" merely to cover the broad category of human activity. This involves fulfilling ritual obligations as well as obligations to neighbor and family. A trouble with simply conceiving of holiness within the ethical range is that a great many entities in the Hebrew Scriptures are referred to as holy that have only a tenuous relation to ethics at best. Times and seasons, places and objects are referred to as holy, yet how these entities relate to an ethic is not clear.

Where the ethical range seems to drop off, the metaphysical range picks up. On the metaphysical view, holiness denotes some underlying quality of an object. Yet this metaphysical reality can be of two kinds. The first species within the metaphysical range, call this the *metaphysical-property* view, takes *being holy* to be an attribute of an object like *being red* or *being spherical*. Mittleman states, "Holy ground would be, on this understanding, qualitatively different from ordinary ground. A holy place such as the *mishkan* or later the Temple has something qualitatively distinct about it."[29] This property is manifested in objects in many cases due to their closeness or proximity to God's presence. As Mittleman states, this view "in its strongest form is conceptually dependent on the idea of divine presence. As presence departs, holiness declines."[30] This component of the metaphysical-property view leads Mittleman to consider a second species of the metaphysical view that has it that holiness denotes the status of an object as being owned or possessed by God, call this the *metaphysical-possession* view. "*Holy* here," comments Mittleman, "functions more like *mine* than *red*; the object is now in God's possession."[31] In sum, we have three ranges of meaning for the term holy: (a) *ethical goodness* and the twin metaphysical ranges, (b) the *metaphysical-property* view, and (c) the *metaphysical-possession* view. These ranges are not mutually exclusive and there is potential for overlap in these ranges.

For my proposal, at the nexus point of metaphysics and ethics in the concept of holiness is divine ownership. Clearly the *metaphysical-possession* view connotes this, but I think the *property* view entails this as well. The property in question might indeed be related to God's presence, but the proximity to the divine corresponds to intensity of ownership. And God can use God's objects to catalyze the holiness of others. But *ethics* is that area of focus on human actions. Hence, the ethical range of holiness on my conception refers to those actions that humans execute that are done so because of the ownership by God of those humans. Humans act holy when they are owned by God, reflecting God's own ownership of Godself.

## CONCLUSION

Holiness is a central feature of the divine, yet it is also an important attribute aptly predicated of a great many non-divine entities. Puzzling as this is, I think a unitary definition of holiness can apply to both. This chapter has offered a prolegomenic foray into offering such an understanding of holiness.

After sketching the overall shape of this monograph, I offered the observation that holiness has not been one of those divine attributes that have much animated recent discussions in systematic or philosophical theology. I also noted that there is indication in some recent publications that perhaps that trend is turning. However, there very much remains room for conceptual exploration of this central idea, both holiness as it pertains to a divine attribute and as it related to a feature of non-divine entities—importantly humans. I have also suggested that finding unitary account of holiness that characterizes the holiness of God and non-God entities would be preferable to a divergent account. One trouble that theorists run into when describing the divine attribute of holiness is how to conceive of the essential or contingent, relational or non-relational statuses of the attribute. I have argued that if one holds with Van de Walle and Webster that holiness be conceived of as an essentially relational attribute, then one runs into a contradiction when this idea is combined with traditional Christian theistic commitments like divine aseity and *creatio ex nihilo*. Rather, I propose that one define holiness as divine ownership. Holy entities belong to God, whether those entities be God, humans, or other objects in the cosmos. For God, this can be an essential attribute, but it can also have a connotation of being a relational attribute, yet God's relation to Godself is the dynamic at work in this idea. For non-divine entities, they are holy when they are owned by God or act in a manner flowing from that ownership or stand as a means by which God brings about God's ownership. In this manner, the proffered definition can account for the ethical as well as metaphysical poles that seem to be operative in engagement with the holiness conceptual sphere.

The rest of this book applies this conception of holiness to various loci of Christian systematic theology. In this regard, what follows is not so much a deductive argument for the truth of the proffered theory as it is an attempt to test the theory for its utility among various doctrines. We might think of this as a rather scientific approach; scientific in the sense of offering a hypothesis (holiness as divine ownership) that is tested in various experiments (discussions of doctrines such as the divine-world relation, theological anthropology, justification, etc.). If the theory proves useful, then I submit that holiness as divine ownership should be considered a central element to discussions of holiness, both divine and human.

## NOTES

1. Rev 4:8.
2. See, for instance, Nicholas Wolterstorff *Acting Liturgically: Philosophical Reflections on Religious Practice* (Oxford University Press, 2018).
3. Most thoroughly in James M. Arcadi, *An Incarnational Model of the Eucharist* (Cambridge University Press, 2018). That text also includes studies of the nature of consecration (making-holy) and the relationship between God's presence and holy locations. Material from that book could have easily fit in this book and I would commend perusing that material in conjunction with the thoughts offered herein.
4. Alan L. Mittleman, *Does Judaism Condone Violence? Holiness and Ethics in the Jewish Tradition* (Princeton: Princeton University Press, 2018).
5. Lenn E. Goodman, *The Holy One of Israel* (Oxford: Oxford University Press, 2019).
6. Mark C. Murphy, *Divine Holiness and Divine Action*, Oxford Studies in Analytic Theology (Oxford: Oxford University Press, 2021).
7. For a treatment of this act of consecration, see Arcadi, *An Incarnational Model of the Eucharist*, chapter 3.
8. Isa 6:3.
9. R.W.L. Moberly, "Isaiah's Vision of God" in *Holiness: Past and Present*, ed. Stephen C. Barton (London T&T Clark, 2003), p. 126.
10. Moberly, "Isaiah's Vision of God," p. 127, emphasis added.
11. Ex 15:11.
12. Ps 99:9, emphasis added.
13. A thorough treatment of this text will come in chapter 6.
14. Bernie A. Van de Walle, *Rethinking Holiness* (Grand Rapids: Baker Academic, 2017), p. 44.
15. Van de Walle, *Rethinking Holiness*, p. 44.
16. Van de Walle, *Rethinking Holiness*, p. 51.
17. John Webster, *Holiness* (Grand Rapids: William B. Eerdmans Publishing Co., 2003), p. 5.
18. Webster, *Holiness*, p. 32.
19. For a discussion and defense of creation out of nothing, see Andrew Ter Ern Loke, "*Creatio Ex Nihilo*" in *T&T Clark Handbook of Analytic Theology*, eds. James M. Arcadi & James T. Turner, Jr. (T&T Clark, 2021), chap. 22.
20. For discussion, see Kevin J. Vanhoozer, "Love without measure? John Webster's unfinished dogmatic account of the love of God, in dialogue with Thomas Jay Oord's interdisciplinary theological account" and Thomas Jay Oord, "Analogies of love between God and creatures: a response to Kevin Vanhoozer" in *Love, Divine and Human: Contemporary Essays in Systematic and Philosophical Theology*, eds. Oliver D. Crisp, James M. Arcadi, & Jordan Wessling (T&T Clark, 2019), chaps. 1 & 2.
21. Murphy, *Divine Holiness & Divine Action*, p. 60–61.
22. Lev 20:26, emphasis added.
23. Philip Jenson, "Holiness in the Priestly Writings" in *Holiness: Past & Present* ed. Stephen C. Barton (London: T&T Clark, 2003), p. 107. See also Philip Jenson,

*Graded Holiness: A Key to the Priestly Conception of the World*, JSOT 106 (Sheffield: Sheffield Academic Press, 1992).

24. For instance, in Leviticus 19:2 cf. chapter 6.

25. Van de Walle, *Rethinking Holiness*, p. 51.

26. Jenson, "Holiness in the Priestly Writings," p. 121.

27. I note that Mittleman has nuanced his views slightly differently in his 2018 monograph from what I am working with here from his 2015 article.

28. Alan Mittleman, "The Problem of Holiness," *Journal of Analytic Theology* vol. 3 (2015), p. 31. Mittleman credits Lenn Goodman's *Love Thy Neighbor as Thyself* (New York: Oxford University Press, 2008) as contributing to his thinking in this point.

29. Mittleman, "The Problem of Holiness," p. 30.

30. Mittleman, "The Problem of Holiness," p. 32.

31. Mittleman, "The Problem of Holiness," p. 30, emphasis original.

*Chapter 2*

# The Holiness of the Panentheistic God

Systematic theologies—rightly, in my opinion—tend to place discussion of the doctrine of God near the beginning of the systematic theological project. Theology proper, as it is at times termed, deals with such issues as the nature of God, the attributes of God, and the relation between God and the world. The next two chapters use the lens of holiness-as-ownership to explore that latter domain, the God-world relation. I have placed my discussion of this area of theology proper in conversation with a view of God known in the literature as panentheism. I am not so much arguing for the truth of panentheism here as much as I am probing how the God-world relation might be construed when one takes holiness to be a guiding light in thinking about this relationship. It strikes me that panentheism—of a certain sort—might fit the holiness data well, but not without reservations.

## INTRODUCTION

*Worship-worthiness* is considered by many to be a necessary attribute for any candidate referent of the concept of God.[1] If one's conception of God does not move one or others to worship the purported referent of this conception, then—so the argument goes—ones does not have a concept of God but rather of some other entity. As we have seen, a fundamental attribute of God that is derived from Scripture is holiness. As this is a fundamental attribute of God and as this is a predicate said of God primarily and not just derivatively, we might think that holiness has a special role to play in ascribing worship-worthiness to God. Whether *holiness* is that attribute that is necessary and sufficient for the referent of a candidate concept of God to be considered worthy of worship is up for debate. But minimally I think we can say that according to Scriptural religion, God is holy, God is worthy of worship, and God's holiness grounds, in some sense, God's worship-worthiness.

However, in Abrahamic religions—if I may be allowed to refer to this category—holiness is not just a divine attribute but is also a description of certain places and objects within the spatiotemporal realm. I argue that within these religious traditions, when an object or location is denoted as "holy," it is because the practitioner of the religion within which the predication takes place believes it to be the case that there is a particular concentration of divine presence or activity at the location of the holy object.[2] Once the connection between holy objects and the divine presence is secured, it becomes paramount to articulate a conception of the relationship between the divine and the world that undergirds the phenomenology of holy objects. I argue here that a panentheistic conception of God might be construed as better able to provide this ontological undergirding than some versions of classical theism. Finally, I turn to consider how the physical realm serves as a sacrament of the divine, thus providing a means for considering the unity of the panentheistic God.

I note that I am working from the phenomenology of religion as a starting point for this investigation. That is, I am not simply working with a rational conception of the divine or transcendence or something devised in philosophy departments. This is much in the same line of proceeding as Rudolf Otto and, more recently, Mark Murphy. I take it that most who are interested in conceptions of the divine are so because of experiences they have of the divine, or experiences that are at least purportedly of the divine. I also take as a starting point the phenomenology of religion paramount in the Abrahamic traditions, most often from the Judeo-Christian stream of this religious tradition. I do this for two reasons. First, this is my own religious tradition and hence I am more familiar with the phenomenology and conceptions of God within this tradition. Secondly, one key aspect of this study is to put panentheism in conversation with classical theism. Although classical theism is not identical with—nor the only version of—the conceptions of God within the Abrahamic traditions, classical theism has in the history of philosophy most often been bound up with the Abrahamic traditions. However, I specify that references to religious practices or religious texts are not necessarily intended to be normative or authoritative. Rather these practices and texts are windows into the phenomenology of these religious traditions. No doubt these practices and texts have shaped the experience of practitioners of these traditions, but these practices and texts themselves have emerged out of experiences of the divine from within these traditions. Hence, my use of them is not to be seen as an appeal to authority, but rather as part of the phenomenological data of which concepts of the divine, in conjunction with philosophical reasoning, must reckon. With these preliminary notions in place, I turn first to examine one important desideratum for any concept of the divine.

## WORSHIP-WORTHINESS

Conceptions of God vary widely across religious traditions. Many religious traditions take God to be the highest or ultimate or maximal being of the universe. Not every practitioner of the world's religions would attest to being an Anselmian, but the concept of God as *that than which none greater can be conceived* rings true in the ears of many of the faithful. If a faithful practitioner of religion has before them two candidate referents for the term "God," A and B, and A is taken to be a greater, higher, larger, or more maximal being than B (in whatever sense the practitioner defines these terms), it would be hard for the practitioner to assent to the truth of the proposition *that B is God*. Whether the notion is that the candidate God is the greatest possible or simply the highest in comparison, the relative greatness of a being is a fundamental aspect of standard conceptions of God.

But is size or greatness really the only metric for evaluating competing conceptions of God? Is this simply an instance of humans seeing something bigger and projecting a divine status on that which is bigger than themselves? Is the greatest possible human, if such a human were to exist, an apt candidate for practitioners of religion to submit to? Or is there something beyond sheer magnitude that makes a candidate apt of the title "God"? I do not think the faithful would consent to the notion that it is size or greatness alone that makes their God the one to whom they order their lives. Rather, the divine-human relationship is marked by something deeper and more phenomenologically rich than a simple acknowledgment of the divine's greatness.

In specifically those monotheistic religious traditions stemming from the Abrahamic tradition, the divine-human relationship is fundamentally characterized by a posture of worshipped to worshipper. God is to be worshipped; humans are to be the worshippers. In this regard, it is a fundamental characteristic of a purported candidate for the title "God" that this entity be an apt target for human worship. Peter Forrest writes that a concept of God:

> is that of a worthy object of worship, where worship is an attitude often expressed by religious rituals, such as the paradigm of prostration before some representation of the object of worship ... it involves both awe at the object and a consequent restraint of the worshipper's actions, expressed by saying, "Not my will but thine be done."[3]

A candidate for God must be, on Forrest's analysis, worthy of worship. But not only this, according to Forrest's definition, a candidate God must be worthy of worship by the submission of one's will to the God. In this regard, there is something of an ownership relation that the worshipped has over the will of the worshipper. Now, I do not think that has to be taken to an extreme, as if the worshipper ceases to be an agent or is obliterated. Rather, Forrest puts a finger on a phenomenon in worship that is characterized as a submission, a giving over of will or desire, a relinquishing of self—to varying intensities—to the worshipped; these are all ownership-related phenomena. So, for Forrest, a worship-worthy entity is one to which a worshipper would hand over some measure of ownership of the worshipper's will.

Could not sheer size or power fit this description? "Bow down before me or I'll annihilate you!" says the God of the popular conception. Or indeed does not Zeus demand that one submits one's will to him, lest they be smitten by one of his fiery bolts? Are not greater size, fear-induction, and submission of the will sufficient relational dynamics for one to be properly said to be worshiping a candidate god? We need a definition of worship in order to determine if it is so.

In a recent work on the nature of liturgical worship, Nicholas Wolterstorff offers a discussion of worship that is germane to the project here. He introduces his analysis by offering the general observation that:

> [W]orshipping someone is a mode of acknowledging that person's worthiness, that person's greatness or excellence. Thus worshipping God is a mode of acknowledging God's worthiness, the excellence of who God is and the greatness of what God has done, is doing, and will do.[4]

Then, speaking specifically from his own Christian tradition, Wolterstorff avers that "in Christian worship we acknowledge the *unsurpassable* excellence of God."[5] Although Wolterstorff refines his definition later in the book, at this point I can point out dovetails with Wolterstorff's conception and my previous discussion. The worshipper, on this conception, recognizes something about the candidate god that is great or excellent, and thus grounds a posture of worship towards that entity. Wolterstorff connects this mode specifically to the Christian tradition, but I think the posture he sketches holds true for all the Abrahamic traditions, as well as the posture typically derived from Anselmian theism. This is that when one worships one acknowledges, as Wolterstorff says, the "*unsurpassable*" excellence of God. That candidate for worship cannot be superseded in excellence by any other possible entity. Again, the God who is worthy of worship must be at the pinnacle of greatness or excellence if this candidate god is to be considered *the* God.

However, Wolterstorff points out that simply acknowledging the unsurpassable excellence of God does not, *prima facie*, yield *worship*. An acknowledgment can be understood to be simply an epistemological assent. Is a practitioner of religion, strictly speaking, worshipping when she simply assents to the truth of the proposition *that God is the most excellent* or *that God is unsurpassably great*? As much as it might pain a Los Angeles Lakers fan to say it, a Lakers fan could assent to the proposition *that Michael Jordan is the best basketball player of all time* without thereby liking, admiring, or honoring Michael Jordan. It seems to Wolterstorff, and myself as well, that there is more to worship than a simple cognitive stance. It seems that cognitive assent to the truth of these—or similar—propositions might be necessary for worship, but this alone does not seem sufficient. What is needed in addition to a cognitive stance toward some proposition about the greatness of God, so Wolterstorff asserts, is a particular "attitudinal stance."[6]

In Wolterstorff's analysis, an attitudinal stance is more than feeling or emotion, although it may contain these. Rather, "an attitudinal stance toward someone is a way of regarding that person."[7] So, the worship of God includes cognitive assent to certain propositions about God and a particular attitudinal stance. This attitudinal stance Wolterstorff specifies as "awed, reverential, and grateful adoration."[8] Any candidate referent of the concept of God must be worship-worthy. As such, in conjunction with Wolterstorff's construal, any candidate referent of the concept of God must be (a) unsurpassably excellent, (b) worthy of awe, (c) worthy of reverence, and (d) worthy of adoration. Hence, at least using Wolterstorff's analysis, it is not enough for a candidate god to be simply larger or fear- and submission-inducing for this candidate to be worthy of worship. An unsurpassably great entity might secure this posture, but Zeus is not worthy of awe, reverence, or adoration, and hence not really worthy of worship. Rather, the God who is worship-worthy is not just great but evokes these attitudinal stances towards the candidate.

One piece of evidence that Wolterstorff uses to corroborate the "awe," "reverence," and "adoration" components to his definition of worship is drawn from a standard component of Christian liturgical worship. The "Trisagion" hymn derives from at least the fifth century and is a standard component in liturgies of the Eastern Orthodox tradition as well as prominent in Anglican liturgies. It is a hallmark of the Christian worshipful attitudinal stance toward God, and is thus archetypal as an instance of Christian worship. The Trisagion is:

> Holy God,
> Holy and mighty,
> Holy and immortal one,
>     have mercy on us.

> Holy God,
> Holy and mighty,
> Holy and immortal one,
> > have mercy on us.
> Holy God,
> Holy and mighty,
> Holy and immortal one,
> > have mercy on us.

That the key phrase of the Trisagion is repeated three times is important for Christians to emphasize the Trinitarian nature of their conception of God. Yet this thrice repetition is also reminiscent of a Scriptural passage we have encountered before in Isaiah 6:1–3. What is key for our purposes here is the manner in which an archetypal instance of worship from the Abrahamic traditions includes clear and direct reference to God's holiness. Thus, I contend that an entailment of Wolterstorff's discussion of the definition of worship is to highlight an important connection between God's holiness and God's worship-worthiness. The worship-worthy God is the holy God.

## HOLINESS AND THE DIVINE PRESENCE

In this next section, I pivot to probe the connection between God's holiness and God's presence in the Hebrew Scriptures. Recall that the endgame is to evaluate whether the panentheistic God is a better candidate referent for the concept of God than what is typically held in classical theism. Notably, these two rival conceptions of God differ with respect to the relationship that obtains between God and the created realm, with this difference most poignantly pertaining to the presence of God in the creation. The route for evaluation was first to provide a rubric for evaluating concepts of God, this I took to be worship-worthiness. But this led to specifying that what makes a candidate referent worship-worthy, at least in the Abrahamic traditions, is the attribute of holiness. Hence, I will here explore the concept of holiness as it pertains to God's presence in order to set up the argument that panentheism better satisfies the stated desiderata than does classical theism.

For practitioners of Judaism and Christianity, the Hebrew Scriptures provide the authoritative venue for conceiving of God. It is without question that in the Hebrew Scriptures God is presented as holy and this attribute serves as a distinguishing feature of the referent of the conception of God here adumbrated. For instance, in Psalm 77:13 the psalmist writes, "Your way, O God, is holy, what god is great like our God?" The God of Israel, according to the psalmist, is the greatest God whose way is holy. Also in the form of a poem or song, what has been come to be called the Song of Moses says, "Who is like you, O Lord, among the gods? Who is like you, majestic in holiness, awesome in deeds, doing wonders?"[9] Isaiah introduces a prophetic word from God in this manner, "For thus says the One who is high and lifted up, who inhabits eternity, whose name is holy."[10] Furthermore, in the book of Leviticus, God is depicted as enjoining holiness among the people because of God's fundamental status as holy. God says:

> For I am the Lord your God. Consecrate yourselves therefore, and be holy, for I am holy. You shall not defile yourselves with any swarming thing that crawls on the ground. For I am the Lord who brought you up out of the land of Egypt to be your God. You shall therefore be holy, for I am holy.[11]

This sentiment is repeated later in Leviticus as well, where God says to the people of Israel, "Be holy as the Lord your God is holy."[12] That God is holy is apparent in the narratives of the Hebrew Scriptures. Moreover, given Wolterstorff's discussion of worship and the concern of these narratives to distinguish the holy God as the one solely worthy of the devotion of the people of Israel, we can draw the connection that the holy God is the worship-worthy God.

I pivot now to focus on how the narratives of the Hebrew Scriptures draw a connection between God's holiness and God's presence.[13] One of the most poignant and clear instances of the connection between holiness and the divine presence occurs in Exodus 3, Moses' encounter with God by way of the Unburnt Bush. What I want to highlight in this passage is the manner in which the location of God's activity and presence becomes or is considered to be holy in virtue of this activity. The narrative of Exodus 3 finds Moses attending flocks in the desert of Horeb. In the midst of this seemingly mundane activity, Moses notices a bush that appears to be on fire but is not thereby burning up. As he draws near to the bush, "God called to him out of the midst of the bush and said, 'Moses, Moses!'"[14] The "midst of the bush," here, seems to be a location of particular concentration of divine activity. And as such, it is a particular location of God's presence. Moreover, God goes on to say, "Do not come near here; take off your sandals from your feet, for the place on which you are standing is holy ground."[15] At this point, the narrative indicates that not only is there a significant measure of God's presence in the midst of the bush, but that this presence has radiated out from the middle of the bush to sanctify—or, make holy—even the ground around the bush.

The concentration of divine presence in the midst of the bush is a concentration of God's activity. God is, according to the narrative, at the location of the middle of the bush, in fact, because God is acting at the location of the middle of the bush. God is here speaking to Moses, God is causing fire to appear, God is preventing the bush from being consumed by flame. Further, as we saw, even the ground around the bush becomes holy because of its proximity to a particular location of divine activity. This activity causes the ground around the bush to become holy. Hence, we have in this vignette an indication of the connection between God's presence and a holy place or holy object.

Another instance of the conjunction of these themes—God's presence, holiness, and the radiating nature of the effects of this—occurs at another significant object as depicted by the Hebrews Scriptures, the Mercy Seat above the Ark of the Covenant. The most relevant description of this for my present purposes is in Exodus 25. Here God instructs the Israelites in a number of guidelines for constructing their worship space.[16] Amidst the various instructions regarding the various Tabernacle accoutrements, God offers these instructions regarding the Ark of the Covenant:

> You shall make a mercy seat of pure gold. Two cubits and a half shall be its length, and a cubit and a half its breadth. And you shall make two cherubim of gold; of hammered work shall you make them, on the two ends of the mercy seat [. . .] And you shall put the mercy seat on the top of the ark [. . .] there I will meet with you, and from above the mercy seat, from between the two cherubim that are on the ark of the testimony, I will speak with you about all that I will give you in commandment for the people of Israel.[17]

God is clearly here indicating that this object will be a point of meeting between God and the people. This object will be a significant place of God's location in the universe. Right between the gold cherubim, just above the Ark, God says that he will be present in a special way. God's presence in this object is because of God's activity at this location. God will meet with the people there; God will speak from there; God will command from there; God will be there as God acts there.

Similar to the Unburnt Bush and the ground around it, the Mercy Seat too is an instance of God's activity radiating out from the center of divine activity, bringing about the holiness of the surrounding area. Typically, the Ark of the Covenant, with the Mercy Seat, rests in the Holy of Holies, which itself is located in the Holy Place. The holiness of these spaces even radiates out to the Court and the perimeter of the entire Tabernacle, all particularly holy locations within the cult of Hebrew worship. To wrap up this section, we see a suggestive conjunction in the religious mindset of this text of the themes of holiness, God's presence, and the radiating nature of the effects of divine activity. The worship-worthy God is the holy God and the holy God acts in certain locations in the universe, thereby making those objects themselves holy.

This account from the phenomenology of the religion of the Hebrew Scriptures can be taken as evidence of a connection between God's holiness and God's presence. When one applies this analysis to some of the paradigmatic holy objects or locations (the Kotel, the Kaaba, the Church of the Holy Sepulchre, etc.), a similar story can be told for these. That is, these objects are holy because they are the loci of particular concentrations of divine activity. The God who is holy in Godself breaks into these spatiotemporal locations in a manner different from God's normal activity in locations throughout the universe. These points of connection where the faithful perceive the activity of God become places for awe, reverence, and adoration of God, in harmony with Wolterstorff's definition of holiness and has played out in countless holy spaces throughout the earth. What remains to be seen, however, is which conception of the divine best provides an ontological underpinning to this phenomenology of God's holiness. The next section probes whether a panentheistic conception best fits these desiderata.

## PANENTHEISM

Defining panentheism has not often proved a straightforward project.[18] Panentheism is a theory about the nature of God and God's relation to the cosmos. However, there does not seem to be a consensus in the tradition or the contemporary literature as to just how to characterize God or the God-cosmos relation. Hence, I want to offer here a brief *apologia* for a deflationary account of panentheism. A deflationary thesis about panentheism simply says that God exists, the cosmos exists, and the relation between God and the cosmos is sufficiently intimate to warrant the attribution of "in" of the cosmos to God. The panentheist can account for intimacy in this relation by a diversity of means: ontological, mereological, causal, axiological, teleological, or others. What I am keen to show, however, is that although how one characterizes the intimacy of this relation has bearing on how one conceives of the nature of God, this bearing need not be taken as necessity. And thus a number of very disparate views on the nature of God and God's attributes can be held in conjunction with the deflationary panentheistic thesis.

### Deflationary Panentheism

Deflationary panentheism can allow for such disparate conceptualizations as either the strong divine immutability of classical theism or the strong divine mutability of process theism, and just about everything in between. The distinction turns not necessarily on the nature of God, but on the nature of the cosmos. If the deflationary panentheistic thesis is granted, and one has a corollary commitment to, say, four-dimensional eternalism, one can still seemingly preserve strong divine immutability. This picture would have it that there exists God and in God is a four-dimensional whole that presently—from the divine present—contains all that there was, is, and will be—from our phenomenal experience. This can be as strongly a hard determinism, with a related strong divine immutability, as one likes. Likewise, on the contrary, one can lodge a presentist view of time with the deflationary panentheistic thesis and articulate a divine that is as changing, shifting, and mutable as the process theist likes. To determine one extreme or the other, or something in between, is not settled by accepting or demurring from panentheism.

A properly Christian appropriation of the panentheistic model of God's relation to the cosmos must remain faithful to the creedal affirmations regarding the Trinity and the Incarnation, as well as the creaturely dependence relation the cosmos has on God as denoted in the first clause of the Creed. A project—such as this present study—that attempts to maintain fidelity to the teachings of the Ecumenical Councils would be inconsistent if it did not maintain fidelity to the non-Christological teachings of those Councils as well. However, assenting to the creaturely status of the creation, does not necessarily rule panentheism out from the start. Rather one can maintain this notion, with an understanding of panentheism as well. Göcke characterizes panentheism in this way: "Although there is a distinction between God, as the ultimate ground of reality and reality itself, a distinction that is epistemologically needed for ultimate explanation, there cannot be a substantial ontological distinction between them."[19] The conjunction of a thesis about God's status as creator and the non-substantial ontological distinction between creation and creator do not need to be seen as entailing a contradiction. Rather, one can hold that the creation was brought into being out of God's own being.

This conception might seem to push against the traditional Christian notion of *creatio ex nihilo*, a key concept discussed in the previous chapter. However, this need not be the case. This standard phrase can easily be interpreted to hold that God created out of nothing distinct from Godself, as if there were some entity or entities co-eternal with God from which God fashioned the creation.[20] One does not need to hold that creation out of nothing entails that "nothing" is some space or area outside of God from whence God created the cosmos. Rather, the concern in this line of inquiry has to do more with God's aseity than the process of creation. The Christian panentheist can maintain God's aseity just as firmly as the classical theist, if she so wished. And hence she can similarly endorse the doctrine of *creatio ex nihilo*—which is ordered to this end—just as much as the classical theist; again, if she so wished.

One plausible mode for explicating the intimacy of the relation between God and the cosmos—an intimacy sufficient for holding the cosmos to be "in" God—is a causal mode. God is in the cosmos in that God is fundamentally and continually causing the cosmos whose existence is necessarily dependent on this divine causal activity. Drawing on my action model of God's omnipresence, Georg Gasser makes the causal relation between God and the cosmos one of the central planks in his account of panentheism.[21] According to Gasser, a traditional way of explicating God's omnipresence has been to see God's presence in a threefold manner: by God's knowledge of all things, by God's providential conservation of all things, and by God's being the author of the nature and existence of all things.[22] My account of omnipresence holds that the second manner, God's causal activity, is all that is requisite to get an explanation of omnipresence off the ground. For Gasser, panentheism is such that, "All of creation is within the sphere of God's creative, sustaining and caring agency or it is not at all."[23] Being "within the sphere of," for Gasser, is sufficient to capture the "in" of panentheism.

## Panentheism and Its Competitors

It is a hallmark of attempts to describe panentheism that it be distinguished on one side from classical theism and on the other from pantheism. It seems easier to delineate panentheism from pantheism. Pantheism simply states that God and the universe are identical. As R.T. Mullins notes, "Pantheism denies that there is a plurality of substances that make up the world. Though it appears that there is a plurality of substances, this is an illusion since there is only one substance."[24] Panentheism does not take this step by holding that there is some aspect of God that is outside of or beyond the universe. Again, Mullins, "Panentheists say that, unlike pantheism, God is not identical to the universe. Instead, God is more than the universe."[25] Thus, panentheism is distinguished from pantheism.

Distinguishing panentheism, especially a deflationary panentheism, from classical theism is a bit more challenging. Here is one way of marking the difference between classical theism and panentheism that pertains to the notion of divine presence. It might seem challenging for the classical theist to hold to a conception of divine omnipresence, even as much as omnipresence is part of the conceptual "hard core" of classical theism.[26] Some classical theists, notably Anselm and Aquinas, hold that the manner in which God is said to be omnipresent reduces to one or a combination of God's purported other attributes, typically knowledge or power. This is to say that God is at a location if God either exhaustively knows what is going on at that location or God is acting at that location, or both. On divine activity at a location, the motivation for omnipresence (God's presence everywhere) is that as the sustainer in existence of the entire universe, God is acting at every location in the universe; hence, God is present at this location. But is simply knowledge of or the exercise of power at a location sufficient to ground the notion of the holiness of certain places in the manner I sketched above?

Rather, it might seem that in the holy places discussed in the Hebrew Scriptures, the holy God is taken as *there* in a more robust sense than simply God's knowing what is going on at a location or God acting at all places. Panentheism may seem to fit better the notion of God's presence as desired by the presence of holy objects and places in the universe. This is because the accounts noted above articulate a specific concentration of divine activity at some locations that is not the same as others. Classical theism is concerned to maintain a strict divide between God and universe, as Aquinas articulated there is no "real relation" between God and the universe. The conjunction of the lack of a real relation and the immateriality of God seems to entail that it is more proper to conceive of the God of classical theism as literally no "where" rather than every "where." But if God is nowhere, God cannot be in certain locations such as the Unburnt Bush or the Mercy Seat or the Kotel or the Kaaba. Yet, this does not match the phenomenology of the practitioners of the Abrahamic religions.

Panentheism, however, stipulates that there is a fundamental relation between God and the universe. Classical theism maintains a strict division between God and the universe, whereas pantheism collapses this distinction. However, in contradistinction from pantheism, on panentheism it is possible to make some distinction between God and the universe, on the order of the difference between a part and the whole of which it is a part (at least as the "in" in pan*en*theism connotes). As I construe panentheism, there is always some remainder of God that exists independently and outside of the universe. That is, panentheism is a mediating position between classical theism and pantheism with respect to the relation between God and the universe. Whereas classical theism posits no overlap between God and the universe and pantheism posits complete overlap between God and the universe, panentheism posits a partial overlap between God and the universe. On this construal, the totality of the universe overlaps with God, but the entirety of God does not overlap with the universe. Pantheism entails the identity of the universe with God, classical theism entails the non-identity of the universe with God, panentheism entails the identity of the universe with part of God.

Given that panentheism is satisfied with a connection—a real relation—between God and the universe, there is ontological grounding for the kind of presence seemingly desired by the accounts of holy places in the Abrahamic traditions. On classical theism, it does not seem as though it can properly be said that God is in any holy object or located at any holy place. But, if God is what is fundamentally holy, and thus worship-worthy, then the derivative holiness of any object in the universe will be an illusion. The panentheistic God need not offer such a ruse. Since God enjoys a real relation with all locations in the universe, all God need do is intensify God's activity in a location. This, then, makes it such that God is more present at some locations than others, and hence that location is more holy than others. God's activity at a location increases God's ownership of that location, thereby increasing the holiness of that location. Granted that the real relation between God and the universe entails that in some sense the entire universe is holy. But as the universe is a part of God, this should neither surprise nor worry. Rather, this conception grounds a kind of sacramental ontology that is the subject of the next section.

However, one might raise two worries about panentheism pertaining to unity that neither pantheism nor classical theism face. The classical theist can easily maintain that God is a consistent unity. On classical theism, God is immaterial, immutable, and wholly simple. Especially given the latter attribute, there is no question that God is unified. As God is completely distinct from the universe, the vast diversity of entities and objects within the universe does not impinge upon the unity of God. The pantheist likewise has resources to maintain the unity of God. For supposing one were a Stoic or Spinozan pantheist, then all that is necessarily is and God is simply identical to the totality of all. In this regard, there is in reality only one entity, and this entity is God. Panentheism, however, is not able to explicate a conception of the unity of God so easily. By borrowing the notion of a sacrament from standard Christian theology, one can point to a unified conception of God that is unified, holy, and worship-worthy.[27]

## SACRAMENTAL ONTOLOGY AND THE UNITY PROBLEM

Arthur Peacocke[28] and Anne Case-Winters[29] have suggested a sacramental explication of the God-world relation. I here follow this suggestion, but to a greater level of specificity and as a potential solution to the unity problem of panentheism. A common definition of a sacrament within the Christian tradition has it that a sacrament is an outward and visible sign of an inward and spiritual grace. For example, one can take baptism as a representative sacrament. The outward and visible sign is the water of baptism and the act of immersing or sprinkling the person to be baptized with the water. This is a symbolic washing with water and a symbolic burying. The inward and spiritual grace purportedly shown forth by the sacrament is the internal cleansing of one's sins and the spiritual identification with Christ in Christ's death, burial, and resurrection. This motif, then, is taken as being representative of any sacramental sign. I do not think that we need to reserve the term "sacramental" for only those activities or ceremonies that have been officially decreed or recognized by some authoritative church body. I am merely appropriating the adjectival sense of the word to denote any instance in which one construes an outward and visible sign as pointing to an inward and spiritual grace. Hence, in the use I am employing here, "sacramental" simply refers to this dynamic of the outward and visible pointing to the inward and spiritual grace regardless of this being within an officially delineated Christian religious milieu.

What is at play in this conception of the holy God in the holy places is that any and all holy places are locations of the inward and spiritual grace of a concentration of divine activity. When God speaks to Moses in the Unburnt Bush, inwardly and spiritually God is present more robustly than in other locations. The outward and visible sign in this dynamic is just whatever holy object is in question. But more than this, on this account of the worship-worthiness of the panentheistic God, the divine activity at these holy locations is indicative of the fact that the God who is active there extends (so to speak) beyond the bounds of that location. The holy object points not just to divine activity at a location, but to the remainder of God that goes above and beyond the spatiotemporal realm. Holy places and holy objects point to a spiritual reality beyond themselves because the God who is beyond, yet connected, to the spatiotemporal realm acts there. Objects owned point to an owner beyond.

Every object independently and jointly with any conglomeration of objects serves as a sacramental pointer to the reality of God that exists beyond the universe. The holiness of God refers to God's self-ownership, which is independent of the creation. The universe itself, or any subsection of it, is not worthy of worship. It is only that which is beyond or outside the universe that is worthy of awe, reverence, and adoration, the attitudinal stance that in conjunction with the epistemic posture that God is unspeakably great forms the basis for worship. The entity that is worthy of this worship is the holy God, the God that stands above and outside of the universe, and yet acts in such a manner as to bring about God's direct ownership and presence in the universe. The God who is worthy of worship is not far, but near, right here in the holy places. "'Am I a God who is near,' declares the Lord, 'And not a God far off? Can a man hide himself in hiding places, so I do not see him?' declares the Lord. 'Do I not fill the heavens and the earth?' declares the Lord."[30] The God who is near is the God who can be awed, reverenced, and gratefully adored.

The remainder of God secures the holiness and worship-worthiness of God, the overlap of God with the universe provides the connection point requisite as an avenue of worship. Holy locations as concentrations of divine activity provide more apt locales for this act. On this picture, it is adequate to be anywhere in the spatiotemporal realm to have a connection point with

God. God is located at all places because all places are in God. However, it would be easier and more apt to worship God in a location wherein God's presence is concentrated, concentrated due to an increase of divine activity at that location. This is just what occurs to Moses at the Unburnt Bush and those who meet with God in the Mercy Seat. Furthermore in the narratives of the Hebrew Scriptures, the Holy of Holies is at the heart of Israelite worship. The entire Israelite worship structure was predicated on the meeting of God and the world that took place in the Tabernacle. It was certainly permissible for the Psalmist to write of encountering and worshiping God in the field or on the hillside, but the Tabernacle—the special locus of divine activity—is the archetypal place of worship. This was the archetypal place of worship because this is where the holy and worship-worthy God was located in a more robust sense than God was located in the field or on the hillside.

This conception of the universe as sacrament for divine activity—the inward and spiritual grace—can account for the unity of God. First, God is taken on this view to be the most inclusive entity of all. The parts of the universe are all in God, pointing to God as the greater reality. There is no segment of the universe that somehow is outside the limits of God. As wholes take a greater precedence over their parts, and the parts of the universe are not exhaustive of God, the unity of God is paramount over the diversity of the universe. Secondly, the entire universe, individually and jointly, point beyond themselves to God. That is, the whole universe is a sacrament and each individual part is a sacrament. In those places where there is a concentration of God's activity, the sacramental presence is more pronounced, but that does not denigrate the fact that there is divine presence in all locations, and hence all objects can point to God. With the emphasis on concentration and intensification of divine activity in holy places, but not an ontologically other category of the holy, the entire universe serves as a unified sacrament of God's presence. In this regard, the part (universe) is in the whole (God), but the whole is also in the part by being the inward and spiritual grace underlying each outward and visible sign.

## CONCLUSION

Within the Abrahamic traditions it is clear that (a) there are holy objects, (b) that God alone is fundamentally holy, and (c) that God is worship-worthy. It could be argued that the classical theist God invokes too strict a divide between the universe and God to ground either the notion of God's omnipresence or the notion of God's special presence in holy objects. Although this God might be considered holy, in retaining God's ownership of Godself, this holiness is of no effect to objects in the universe. This contradicts the phenomenology of the religious traditions it is typically associated with. However, the God of deflationary panentheism is not only holy, but also really present and really related to the universe and as such bestows a baseline measure of holiness to the entire universe. The panentheistic God merely intensifies God's activity at certain locations, not bridging any ontological divide, in order to bring about a concentration of divine presence and thus holiness at these locations and in these objects. In this way, the entire universe functions as a sacrament of God's inward and spiritual grace, with holy objects serving as outward and visible signs of more pronounced instances of the holiness of the panentheistic God.

## NOTES

1. See, for instance, the discussion in Peter Forrest, "The Personal Pantheist Conception of God," in *Alternative Concepts of God: Essays on the Metaphysics of the Divine* eds. Andrew A. Buckareff and Yujin Nagasawa (Oxford: Oxford University Press, 2016), pp. 21–40.

2. I will tend to use the term "object" to refer to any location in the spatiotemporal realm that can be the subject of the predicate "holy" as in, "This object is holy." This term is intentionally broad enough to include a myriad of items standardly considered holy in the Abrahamic religions: small human-fashioned artifacts like a Temple accoutrement; a natural object like the breast of a ram (Exodus 29:17); large human-fashioned objects such as the Kotel (the Western/Wailing Wall) or the Kaaba; a place such as the Church of the Holy Sepulchre, the Temple Mount, or the St. Peter's Basilica; a day such as the Sabbath (Genesis 2:3). I will, at times, use "object" and "location" interchangeably. I am not, in this chapter, interested in how to explain the holiness of humans, that will come in a later chapter.

3. Forrest, "The Personal Pantheist Concept of God," p. 21.

4. Nicholas Wolterstorff, *The God We Worship: An Exploration of Liturgical Theology* (Grand Rapids, MI: William B. Eerdmans Publishing Company, 2015), p. 23.

5. Wolterstorff, *The God We Worship,* p. 24, italics original.

6. Wolterstorff, *The God We Worship,* p. 24.

7. Wolterstorff, *The God We Worship,* p. 25.

8. Wolterstorff, *The God We Worship,* p. 26.

9. Ex 15:11.

10. Isa 57:15.

11. Lev 11:44–45.

12. Lev 19:2.

13. For an account of God's presence as God's action and the implications of this for an account of omnipresence, see Arcadi, *An Incarnational Model of the Eucharist,* chap. 3.

14. Exodus 3:4.

15. Exodus 3:5.

16. A quick aside: even that the Israelites would follow the instructions of God in this instance by constructing a worship space for the worship of this God indicates that they considered the God who was giving these instructions to be worship-worthy.

17. Exodus 25:17–18, 21a, 22.

18. For helpful efforts to this end, and concurring opinions of the difficulty of the task, see, Benedikt Paul Göeke, "Panentheism and Classical Theism," *Sophia* 52 (2012): 61–75 and R.T. Mullins, "The Difficulty with Demarcating Panentheism," *Sophia* 55 (2016): 325–346.

19. Benedikt Paul Göcke, "Concepts of God and models of the God-world relation," *Philosophy Compass* 12 (2017): 1–15, p. 6.

20. Here the recent discussion around the relation between God and abstract objects is paramount. See, for instance, William Lane Craig, *God Over All: Divine Aseity and the Challenge of Platonism* (Oxford: Oxford University Press, 2016).

21. Georg Gasser, "God's omnipresence in the world: on possible meanings of 'en' in panentheism," *International Journal for Philosophy of Religion* 85 (2019): 43–62 and James M. Arcadi, "God is where God acts: Reconceiving divine omnipresence," *Topoi* 36.4 (2017): 631–639.

22. Gasser, "God's omnipresence in the world," p. 57.

23. Gasser, "God's omnipresence in the world," p. 60.

24. Mullins, "The difficulty of demarcating panentheism," p. 333.

25. Mullins, "The difficulty of demarcating panentheism," p. 335.

26. Mullins, "The difficulty of demarcating panentheism," p. 327.

27. One might wonder, is this really panentheism? In a sense, perhaps we have descended into a semantic—or, worse, marketing—debate. It might be that the kind of state of affairs I am sketching here could easily be adopted by a modified classical theism or a theistic personalism, without the need for emphasizing an overlap between God and the cosmos. Moreover, most contemporary panentheists wish their panentheism to entail a changing, dynamic, responsive God, which is not at all required by this picture I sketch here. At some point modified classical theism and deflationary panentheism might coalesce. This is fine with me. It is not so much the label I am interested in here as the nexus point between God and the universe, specifically between God's holiness and the holiness of objects or locations in the cosmos. These objects or locations are holy because God has acted to take ownership of them. This, to my mind, requires a tighter connection between God and these objects that is seemingly allowed on some extreme forms of classical theism. But if panentheism is not the term to describe this phenomenon, I will have no attachment to using it.

28. Arthur Peacocke, *Paths of Science Toward God: The End of All Our Exploring* (Oxford: One World, 2001).

29. Anne Case-Winters, "Rethinking Divine Presence and Activity in World Process" in *Creation Made Free: Open Theology Engaging Science* (Eugene, OR: Pickwick Publications, 2009), 69–87.

30. Jer 23:23–24.

*Chapter 3*

# A Panpsychist Panentheistic Incarnational Model of the Holy Eucharist

The God-world relation is a difficult conceptual area to map, the mind-body relation perhaps even more so. The previous chapter argued that attention to the relation between God's holiness and the holiness of objects and locations in the universe might motivate one to opt for a deflationary panentheism. This chapter adds to that picture some reflections on the mind-body relation and the implications of these conceptions on one's understanding of the Eucharist, some of those objects considered most sacred in the Christian tradition. In a sense, then, this is another hypothetical chapter. Suppose one wished for a tight connection between God and world such as one deflationary panentheism offers. Suppose one also wished for a tight connection between mind and body such as panpsychism offers. Suppose one also wished for a robust manner for conceiving of the holiness of the bread and the wine of the Eucharist. The sort of metaphysical picture that might emerge out of this crowded intersection is what I wish to sketch in this chapter. Again, as with the previous chapter, I am not here committing myself to panentheism or panpsychism, or even a robust metaphysics of the Eucharist. However, I think these are all conceptual points worth taking seriously. One way of taking these points seriously is by making connections and drawing out implications of these connections in order to evaluate the whole even as we analyze the constituent parts of the whole as well.

## INTRODUCTION

According to the guidance of the seven Ecumenical Councils as explications of the Christian Scriptures, Christianity teaches not only that there is a God, but that this God is triune and that one member of this Trinity has become incarnate in the person of Jesus Christ. Traditional explications of this teaching show Christ as being both fully God and fully human, while remaining only one person. That is, whereas most everything else in the cosmos only has one nature, Christ is unique among entities in having two natures—divinity and humanity. Hence, Christ is properly named "Emmanuel," "God with us." When one turns to Christian practice to find those instances wherein humanity's encounter with God is most profound, the Eucharist is that holiest moment in Christian practice because of a direct encounter with God. This is because the majority opinion teaching of the Christian tradition has it that in some fashion Christ—the God-human—becomes so related to the mundane elements of bread and wine, that the predications, "This is the body of Christ" or "This is the blood of Christ" are warranted. Hence, the tradition teaches an increasing concretizing of God's being with humanity: in the cosmos, in Christ, and in the Eucharist.

What is not laid out explicitly in the Christian Scriptures or the pronouncements of the Councils, are specific statements regarding the ontology of the cosmos. The Christian theologian, then, is free to pursue fine-grained expositions of ontology that can be said to fall within the more thick-grained determinations of these authoritative sources.[1] Hence, well-intentioned Christians have pursued such radically distinct fundamental ontologies as idealism, dualism, and materialism as possible ideologies within which to make sense of the Scriptural and Conciliar material. This chapter proposes a route for explicating a model of the Holy Eucharist—and its Christological infrastructure—within a panpsychist panentheistic ontological framework. Hence, the model offered here is a hypothesized conclusion of the conjunction of numerous conceptual data points (all of which will receive further elaboration anon), including:

1. The Christological determinations of the seven Ecumenical Councils.[2]
2. A Corporeal Mode model of Christ's presence in the Eucharist.[3]
3. Deflationary Panentheism.
4. Panpsychism.

In order to explicate this model of such a holy "site" as the Eucharist, each of the aforementioned data points must be laid out and explained. Since a description of the Eucharist's holiness is the *telos* of this chapter, I will first set out some key distinctions and desiderata within the Eucharistic sphere of inquiry. Because the model of the Eucharist I favor utilizes the metaphysical infrastructure of Conciliar Christology, in the following section I will discuss these conceptual guidelines and show how they are brought to bear on the Eucharist. Subsequently, I will briefly discuss both panpsychism and panentheism. This will give rise to a discussion of how the Incarnation may be understood within a panpsychist and panentheistic framework. Finally, I bring all the data points to bear on the Eucharist in order to construct a panpsychist panentheistic incarnational model of the Eucharist, a holy place for the holy God to be.

## PRELIMINARY FRAMEWORK

### The Eucharist

According to the accounts of Christ's life from the Synoptic Gospels, Paul's letter to the Corinthians, and in light of the liturgical traditions of broadly catholic Christianity, on the night before he was handed over to suffering and death, Jesus Christ took bread, blessed it, gave it to those with him and said, "Take, eat, this is my body." Likewise, Christ took some wine, similarly blessed it, similarly gave it, and similarly said, "Drink this all of you; this is my blood of the new covenant."[4] How properly to understand these locutions, however, has been the subject of no small amount of controversy over the course of the history of Christian theological reflection.

As I see it, the traditional explanations of these words fall into three main families. First, we might designate those interpretations that join the bread and the wine in a metaphysically robust sense to the body and blood of Christ. These are, as I term it, Corporeal Mode explications of Christ's presence in the Eucharist. This is the majority opinion family of views in the tradition and the genus under which my specific model will fall, hence further discussion of this family will come further on.[5] Another family of views on the relation between Christ and the elements of bread and wine is the Pneumatic Mode.[6] This family emphasizes a spiritual connection between either Christ and the elements or Christ and the recipient by means of the elements. Finally, a third family of views I refer to as the No Non Normal Mode.[7] This mode states that there is no more significant connection between Christ and the elements or Christ and the recipient of the elements by means of the elements than is found in any other locale in the cosmos. Perhaps one or more of these modes would fit more or less easily within a panpsychist panentheistic framework, but due to its popularity in the tradition, this essay pursues a species of a Corporeal Mode explication of Christ's presence in the Eucharist.

The Corporeal Mode family of views can be further subdivided into three main descendants, transubstantiation, consubstantiation, and impanation. The former can be defined as holding to the twin beliefs that after the consecration of the bread and the wine, the consecrated object is (a) no longer bread or wine, yet is (b) the body or blood of Christ, respectively. These metaphysical claims, however, obtain with no corollary empirical change in the consecrated objects. The objects remain empirically the same prior and subsequent to the consecration of these elements. What does change is the underlying reality of the objects. The proponent of consubstantiation—found not by that name in many Lutheran quarters—holds (b) with the transubstantiation theorist, but does not endorse (a). That is, the consubstantiation theorist holds that the body and blood of Christ come to be located "in, with, and under"[8] the bread and the wine. Yet in addition to retaining all their empirical qualities, the consecrated objects remain bread and wine. Finally, like consubstantiation, the impanation theorist holds to (b) but not (a). However, what differentiates impanation from consubstantiation is the desire of the proponent of impanation to offer an account of the union between the bread and the body of Christ—or the wine and the blood of Christ—in a manner patterned after the Incarnation. It is my contention here—as elsewhere—that impanation is to be preferred as most adequately satisfying the Scriptural, liturgical, linguistic, metaphysical, and theological desiderata pertaining to the presence of Christ in the Eucharist.[9]

Although transubstantiation, consubstantiation, and impanation are all Corporeal Mode cousins, there are subtle differences between them. What is desired by Scripture and the liturgy is a metaphysical state of affairs such that it is apt to say of the consecrated bread, "This is the body of Christ."[10] Each Corporeal Mode view attempts to offer such a metaphysical state of affairs. The transubstantiation theorist holds that the best way to secure the aptness of this predication is to hold that the post-consecration consecrated object is no longer bread. Oftentimes, in the Roman Catholic tradition this phenomenon is exposited with recourse to an Aristotelian substance ontology. However, this is not a necessary feature of the official Roman Catholic position. What is necessary for the Roman Catholic is the denial of the continued presence and existence of the bread, post-consecration.

My purpose here is not to show the necessary falsity of non-impanation views of the Eucharist. Hence, I briefly just gesture in the direction of a response to the transubstantiation model. I do so by raising the question of: to what does "this" in the sentence "this is the body of Christ" refer? It is not the object empirically and phenomenally present to potential recipients, for that is merely the empirical features of bread, which the object no longer is. If the indexical refers to the body of Christ, we might reasonably ask about just where this body is? Aristotelian substance ontology has been deployed to argue that while the accidents of the bread remain where and what they always are, the substance of the bread changes to become the substance of the body of Christ. But then one is forced to accept the severing of the relation between substance and accident that is the bedrock of that ontology. Absent this modification to this ontology, we are left wondering just what "this" is.[11]

A similar linguistic—and then by extension metaphysical—query can be raised in regard to the consubstantiation theory. The theorist in this camp typically holds that the body of Christ comes along with the consecrated bread to be consumed by the recipient. What is oftentimes lacking in this sphere of explanation is a robust account of the union between the consecrated object and the body of Christ. "With-ness," if it even meets the vagueness objection, does not seem to be any more intimate a relation than co-location. While this view can provide for the reality of the empirical features of bread in the consecrated object—because it is still indeed bread—it does not seem as though this view can countenance the predication that this object, "this," is the body of Christ. Rather, on this construal, "this" refers to some imperceptible entity co-located with the bread. Yet, the bread is what draws the attention of the recipients, and the bread is that which the minister holds and says, "*this* is the body of Christ." More specifically speaking, if this metaphysical situation were apt, the minister should refer to the bread and say, "the body of Christ is around here." But this, of course, is not what ministers following the catholic liturgies, following the words of Scripture, in fact say.

By contrast, impanation has the virtues of both countenancing a natural interpretation of the indexical and reusing a metaphysical infrastructure with the weight of Ecumenical Councils behind it. According to the traditional teaching regarding the Incarnation, the faithful are to say both that Jesus Christ "is God" and that he "is a human being," while remaining one person. Hence, unity and duality are at the heart of the traditional teaching; Christ is unified in personhood, but dual in natures. In like manner, the impanation theorist holds that post-consecration the consecrated object is both bread and the body of Christ yet remains unified by being only one object. In the Incarnation, the notion of the hypostatic union is deployed to describe the union between the divine nature and an instance of human nature. In a similar manner in impanation, the notion of a sacramental union is deployed to describe the union relation between the bread and the body of Christ. Hence, the impanation theorist holds that the metaphysical state of affairs undergirding the predication of the bread that "this is the body of Christ," is parallel to the metaphysical state of affairs undergirding the predication of Jesus Christ that "this is God." As, however, should be clear by this paragraph, since impanation is based on a traditional explication of the Incarnation, we must first offer an examination of that doctrine.

## The Incarnation

Anyone who reads the Christian Scriptures with the grain of the determinations of the seven Ecumenical Councils will see that Christians think that

Jesus Christ is both God and a human being. For instance, the so-called, "Definition" of Chalcedon states:

> Jesus Christ is one and the same Son, the Same perfect in Godhead, the Same perfect in manhood, truly God and truly man, the Same [consisting] of a rational soul and a body; homoousious with the Father as to his Godhead, and the Same homoousious with us as to his manhood . . . made known in two natures [which exist] without confusion, without change, without division, without separation . . . concurring into one Person and one hypostasis—not parted or divided into two persons, but one and the same Son . . . the Lord Jesus Christ.[12]

This statement, among others in Scripture and the proceedings of the Councils, gives rise to the two-natures doctrine—that one member of the Trinity is incarnate as Jesus Christ, being one person with two natures. How to understand this doctrine, and defend the logical coherence of it, has been the focus of much recent work in analytic theology.

In tracing the conceptual frameworks in the analytic literature's discussions of the two-natures doctrine, we can see a number of streams of explication. For instance, Jonathan Hill delineates a first branching of the Christological tree between those who hold to *transformationalist* models of the Incarnation from those who hold to *relational* models of the Incarnation. For the transformationalist, when the Christian tradition says that the second person of the Trinity became human, "to *become human* means being *transformed into a human* . . . just as a caterpillar becomes a butterfly by being transformed into one."[13] However, one worry that might be raised to this explanation is that, on the analogy of a butterfly, once the caterpillar is transformed into a butterfly it ceases to be a caterpillar. If the second person of the Trinity were transformed into a human and yet ceased to be divine, then we would no longer have a two-natures doctrine of the Incarnation, as Conciliar Christology seems to require. Moreover, following the theo-logic of deflationary panentheism, we might see the transformationalist view as not being apt. On panentheism, much of God remains beyond or outside the cosmos, but then by application to the Incarnation, in the Incarnation we would want some or much of God to remain beyond or outside the human nature in Christ.[14] Hence, the two-natures proponent may go looking for other models to describe the Incarnation.

A second family of views on the Incarnation in the recent analytic literature are called *relational* views. These views typically hold that the second person of the Trinity—in the Incarnation—comes to be related in a particularly intimate way with a concrete particular that is an instance of human nature. Hence, on this view, Christ is composed of two concrete natures, the divine nature and an instance of human nature. Thus, this view is also termed "concrete-compositionalism." Given the panentheistic framework to be sketched, we must specify that this view is relational by God in Christ being more intimately related to a segment of the cosmos than is God's normal *modus operandi*. The panentheist is always going to think that God is related to the cosmos in a particularly intimate way (more on this anon). What occurs in the Incarnation, then, must be either of a different kind or different intensity of relation than is God's relation to other parts of the cosmos. Yet, just what this relation is and how it might differ from God's general relation to the cosmos remains a bit obscure.

There is a potential mediating position between transformationalist and relationalist views, even as it might be characterized as one or other of the two. This view can be referred to as an *"additionalist"* perspective.[15] The idea here is that the second person of the Trinity merely "adds on" whatever necessary and sufficient features for being human are requisite. In this manner, the second person need not transform into a human and thus cease to be divine. Nor, however, does one need to hold that the second person becomes related to something somehow somewhat independent of the second person. Rather, whatever it is to be a human can be added on to the second person of the Trinity such that this person can properly said to be both divine and human. As will be seen further on, this is the most promising route of explication for Conciliar Christology within a panpsychist framework.

## Deflationary Panentheism

I turn now from Christology to panentheism. In the previous chapter, I proffered deflationary panentheism as a profitable way to go forward in describing panentheism as one theory about the God-world relation. I also suggested—what I call—the causal account of panentheism as being particularly helpful in characterizing God's presence at holy locations. The causal account of panentheism is but one among many ways of characterizing deflationary panentheism, but as it was generally useful for characterizing God's holy presence, so too do I think that it will be particularly useful for my explication of the Incarnation and the Eucharist within a panentheistic framework. However, before we turn to the task of conjoining panentheism, the Incarnation, and the Eucharist, I have next to discuss the final data point of this hypothesis, panpsychism.

## Panpsychism

Similar to panentheism, if one asks ten philosophers of mind about the nature of panpsychism, one will likely get a dozen different answers.[16] Hence, all I can do here is to adopt a version of panpsychism that seems to have particular potential for my sacramental aims. The fundamental tenet of this ideology is that each and every object in the cosmos is composed of or constituted by mentality (or proto-mentality) and physicality. Call this a monism, call this dualism all the way down, call this something else, but the basic idea is that mentality is ubiquitous in the cosmos. The basic motive for panpsychism is that it certainly seems as though we humans have phenomenal consciousness that is not reducible to mere physical explanation. However, a pure or simple dualism is fraught with many issues. Hence, if like comes from like, then this consciousness or mentality or proto-mentality must be a part of the whole cosmos since it is part of at least one part of the cosmos, namely humans.

I take it that on this view the microexperiences of less complex objects can fuse together into more complex objects with governing macroexperiences. In an analogous manner as we think of the human body as a complex system of nerves, bones, blood, and flesh, the human mind (related to these bodily parts) arises as a macroexperiencer out of the microexperiences of its constitutive parts. This entails, however, that one can find consciousness or proto-consciousness at all manner of varying levels of complexity. Whether objects vastly less complex than animals like rocks, bread, or wine actually have consciousness is up for interpretation and debate, but the determination of this discussion is not relevant for my purposes. All that is needed is that mundane objects have at least some level of mentality or protomentality that can be incorporated into larger complexes that do clearly have macroexperiences.

## Conjunction of the Preceding

In what follows I draw together the various conceptual strands relating to panpsychism, panentheism, Christology, and the Eucharist.

## PANPSYCHIST PANENTHEISM

As there are multiple ways to construe panpsychism and there are multiple ways to construe panentheism, so too are there multiple ways to construe a panpsychist panentheism. I suggest but one way here which, *prima facie*, fits the other conceptual data points of the current chapter as it pertains to God's holiness *qua* ownership.

When we discuss deflationary panentheism, we are inquiring into how the cosmos is in God. When we fuse this view to panpsychism, we begin to inquire how God is in the cosmos. As indicated above, one plausible way to construe panentheism is through the continuous and fundamental causal activity of God at every location in the cosmos. This would entail that God is causally active on each and every object in the cosmos, no matter how simple or complex, small or large. I propose that at least one action God performs on the cosmos is to push simple objects into configurations of greater complexity. That is, God acts teleologically on the cosmos to push (or pull) a trajectory of ever-increasing complexity. One could easily overlay this story onto an evolutionary narrative whereby the history of the cosmos includes the emergence of ever increasingly complex animals and systems, presently culminating in humans as the most systematically complex entities in the cosmos (so far as we know). On this view, everything is in God because God is in everything causally pushing (or, one might say, teleologically pulling) the fundamental mentality or proto-mentality of all objects toward greater complexity.

However, given the theism of Scripture and the Ecumenical Councils, since God is the fundamental entity, and God is a mental entity, it might seem as though it would be God's mentality that is at the core of every mental-physical object. How can a panpsychist panentheism avoid the entailment that there is only God's mentality in the cosmos and the presence of non-divine mentality is merely an illusion? What blocks panpsychist panentheism from collapsing into pantheism? I propose that one way to block this entailment is to hold that in order for a system to be identified with an agent, that agent itself must *identify* with the system and take *ownership* of the system as its own. Systems of higher complexity—say, humans—are capable of incorporating systems of lesser complexity into their system. This routinely happens when humans use tools and also occurs in such mundane instances as wearing clothes, eating breakfast, and brushing one's teeth. The incorporation of other objects into one's own human system occurs by means of a causal connection between the agent and the object. When the object is in use by the agent, the object becomes part of the agent's system and—even if for a time—is a constitutive component of a system more complex than itself.

A sycamore tree in my yard has, on the panpsychist proposal, mentality or proto-mentality. If, however, I were to take a branch from the tree, adhere it to my body and utilize it as another leg, that branch would be incorporated into my body. As I had taken ownership of the branch, I could then identify it as part of me and it would indeed become part of my psycho-physical system. In my causal connection to the branch, taking ownership of and identifying with the branch, it would be proper to say of the branch that it is part of me, and that it is me. Conversely, with the cosmos and God, although God is continually acting on each and every object in the cosmos, supplying it with existence, mentality, and pushing it toward greater complexity, God does not identify with or take ownership of each and every object. But were God to do so, then that object would indeed become God. Since God is the source of each and every object in the cosmos, so I propose, God reserves the prerogative to intensify God's causal union with each and every object and take the requisite kind of ownership needed for God to identify Godself—at least in part—with the newly owned object. When God does so, the holiness of the object increases. On this hypothesis, God is continually acting on the created realm. God does this (a) in order to sustain it in existence, (b) to provide the mental component that is paired with the physical as is necessary in the panpsychic worldview, and (c) to push the creation "upwards" into greater complexities of macroexperience, culminating in human beings. When fusing this view with traditional Christology, we arrive at one particular human being on whom this activity reached a unique height, the height of Incarnation.

## PANPSYCHIST PANENTHEISTIC CHRISTOLOGY

Traditional Christology has it that the phenomenal experience had by Christ was and is had by God. In fact, this statement is a tautology for the one who accepts Conciliar Christology. A panpsychist panentheism opens up the conceptual space to show how God could take on the consciousness of any component of the cosmos. There is no requirement that God take on the experiences—micro or macro—as God's own of the cosmos. But there is no prohibition either. Demurring from a Thomist *actus purus* conception of God, God is free to act as much or as little as God likes in any given situation. Because of the radical dependence relation of the creation on the creator, God could simply cease acting on some segment or other of the cosmos and it would cease to exist. However, conversely, God is able to intensify God's actions as well, by means of a greater concentration of divine attention or focus at a particular location. And this intensity could reach the point at which God even took on the phenomenal experiences of some complex segment of the cosmos as God's own. This, we might say, would be a divine incarnation. And if it were to occur by way of a complex segment of the cosmos that meets the necessary and sufficient conditions for being human, this would be a divine-human incarnation. When we say that a divine-human incarnation has in fact occurred in the person of Jesus Christ, then we have finally arrived at the Incarnation of Christian teaching.

Within the contemporary analytic literature on Christology, this would be an additionalist model of the Incarnation. God could add on any segment of the cosmos as God likes in this incarnational manner. God does not need to transform into some segment of the cosmos, but nor does it need to be said that God merely becomes related to some segment of the cosmos. Rather, the additionalist conception of Christology has it that God adds on the phenomenal perspective of the human nature of Christ. Moreover, the additionalist

Christological motif might in some way even parallel how the panentheist tends to think of the relation between God and the cosmos. We might say that God adds on the cosmos to Godself, within Godself. Just as the second person of the Trinity additionally becomes human, so too at creation does God additionally include the cosmos. Consequently, we have a harmonious conceptual framework for thinking of both the divine-cosmos relationship and the relationship between the divine and human natures in Christ.

Here, then, is a panpsychist panentheistic just-so story of the Incarnation: God, from Godself, creates the cosmos and continually exercises causal power on each and every object in the cosmos. These created entities are mental/physical hybrids, which are ontologically dependent on the causal power supplied to them by God. The microexperiences of the most simple objects can join together to form macroexperiences when the simple objects are joined up into a system of greater complexity. Such is, then, the emergence of human consciousness as a complex system. As the ontologically highest entity in which the cosmos has its being, God has the fundamental right to take ownership of each and every object and identify its phenomenal experiences as God's own. God does this by intensifying God's causal power exercised at the location of an object. God is present by causal power, and hence God can be more present by causal power, by causing the physical objects to move in specific ways or causing a greater influence on those objects. If God were to intensify God's causal power at a location to the point of taking ownership of the object at that location, that object would become God. This could happen with as simple or as complex a system as God likes. This has occurred in the person of Jesus Christ. God has added on the complex human system with its attendant macroexperiences that is the human nature born of the Virgin Mary. That object, the human nature born of the Virgin, remains a human nature despite its incorporation into the divine in a unique way. But the incorporation that is incarnation also makes it such that it is proper to point to Jesus Christ and say, "This is God" in a manner inapt for other objects in the cosmos. Hence, it could be said on this model that the panentheistic God has become incarnate in the panpsychist complex that is the human nature of Jesus Christ. Jesus Christ is holy because God added on the human nature of Christ. God was always in us, as we are always in God, but in the Incarnation God became *with* us, as God became one of us, in Emmanuel.

## A PANPSYCHIST PANENTHEISTIC INCARNATIONAL MODEL OF THE EUCHARIST

With a brief account of the Incarnation within a panpsychist panentheism in place, we can finally apply all the preceding data points to the Eucharist. In the Eucharist, God is not just with us in a general causal sense; God is with us in a specific sense in the consecrated bread and wine. As indicated previously, I find the impanation view the most satisfying for a variety of reasons, not the least of which is the manner it comports with incarnational thinking. This is what will be expounded here. However, there are at least two routes by which one might apply the preceding to the issue of the presence of Christ in the Eucharist. Elsewhere I have called versions of these two routes "Hypostatic Impanation" or "Type-H Impanation" and "Sacramental Impanation" or "Type-S Impanation."[17] Since I have not heretofore systematically deployed the terms "hypostatic" or "sacramental," I will use "Type-H" and "Type-S" for convenience. I will here describe each view in kind and then offer a brief assessment.

## Type-H Impanation

Above I sketched the notion that God has the ultimate prerogative to take ownership of any segment of the cosmos and identify it as God's own self. God does not do this in order to preserve the distinction of (most) of the cosmos (save Christ) from Godself and thus not entail pantheism. Yet, this is just what the second person of the Trinity does in the Incarnation. God intensifies God's causal activity at the location of the human nature of Jesus Christ, takes ownership of it, and identifies with it such that it warrants the predication, "This is God" when spoken of Christ.

The same situation could apply to consecrated bread and wine and this is just what Type-H avers occurs in the Eucharist. Through the second person of the Trinity, God intensifies God's causal activity at the location of the bread and wine, takes ownership of it, and identifies with these objects. God would then take ownership of the phenomenal perspective offered by these objects, and this perspective would become God's perspective. This might be termed another incarnation of God in another location in the cosmos. The structure and relative complexity (or relative simplicity) of the bread and wine would dictate what God could do with the bread and wine. A human body, like what God adds on in the Incarnation, is a complex system that would allow God to walk, talk, eat, sleep, and do all manner of human activities as a human being. Bread and wine have no such complexity, nor potential actions. Nevertheless, this model grounds the traditional Christian notion that God is specially present in the consecrated bread and wine of the Eucharist.

## Type-S Impanation

The Type-S theorist worries, however, that the Type-H view circumvents the human nature of Christ. On the Type-H view, God can intensify God's presence at any and every consecration. But this happens only on an analogy with the Incarnation, not because of or related to the Incarnation. Type-H seems to result in predications of the consecrated objects like, "This is bread" or "This is God" or even "This is the body of God." But it depends on what one means by "Christ" whether Type-H is able to deliver on the Scriptural and liturgical utterance, "This is the body of Christ." If one took "Christ" to refer to the specific instance of Incarnation that is the adding on of the human nature of Christ's phenomenal experiences to God, then Type-H would not supply the metaphysical story for the state of affairs expressed by "This is the body of Christ," but Type-S would.

Type-S wishes to draw a specific connection between the human nature of Christ and the consecrated bread and wine. How would this work? God would need to conjoin the microexperiences had by the bread and the wine to the system that is the human nature of Christ. Christ's human nature, then, would be extended beyond the bounds of its organic human body to include objects non-organically connected to his human body.[18] Despite these objects' distance from the human body of Christ, they would nonetheless be joined by divine power to the human phenomenal experience of Christ. As the human body just is the locus of human phenomenal experience, then these objects would properly be considered parts of the human body of Christ. This would, of course, then sanction the liturgical utterance made of the consecrated bread, "This is the body of Christ."

The symmetry of this model with my illustration of the sycamore tree branch above should be clear. The consecrated bread and the wine become instruments or tools of the human nature of Christ. In this manner, as in other instances of bodily extension or prosthesis use, the instruments become parts of the body of Christ and are aptly named as such. The distinction, however, between the Type-S explication of Eucharist and the sycamore branch illustration is the lack of physical contiguity between the consecrated elements and the human nature of Christ. However, I do not see the lack of physical contiguity as an obstacle for the view. Given a panpsychist and panentheistic framework, God merely needs to conjoin the phenomenality of the consecrated elements to the phenomenality of Christ's human nature. This fusion of mentality or proto-mentality of seemingly discontinuous objects, then, fuses the objects themselves. When this conjunction is instantiated and a causal connection between Christ and the consecrated elements occurs by means of this conjunction, the liturgical utterance is warranted: *this*—this bread—is the body of Christ.

## Assessment of Both Views

Both of these impanation theories are able to deliver on a concentration of God's presence at the location of the consecrated bread and wine. Both, in different senses, would be able to deliver on the conception of the bread and wine being the body of God. Type-S is to be preferred, however, if one holds "Christ" to be a specialized term denoting *only* the incarnate activity of the Second Person of the Trinity in the human nature of Christ. If one is attempting to draw a tight connection between the historical body of Christ (born of the Virgin, suffered under Pontius Pilate, raised on the third day, etc.), then, for my money, Type-S is the preferred route. However, Type-H is not without merit and is worthy of consideration. Here I simply raise two other brief considerations.

First, one might wonder whether having the phenomenal experiences of consecrated bread and wine would entail feeling great pain at being chewed and digested. However, there should be no worries about Christ feeling the pain of being manducated. The sensation of pain—so far as we understand it—requires a much more complex configuration of matter than we see in the combination of flour, water, yeast, oil, and salt. The human body that the second person of the Trinity assumed at the Incarnation provided an appropriately complex configuration of matter such that in virtue of his human nature Christ did feel the pain of the Passion. But there is no requirement on the present Eucharistic model—or any model of impanation—that Christ feel pain by way of the faithful's teeth. Bread and wine just cannot supply that kind of phenomenal experience as an actual human body can.

Second, given the incorporation of the bread and wine into the body of Christ, does the bread and wine cease to be bread and wine? That is, do the impanation models I have sketched collapse into transubstantiation? From one angle, I see no reason the transubstantiation theorists could not help themselves to much of what I have described as impanation within a panpsychist panentheistic incarnational framework. They too could argue that the predication "this is the body of Christ" is apt due to the requisite concentration of divine activity that "elevates" the microexperiences of the elements to a sufficiently high level. However, at this point in the analysis it does not seem that the distinction between transubstantiation and impanation can be made on the basis of philosophical reasoning alone. Rather the transubstantiation theorist will assert the determinations of the Roman Catholic magisterium to say that we may no longer call the consecrated object "bread" post-consecration. On the contrary, the impanation theorist will aver that the theo-logic of the Incarnation that provides the metaphysical infrastructure for the aptness of the predication pushes the faithful to maintain the reality of the bread in the same way as Christ is both God and a human being. The dispute here, to me, seems intractable and one will simply have to choose whether they will choose the conception of their ancestors, or the view of those in whose land they dwell. But as for me and my house, we will choose a version of impanation.

## CONCLUSION

Panentheism—even deflationary panentheism—teaches that God is in us insofar as we and all things are in God. Christianity teaches Emmanuel, that God is with us in the person of Jesus Christ. The Eucharist has long been held to be a unique way that God is with humanity. Hence, as indicated from the outset, this progression from panentheism to Incarnation to Eucharist indicates an ever concretizing and ever localizing experience of God's presence with humans. Although in some sense any view of the divine that includes the attribute of omnipresence entails the possibility of encounters with God anywhere, Christian teaching has it that the Eucharist is a direct encounter with God; the Eucharist is literally an instance of Emmanuel, of God with us. This essay has sketched how this might be said to be so within a panpsychist panentheism. It should not be forgotten, however, that in addition to making it such that God is with us, the Eucharist is intended by Christ to be consumed by the faithful. Thus, the Eucharist becomes a unique way that—even as we are in God—God is in us.

This has profound implications for how we think about holiness, on the ownership model of holiness. God has ultimate ownership of all that is in the cosmos in virtue of God both being the creator of the universe and being that from which the universe came. God also acts at all locations in the cosmos, minimally simply keeping them in existence. In certain instances, God intensifies God's causal activity and takes greater ownership over certain objects of the cosmos. This entails a greater holiness of those objects. The human nature of Christ is one such object. Indeed, given the level of intimacy between God and the human nature of Christ—the hypostatic union which in fact identifies God with Christ—on this model, Christ is the holiest object in the cosmos. But, moreover, a Corporeal Model of the Eucharist holds that the bread and wine of the Eucharist are Christ's body and blood. This requires a similar, if derivative, divine causal activity as occurs in the Incarnation. Hence, this state of affairs results in the profound holiness of the elements of the Eucharist as well.

## NOTES

1. On the distinction and relation of fine-grained and thick-grained explanations in theology, see Arcadi, *An Incarnational Model of the Eucharist*, pp. 148–152.
2. What has been called in the recent analytic theological literature, "Conciliar Christology." See Timothy Pawl, *In Defense of Conciliar Christology: A Philosophical Essay* (Oxford: Oxford University Press, 2016).
3. This terminology will be explicated further on and is derived from James M. Arcadi, "Recent philosophical work on the Eucharist," *Philosophy Compass* 11.7 (2016): 402–412. For a discussion of models of the Eucharist within an idealist ontological framework—and hence, support for the claim that one may realize at least one aspect of the traditional teaching of Christian theology within different ontological frameworks—see James M. Arcadi, "Idealism and participating in the body of Christ," in *Idealism and Christian Theology*, eds. James Spiegel, Joshua R. Farris, and S. Mark Hamilton (New York: Bloomsbury Academic, 2016), pp. 197–215.
4. The most relevant Scriptural pericopes are: Matthew 26:26–28, Mark 14:22–25, Luke 22:17–20, I Corinthians 11:23–26.
5. Specific communions that tend, either implicitly or explicitly, to endorse proposals in this family are the Eastern Orthodox, Roman Catholic, Lutheran, and some Anglican traditions.
6. Representative examples from the traditions of views falling in this family are the Reformed theological descendants of John Calvin, some Anglicans, and some Methodist theological descendants of John Wesley. It is a point of dispute in the history of interpretation, but I would place views inspired by the 20th century Roman Catholic theologian Edward Schillebeeckx in this latter category as well. An application of this view to discussion of human holiness forms the basis of chapter 7.
7. This view is largely found among the theological descendants of Ulrich Zwingli including—but not limited to—Baptistic, Pentecostal, and Free Church traditions.
8. As the traditional Lutheran quip goes.
9. This is, of course, absent the constraints of the official teaching of the Roman Catholic magisterium.
10. I will here focus on the bread and the body of Christ; a similar analysis applies, *mutatis mutandis*, for the wine and the blood of Christ.
11. Of course, modifying Aristotelian substance ontology is just what the medieval schoolmen did. See Marilyn McCord Adams, *Some Later Medieval Theories of the Eucharist: Thomas Aquinas, Giles of Rome, Duns Scotus, and William Ockham* (Oxford: Oxford University Press, 2010). Again, my purpose is not to show the necessary falsity of non-impanation views, but rather to show that there are more attractive features to this view in just those places where others are less attractive.
12. Sarah Coakley, "What Does Chalcedon Solve and What Does It Not? Some Reflections on the Status and Meaning of the Chalcedonian 'Definition,'" in *The Incarnation: An Interdisciplinary Symposium on the Incarnation of the Son of God*, eds. Stephen T. Davis, Daniel Kendall, and Gerald O'Collins (Oxford: Oxford University Press, 2002), p. 143.

13. Jonathan Hill, "Introduction," in *The Metaphysics of the Incarnation*, eds. Jonathan Hill and Anna Marmodoro (Oxford: Oxford University Press, 2011), p. 8.

14. The notion of the second person of the Trinity extending beyond the human nature sometimes falls under the doctrinal heading of the (somewhat anachronistically termed) *extra Calvinisticum*. For a helpful historical theological examination of this doctrine, see, Andrew M. McGinnis, *The Son of God Beyond the Flesh: A Historical and Theological Study of the* extra Calvinisticum, T&T Clark Studies in Systematic Theology vol. 29 (London & New York: T&T Clark, 2014).

15. See discussion in James M. Arcadi, "Recent developments in analytic Christology," *Philosophy Compass* 13.4 (2018): 1–12.

16. For discussion and introduction, see Godehard Brüntrup and Ludwig Jaskolla, eds., *Panpsychism: Contemporary Perspectives* (New York: Oxford University Press, 2017).

17. See Arcadi, *An Incarnational Model of the Eucharist* and James M. Arcadi, "Impanation, incarnation, and enabling externalism," *Religious Studies* 51.1 (2015): 75–90.

18. This might seem a stretch, but the literature on the Extended Mind Thesis (EMT) is now vast and has obvious points of contact with the narrative adduced here.

*Chapter 4*

# God the Holy Person

The Holy God's relationship to the cosmos is, as noted, a challenging conceptual area. The last two chapters explored this relationship in conversation with two, shall we say, less than typical ideologies. Both panentheism and panpsychism refer to particular ways of conceiving of the relationship between spirit and matter, mind and body, God and cosmos. Panentheism in particular has gained traction in recent literature as proffering a more intimate connection between God and cosmos than—it is alleged—the classical theist's perspective on this relation (or lack thereof). Moreover, it might seem that taking God's holiness as a guiding attribute could lead one to prefer a version of panentheism to more classical or traditional ways of modeling the God-world relation. Yet, even as panentheism might appear to bring God more near to us humans, the other side of the panentheist coin might be to make God appear much less like us. This is because these panentheistic reflections on God's holiness might seem to make God much less personable, perhaps more mechanical like a natural law, perhaps not even a person at all. Granted the panentheist might wish not to reduce God to an impersonal force or mere cosmic causal power, but this conceptual trajectory is discernable and ought not be brushed aside. In what follows in this chapter, I continue to explore the implications of the holiness of God, specifically as it pertains to the relation between God's holiness and God's personhood.[1] Rather than seeing an emphasis on God's holiness lead in a depersonalizing direction, the holiness of God gives us good reason to think that God is in fact a person.

## INTRODUCTION

God, religion and philosophy tell us, is both similar to and different from the persons we know best, human persons. Anselmianism tells us that God has those attributes it is better to have than not to have and that God has them to the maximal amount—or at least the maximal compossible amount. So, since it is said that it is good to be able to exercise some power or ability, then God would be all-powerful or omnipotent. It is said that it is good to know some things, then God would know all things or be omniscient. It is said that it is good to be in some places, then God would be in all places or omnipresent. Although finite and limited in a manner God is not, humans possess some of these goods as well. It does not seem possible for a finite mortal human to be omnipotent, but humans have some power or abilities. The human brain is a wonder, full of potential, but does not seem able to know all things, yet humans do know some things. And while human bodies are limited in size and location, and thus are not omnipresent, human bodies are in some places. In this regard, there are similar attributes that the persons we know best share with God, even while there are great differences in the amount or extent of these similar attributes when comparing humans to God. Moreover, the Judeo-Christian tradition following Genesis 1 further undergirds the notion that there are similarities between God and the persons we know best. Genesis 1:27 describes God as making humans "in the image of God" and, in fact, Genesis 1:26 states God's desire to make humans in the image and, indeed, *likeness* of God.[2] If these words are a reliable indicator of reality—which traditional Christians take them to be—then we have good grounds for thinking that there are at least some similarities between God and humans.

## God as a Person?

The proposition *that God is a person* is the topic under examination in this chapter. God's personhood is often taken for granted in theistic circles. For, is it better to be a person or not a person? God's personhood might be seen to follow easily from Anselmianism. Yet, it is also admitted that God is surely a different kind of person than the persons we encounter in our friends, families, and neighbors. This similarity and difference is what gives rise to the investigation in the first place. Humans tend to point to themselves and/or other humans as paradigm examples of what entities fall into the category of *person*. When humans who consider ourselves persons encounter other humans, we have no difficulty in attributing sameness to these other humans, at least sameness that rises to the level of thinking that these others are also persons like ourselves. This attribution of personhood to other humans occurs even when we encounter humans that we recognize have a great degree of difference from ourselves. These differences might be physical, emotional, behavioral, or otherwise, yet these differences—on the whole or for the most part—do not cause us to question the status of other humans as persons. More limit cases arise when we consider the similarities and differences between ourselves and other occupants of the cosmos. A wax statue of myself would exemplify a good many superficial physical similarities. Yet, only a moment's investigation would show that the differences between a wax statue of myself and the person I know best are so great as to determine decisively that the statue is not a person. Certain animals, apes or dolphins for instance, exhibit several behavioral traits that serve to differentiate them from other animals and also show them to be similar to the persons we know best. Yet again, despite some behavioral similarities, the behavioral (not to mention physical, emotional, and cognitive) differences between these animals and ourselves lead most to conclude that these animals are not persons. This is even as we might agree that their similarities to persons go far beyond the similarities to a person that a wax statue exemplifies. Whether the similarities between humans and God extend to the point of holding that God, like humans, is to be credited with the status of being a person is, as mentioned, the topic of this chapter.

## God as Holy?

The proposition *that God is holy*, as we have seen, is a hallmark component of the major monotheistic religions of the world. My previous comments in this volume have shown that this proposition is very secure as a core component of the Scriptural conception of God. Recall, once more, a scene such as Isaiah's vision. During this vision, the prophet sees God seated on a throne in a high and exalted state. Around this visual manifestation of God are the seraphim who call to one another:

> Holy, holy, holy is the Lord Almighty;
> the whole earth is full of his glory.[3]

God is here described as not just holy, but thrice holy. This same predication is made by the four living creatures in the apocalyptic vision of St John:

> Holy, holy, holy,
> the Lord God the Almighty,
> who was and is and is to come.[4]

These Scriptural allusions are also referenced weekly in the service of Holy Communion for those Christians that include the *Sanctus* as part of their liturgical tradition.

> Holy, holy, holy, Lord God of power and might,
>     heaven and earth are full of your glory.
> Hosanna in the highest.
> Blessed is he who comes in the name of the Lord.
> Hosanna in the highest.

Hence, *that God is holy* seems to be a proposition on solid ground as being an important feature of God.

## The Task of This Chapter

I have argued that analytic theology—of which I take this monograph to be an instance—can follow the lead of one of its theological ancestors from the fourteenth century known as declarative theology.[5] One of the tasks for the declarative theologian is to attempt to make clear some of those aspects of the faith that are opaque or unclear by means of those things that are more clear. For instance, the doctrine of divine simplicity might be an article of faith the content of which is challenging to understand, but the unity of God—as described in the *Shema* of Deuteronomy 6:4—is a bit more easy to understand. The declarative theologian might show how one can move from the unity of God to the simplicity of God as that theologian helps the faithful move from more clear and more easy to understand to less clear and less easy to understand issues of the faith.

Hence, in this chapter, I offer two arguments for the personhood of God that take as a key premise the proposition *that God is holy*. The hope here is that by thinking about a more clear or easier to grasp notion like the holiness of God we will be able to shed conceptual light on a less clear or more challenging notion like the personhood of God. The first argument for the personhood of God arises from the conjunction of the premise *that God is holy* and a certain understanding of the unitive feature of the holiness of God. If we understand the kind of unity sketched in a unitive understanding of holiness as being of the highest kind for persons like humans, then I would argue that the highest kind of unity is that between persons and indeed God would need to be a person in order to be a participant in such a unification. To make this case, I draw on the recent work in the analytic theological literature, first on divine holiness from Mark Murphy and, second, on the union of persons from Eleonore Stump. The second argument for God's personhood comes from an explication of one aspect of the ethical pole of the holiness conceptual range. If God's holiness is to entail some ethical considerations that have bearing on human ethics, then, so the argument goes, God must be a person. For this case, I draw on the reflections on the ethics of holiness by Alan Mittleman. In this next section, I will engage with Murphy's discussion of holiness that attempts to be an explication and expansion of the groundbreaking work on holiness from the classic text, *The Idea of the Holy* by Rudolf Otto.

## MURPHY'S OTTOIAN ACCOUNT OF HOLINESS

Although I do not share exactly the same view of holiness as Mark Murphy, he has presented a creative and sophisticated discussion of holiness, both as a divine attribute and as found in other entities. The former Murphy refers to as "primary holiness," while the latter is correspondingly termed "secondary holiness." In this manner, Murphy, like myself and many other commentators, wishes to see the holiness of humans, objects, times, or any created entity as derivative from the holiness that is properly predicated of God. For Murphy, God alone is holy in Godself and any other apt candidate for that predicate is such because of a relationship to or with God. For our purposes here, we are interested in how assenting to the aptness of predicating the attribute of holiness of God might lead us also to endorse God's status as a person.

Otto and Murphy adopt something of a phenomenological approach to the study of holiness. In this regard, they attempt to describe holiness as that which evokes a particular attitudinal response in us humans. This is a daunting task for the very entity that they are trying to describe, God, is so very unlike us humans. Murphy alludes to this when he references Marilyn McCord Adam's description of the "metaphysical size gap" between God and humans,[6] but what I think this refers to, in more properly theological terms, is the creator-creature distinction. Quite simply, God is God and humans are not. Humans are instances of creation; God is the creator. This presents an inevitable—and perhaps necessary—distinction, distance, and divide between God and humanity, indeed between God and any instance of creation. Call it a metaphysical size gap, a conceptual glass ceiling, a Kantian divide, or what have you, God cannot be reached by the human from the human's own powers alone. Yet, for Otto, it is clear that we are not left adrift without any hope of intimacy with God, for God has reached across the divide in creation, in divine activity, and, in a proto-charismatic move, through the Spirit we term Holy.

This is what we measure by our senses of the holy, our premonitions, our insights, even our fears. Otto takes seriously the *feelings* humans have when they are in certain spaces or at certain times. Here is Otto describing an angle into his methodology early in his text:

> It will be our endeavor to suggest this unnamed Something to the reader as far as we may, so that he (*sic*) may himself *feel* it. There is no religion in which it does not live as the real innermost core, and without it no religion would be worthy of the name. It is pre-eminently a living force in the Semitic religions, and of these again in none has it such vigour as in that of the Bible. Here, too, it has a name of its own, viz. the Hebrew *qādôsh*, to which the Greek ἅγιος and the Latin *sanctus*, and, more accurately still, *sacer*, are the corresponding terms

[. . .] And we then use the word "holy" to translate them. But this "holy" then represents the gradual shaping and filling in with ethical meaning, or what we shall call the "schematization," of what was a unique original *feeling-response*, which can be in itself ethically neutral and claims consideration in its own right.[7]

For Otto, as for Murphy who follows him, there is some sort of affective response, a feeling that humans have evoked in them when they are in the presence of the holy that is due to being in the presence of the holy. For Otto, this is a transcultural and trans-religious feeling. Although he here in this quotation describes the "Semitic religions," by the languages used I take it that he means Judaism and Christianity, Otto sees this feeling manifested throughout the human experience. For Otto, all humans at times have the sense or feeling that they are in the presence of the Holy. The task of the holiness theorist is to draw out from that feeling something of the nature of the one that evokes it.

If I might be allowed a brief literary interlude, I think three characters in Charles Williams' novel *Descent into Hell* share an exchange that well captures the motive for a phenomenological approach to the study of holiness in an Ottoian vein. This scene includes two young women, Miss Fox and Pauline, and an older man, Mr. Stanhope:

> "Nature's so terribly good. Don't you think so, Mr. Stanhope?"
> . . .
> "that Nature is terribly good? Yes, Miss Fox. You do mean 'terribly'?"
> "Why, certainly," Miss Fox said, "Terribly—dreadfully—very."
> "Yes," Stanhope said again. "Very. Only—you must forgive me; it comes from doing so much writing, but when I say 'terribly' I think I mean 'full of terror.' A dreadful goodness."
> "I don't see how goodness can be dreadful," Miss Fox said, with a shade of resentment in her voice. "If things are good they're not terrifying, are they?"
> "It was you who said 'terribly,'" Stanhope reminded her with a smile, "I only agreed."
> "And if things are terrifying," Pauline put it, her eyes half-closed and her head turned away as if she asked a casual question rather of the world than of him, "can they be good?"
> He looked down on her. "Yes, surely," he said with more energy. "Are our tremors to measure the Omnipotence?"[8]

At this point, the conversation is abruptly interrupted. I interpret this move by Williams to highlight the importance of this last question for the characters in the novel, a question the rest of the novel goes on to answer in the affirmative. Or at least so I think. For Stanhope here, and nascently for Pauline, the goodness inherent in nature is derived from the creator of nature, the "Omnipotence." As such, nature is, say, charged with some of the quality of its origin, which is God. But this means that there is something actually *super*natural about the natural world, which can confront the astute observer with a sense of terror or dread. The "tremors" that one at times feels in response to some "natural" phenomenon, for Stanhope, points to the supernatural Other from which all has come. Given the fact that humans are creatures, it stands to reason that humans might feel this terror or dread or simple otherness when presented with such stimuli. The phenomenology of the experience of otherness is precisely the foundation on which Otto and Murphy erect their theories of holiness.

The key Ottoian concept that Murphy uses as the north star of his discussion of the holiness of God is that God's holiness is the "*mysterium tremendum et fascinans*."[9] Holiness is that mysterious quality of God that provokes in humans a two-fold response: (1) a desire for the holy (the *fascinans*) and (2) a sense of one's unfitness for the holy (the *tremendum*). For Murphy, the *fascinans* aspect of the holy connotes that it is attractive or desirable, and the perceiver of the holy sees it as a great good that the perceiver be related to the one who is holy. This, however, is tempered by the realization that the ones who see the one who is holy see themselves as profoundly unfit to be related to the one who is holy—the *tremendum* aspect of the formula.[10] This arresting paradox is at the heart of the phenomenology of holiness. Humans both want the holy and feel unfit to have the holy. I wish here to focus on the *fascinans* feature—the attractive or desirable—in the concept of holiness.

God's holiness is *fascinans* on this Ottoian/Murphian conception. As Murphy puts it, "to experience something as holy is to experience it as something a certain sort of relationship with which is exceedingly desirable for one."[11] As with Stanhope's sentiments described above, although the "Omnipotence" induces terror in humans this is because it is "terribly good." A good is, minimally, some such thing that one desires, something that attracts. A good is likely more than that and it might be the case that one might not desire what one ought, but—on the whole or for the most part—goods are those things that serve as the object of one's desires. For Otto, corroborating Stanhope, the holy "may appear to the mind an object of horror and dread, but at the same time it is no less something that allures with a potent charm, and the creature, who trembles before it . . . has always at the same time the impulse to turn to it, nay even to make it somehow his own."[12] So, for Murphy characterizing the Ottoian "feeling-response," to feel that something is holy is to feel it as something with which one wishes to have a relationship.

Of course, we are not talking about some kind of mundane relationship that is the subject here. The "potent charm" of the holy causes one to "turn to it" and even, as Otto puts it, "make it somehow his own." On the Ottoian/Murphian framework, the holy attracts, causes one to wish to draw near, causes one to wish for deeper and deeper relationships with the holy. As

Murphy describes, "The relationships in question are, pretty plainly, those of *unity* with the holy being."[13] The holy is that which is *fascinans* for humans: attractive, desirable, and that with which humans desire to unite.

## UNITY RELATIONS

For Murphy's Otto-inspired account of God's holiness, God's holiness is such that humans have a deep desire for unification with God that is provoked by this attribute. This is even as humans also have almost an aversion to unification because of their sense of their own unworthiness for said unification. But, what kind of union are we talking about with respect to this desired union between humans and the holy God? What are the conditions needed in order for such a union to obtain?

We can see union relations in many aspects of our normal experience. When the artist dips a paintbrush in paint and sweeps it across the canvas, there is a union of paint and canvas. Or we might observe that there are relations of union between humans and non-human entities. For instance, suppose when surfing I wish to carve a wave while remaining on the surfboard. I might in this instance desire a physical union with the board, a connection between feet and board facilitated by wax. The good of carving the wave is here achieved by actualizing the good of uniting with the board. Moreover, we see varying levels and kinds of union relations obtaining between humans and other humans in friendship, family, work, sport, and all the many other human-to-human relationships in which we find ourselves.

Since both Otto and Murphy begin with the phenomenology of *human* experience, and it is indeed this *human* feeling that gives rise to the categorization of the feeling stimulus as "holy," then we already have insight into one *relata* of the holy-to-human relation of unity. Whatever "the holy" is, we know a few things about the human side of the relation. And at least one thing we know about humans is that humans are persons. Hence, any relation between a human and another entity will minimally be a relation of the category "person-to-X" where X might be a person or might not. We could categorize various instances of union relations as follows:

- **Non-personal union**: a union between two non-personal entities: $X \cup Y$ (e.g. paint and a canvas)
- **Personal union**: a union between two entities one of which is a person: $P \cup X$ (e.g. James and a surfboard)
- **Person-to-person union**: a union between two (or more) entities both (or all) of which are persons: $P_1 \cup P_2$ (e.g. James and Francisco)

- **Human union**: a union between two entities one of which is a human: H ∪ X (e.g. James and a surfboard)

Human unions are a subcategory of personal unions, for all humans are persons, so we can specify:

P(H) ∪ X (e.g. James and a surfboard)

Human-to-human unions are also instances of person-to-person unions. The pressing question for this chapter is under what category does the union between a human and the holy God fall? Is this a mere personal union (perhaps denoted as P(H) ∪ G) or a person-to-person union (perhaps denoted as P(H) ∪ P(G))? I contend that person-to-person relations of unity are the highest kinds of unions for human persons and hence it stands to reason that God too is a person.[14]

## UNITING WITH PERSONS

Why think that the highest or deepest kinds of union relations that human persons can have are with other persons? Are there not many entities with which a human could unite? The imagination could run wild populating answers to this question with any number of items in the cosmos. I could have a union relation with my chair, my shirt, the Río de la Plata, the Milky Way galaxy, my dog, my colleague down the hall, etc. But which of these union relations can be the most unifying, deepest, or most intimate? My intuition is that the most intimate union relations I as a human person can have are with other persons. My suspicion is that the basis for this intuition lies in the potential for a mutually reciprocal dynamic that can occur between persons, which is not available in person-to-non-person union relations.

For, suppose I mount a surfboard, paddle out on the Pacific coast, and catch a wave. During these actions, I would form a relation of physical unity with the board. This, of course, is a momentary unity, easily concluded by my losing my balance. Yet, for the purposes of riding a wave, my body would form a unity with the board such that we might even consider the board becoming an extension of my body. This unity relation, however, seems less intimate than the kind of unity I might form with my dog. My dog can sit on my lap, forming another instance of a physical relation of unity. But my dog and I can also have some semblance of reciprocity in our relationship. I can offer a treat and say, "sit." He responds by sitting (most of the time) and then I in turn reciprocate by giving him the treat. My dog's responsive interactivity creates a dynamic wherein there is potential for deepening our union beyond what was available between my body and an inanimate object like a surfboard. It strikes me that the greater level or potential level of reciprocity available in a relation of union, then the greater potential for intimacy in that union. Since persons seem best able to offer reciprocity with other persons, it would seem that the most intimate relations of union that persons can have are with other persons. In order to deepen this observation, I turn in the next section to probe Eleonore Stump's reflections on the nature of personal unions.

## A Stumpian Account of Personal Union

Over two monumental volumes, Eleonore Stump has made significant contributions to the Christian understanding of suffering and of the atonement. *Wandering in Darkness: Narrative and the Problem of Suffering* presents her angle on an aspect of the Scriptural response to the problem of evil, while her *Atonement* is her theory of that central Christian doctrine.[15] Along the way, she offers keen insight into such perennial areas of the nature of our knowledge of other persons, the nature of guilt, and the nature of love. Under the latter heading is where she develops a Thomistic-inspired account of love whose discussion of union is particularly apropos for filling in the union aspect of the Ottoian/Murphian conception of the *fascinans* component of holiness.

On Stump's Thomist theory of love, love consists of two desires: (1) the desire for the good of the beloved and (2) the desire for union with the beloved.[16] My interest is in the second desire as it is parallel to the *fascinans* aspect of the nature of holiness.[17] For Stump, the relation of union requisite for satisfying the desire of love is one that will be characterized by "closeness" and "presence."[18] A component-like presence might be problematized by the immateriality of God, an attribute supposed in most traditional accounts of God.[19] However, physical proximity is but one way for entities to be present to one another. In fact, for human persons, physical proximity is neither a guarantee of union nor a necessary prohibition of union. I can feel a great sense of absence from another person even if that person is in the same room if that person is aloof or engaged in other activities. Or I can feel a great sense of union with, say, a family member on the other side of the country were we to be speaking on the phone or videoconferencing. Rather, presence and closeness refer to the manner in which persons open their thoughts, feelings, and experiences to one another in acts of unifying reciprocity. These instances of revelatory openness seem only available to persons who have minds and wills that can be shared with other persons.

Regarding closeness, Stump states that it is clear this can come in degrees, and it requires "openness of mind of one person to another."[20] Her discussion centers on psychological studies of joint and shared attention, and specifically acts of empathy whereby an individual comes literally to feel similar emotional states of another. When a friend is injured, we wince and share a similar emotional response as though we ourselves endured the injury. This kind of empathetic response to the emotional states of another creates a reciprocating dynamic that draws persons together in unity. As I open myself to another and receive the openness of that other, we both feel some of the sameness that begins to overcome our difference. And this is unifying.

## UNITING WITH THE HOLY PERSON

Stump's claim, and mine with her, is that these unifying relational dynamics that occur in human-to-human relationships also play out in human-to-God relationships. From the phenomenological approach of Otto and Murphy we adopt the methodology of attending to the human feelings we have in the presence of the holy. For Otto and Murphy, the Holy God is the most attractive, most desirable, that with which we most want to unite. Given that as persons we can unite best with other persons, and that the Holy God is that with which we can most intimately unite, then God is a person with which we can most intimately unite. But this deepest sense of unification is not unilateral. Rather it requires the reciprocity inherent in closeness. As Stump says, "*Mutual* closeness is necessary for the union desired in love, and so union between God and a human being Jerome requires not only that God be close to Jerome but also that Jerome be close to God."[21] Uniting with the holy entails that we open ourselves to the holy as the Holy has opened Godself to us.

But has this occurred? Has God opened Godself to humans? Christian doctrine, but also an idea in the other Abrahamic traditions, specifically states that God has revealed Godself to humans through creation and Scripture. God's acts in making and sustaining the world are acts of the openness of God, showing God's values, desires, and thoughts (even if these terms are understood analogously). Stump accepts this as well, "insofar as God puts a revelation into history . . . God reveals his mind and will to human beings; and in this respect God meets one of the conditions for allowing human beings to be close to him."[22] This revelation comes through Scripture, and for Christians the Incarnation. But as Stanhope and Pauline were exploring at the outset of this essay, our senses of the Omnipotence come even through the "natural" world, as a revelatory act of the Holy Omnipotence. In this regard, what is needed most for the unification to occur is for humans to pay attention to their "tremors" in order to see these as opportunities for the kind of mutual openness with God that leads to the mutual closeness of unification.

## POTENTIAL OBJECTIONS

I began by noting that when we humans observe other entities we notice sameness and difference. We notice other humans and despite noting the difference between them and us, we acknowledge that they are the same as us in being persons. Likewise with God, we also notice sameness and difference. Like God, we humans have knowledge, but unlike God we do not have all knowledge. I have argued that if we are to hold that God is holy—as it seems we are enjoined to by the Scriptural tradition—then we ought to identify personhood as a feature of sameness between humans and God.

However, could it be that the likeness/difference joint could be carved along another line? Perhaps God is like us in being human, but not a human *person*? This seems to be a dead end. When we say that any representative humans like Francisco and Juan are humans, we take it as analytic that they are also in fact persons. Moreover, when we say that Francisco and Juan are humans, we take it that we are predicating the kind of entity they are. This seems to leave us with three options regarding God, either (a) God is human, and thus a person, (b) God is divine and like us in being a person, or (c) God is divine and not like us in being a person. On this analysis, both (a) and (b) deliver the conclusion that God is a person. Option (c) would only be the case if we either deny that person-to-person union is the highest kind of union for human persons or that the Ottoian/Murphian concept of holiness is inapt in its inclusion of the phenomenon of the desire for union with the holy one.

Could it be that some humans do not have relations of union with God or that they have more intimate relations of union with other persons who are not God? The argument I have proffered does not entail that a human person cannot have a more intimate union with another human person than a human person can have with a divine person. Other humans are both similar to and different from us. We can desire to overcome some of the difference by uniting with them. And it may be that this union is a highly desirable state of affairs. I do not think that the argument need entail that humans do not desire union with other human persons in addition to union with a divine person. Neither would this situation entail that a human person would necessarily hold another human person to be holy. On the Ottoian/Murphian conception in order for an entity to be holy, it must provoke both an apt feeling of a desire for union and an apt feeling of one's unfitness for this union. Such a human-to-human relation would seem to be beyond the pale of psychological health. However, with God, fear or a recognition of one's unworthiness is just the sort of response one might expect if one took God to be transcendent in a manner that aptly characterizes the creator-creature distinction noted earlier. Our tremors are to measure the Omnipotence precisely because the holy one transcends normal means of measurement. This is a great difference, the likes of which are impossible to see in human-to-human relations. So, this argument does not conclude that some humans are more holy than God, even if one's desire for union with a particular human in a particular moment might feel stronger than one's desire for union with the Holy One.

## AN ETHICALLY HOLY PERSON

I have argued that there is both a metaphysical pole and an ethical pole to the semantic ranges of holiness. I would take the preceding reflections to be related to both poles. One could take unification to be a more ethically sided phenomenon. Where, recall, I understand "ethics" in very general and broad sense simply to be referring to the behavior of agents. As humans, the unifying feature of God's having shared attention with us can produce behavioral changes, in a similar manner as peer pressure can produce behavioral changes in young teenagers. When we humans attend together, our actions here influence our behavior. Likewise, *mutatis mutandis*, attending with God can influence our behavior as well. So, we might simply say—if the arguments of this chapter are sound—persons attending together can influence the behavior of persons. Yet, a case could be made that these ethical and behavioral implications of the unifying aspect of God's holiness have metaphysical or ontological entailments. I will explore these entailments further in this book under the heading of sanctification and the indwelling of the Holy Spirit. For current purposes, I am interested in how the ethical pole of holiness might shed light on the personhood of God. In order to do this, I will here relay some of Alan Mittleman's reflections on holiness, some of which strike a familiar tone to Stump's in what he borrows from contemporary evolutionary psychology. First, I offer some contextualizing comments on Mittleman's project as a whole. Then I engage specifically with his comments on holiness and ethics.

### Mittleman on Ethical Holiness

One aspect of Mittleman's theory of holiness is to see holiness as a value of "striving toward an ideal of conduct and character [. . .] a [. . .] project of self- and communal transformation."[23] This aspect of his theory is what brings the discussion of holiness into the realm of the ethical. But to merely identify the holy with the good is a dead end, even as they are entangled. Morality, Mittleman avers, emerges out of the value humans place on the other, especially insofar as this value assignment is conducive to human survival. Although Mittleman sees himself as advocating for a modern naturalist conception of holiness, he does gesture to a something beyond in this project of transformation. The striving of holiness moves humans more deeply, more strongly to pursue the good of the other because holiness tells us that there is a "good beyond our own good."[24] This is a transcendent turn, with its apparent nod to Kant, that endows all creation with an infinite and radiating goodness.

However, following this Kantian move is not necessary to glean resources from Mittleman's theory. Rather what is helpful for our purposes is his grounding holiness as ethics in the relational interplay between humans. As he puts it, "The most fruitful naturalist claim, I should think, is that, in line with our gifts of shared intentionality and empathy, the capacity for cooperation and coordination has tremendous survival value [. . .] Whenever possible, we should opt for cooperation over domination, alliance over aggression."[25] Actions like cooperation and coordination, feelings like empathy and sympathy, all contribute to the ethical project of holiness. Indeed, Mittleman points to the gaze of a mother upon her child, the "cherishing"[26] that is apparent there, as the grounds of this. But more than recognizing the good of her child, the mother-child bond is sacred. For Mittleman, "The fact/value dichotomy collapses in the face of the newborn."[27] Central to the ethical project of holiness is relationality.

On the human level the prospect of our survival depends on our being relationally connected and cooperative with one another. A foal might be able to stand on its own two hours after birth, but human babies cannot forego interdependence quite so easily. Rather ethical action that is motivated by a transcendent pull starts in "shared intentionality . . . the sense that others are like me—they are beings with minds like mine."[28] For Mittleman, the ground and heart of ethical holiness is personal relationality.

## God's Ethical Holiness

Whereas Mittleman leaves his reader with a naturalized conception of the divine—or, at best, the God of the Kantian posit—I am inclined to accept the full reality of the God of Christian theism. This God, then, exists and is a firmer ground for our reflections on the ethics of holiness. While I do think God's reality better motivates human-to-human interactions, God's holiness serves to ground another reality that is the remit of this chapter, God's personhood. God says to God's people, "You shall be holy, for I the Lord your God am holy."[29] This warrants, at least to some extent, comparing the holiness of humans with the holiness of God. It does not seem that an impersonal God would be able to enjoin persons to be ethically holy as God is holy if it were not at least analogously true that God were of some kind of sameness with humans. We have already seen that this sameness ought not apply to the level of nature; if God is a human, then God is a person anyway. Rather, what God and humans share is personhood.

However analogously, God the holy person exemplifies such characteristics as empathy and sympathy, even to the point of, it might be said, cherishing human life. In Psalm 139, David praises God that God discerns the thoughts of humans. Moreover, God knit humans together in the wombs of their mothers. And in Psalm 8 relates that God is mindful of humans even as God is sovereign over all creation. In countless instances in Scripture, God attempts to get humans to share intentionality with God. If the people would turn from other gods, if the people would turn from preoccupation with themselves, if the people would but see things as God sees them, then God would be able to share intention with them. And when the people or individuals do so, their holiness is increased.

God, as I understand God, needs no striving. God is not engaged in a project of self-transformation. This is the static aspect of God's holiness. God is, however, in a project of communal transformation. The "whole communion of saints" is under transformation by being engaged with the presence of God. But God is holy and God's holiness grounds the holiness of the "whole communion." One might even think that the ethical side of the narrative of Scripture is God attempting to get God's people to share attention and intention with Godself. And if the ethical aspects of the holiness of humans is of a variety that pertains to persons, the same applies to God as a person.

## CONCLUSION

God is holy; this much is clear from the Scriptural tradition. This proposition likely has many entailments. Two entailments we have been examining in this chapter relate to the unitive feature of God's holiness and the ethical aspects of holiness. Both of these aspects of holiness have a dynamic relationality to them. From a phenomenological starting point like Otto and Murphy utilize, we see that humans best and most deeply unite with other persons. This seems to entail God's personhood as well. Moreover, attending to the ethical side of holiness shows that human morality has shared intentionality and empathy with other persons at its foundation. God too, in whose holiness humans share, can be seen to exhibit these traits as well.

In this regard, these two entailments seem to coalesce. The unitive and ethical features of God's holiness relate to the manner in which persons are joined with one another. Under the unitive heading alone, this is akin to the manner that persons love one another, on the Stumpian-Thomist perspective. Under the ethical heading, the union that humans have with the other motivates their treating the other with the value and respect that another person deserves—the value and respect that a holy person, in fact, deserves. Whether that is a holy human person or the Holy divine Person, the unions of empathy, sympathy, joint intention, and joint attention draw persons closer to one another. For human-to-human unions, this motivates moral behavior. For the human-to-divine union it motivates moral behavior that accords with the "You shall be holy, for I the Lord your God am holy" utterance of Lev 19:2. Union and ethics join in the holiness of God.

Are our tremors to measure the Omnipotence? Perhaps so, and perhaps especially so when we are confronted with the *tremendum* side of the holiness coin. But, also, are our attractions to measure the Omnipotence? Indeed so if the *fascinans* aspect of the Ottoian/Murphian conception of holiness is apt. Are our joint attentions to measure the Omnipotence? Indeed so if the ethics of God's holiness are worth emulating. We have seen that the Scriptural tradition has given us good grounds for thinking *that God is holy*. This is one of those propositions of religion or philosophical theology that is fairly easy to accept. I have offered the Ottoian/Murphian conception of God's holiness as a reasonable and well-worked through framework for thinking about God's holiness. One key feature of their framework is that "the holy" is something for which humans feel a deep sense of attraction towards. The holy is that which one desires deeply and desires deeply to be united with. But when we think about what humans can be united with, it seems that the highest or deepest kind of unity for human persons is to be achieved with other persons. This is in part due to the component of mutual closeness that is inherent in person-to-person relations of unity. Moreover, to pursue holiness in an ethical key is likewise to be motivated by empathy and shared intentionality. Not only does God exemplify this as we do, but our acting in a holy manner further unifies us with God. This then provides strong motivation for holding to a theological proposition perhaps more difficult to accept, *that God is a person*.

## NOTES

1. The tension between an emphasis on God's holiness and the acceptance of God's status as a person also animated Rudolf Otto in his, "The Supra-personal in the Numinous." For discussion of this essay and a constructive proposal, see Melissa Raphael, *Rudolf Otto and the Concept of Holiness* (Oxford: Clarendon Press, 1997), chap. 4.

2. For reflections on what it means for humans to be in the image of God as it pertains to the human vocation of extending God's holiness, see chapter 5 in this monograph.

3. Isa 6:3.

4. Rev 4:8.

5. Oliver D. Crisp, James M. Arcadi, and Jordan Wessling, *The Nature and Promise of Analytic Theology* (Leiden: Brill, 2019), chap. 2.

6. Murphy, *Divine Holiness*, pp. 43, 112.

7. Rudolf Otto, *The Idea of the Holy: An Inquiry into the non-rational factor in the idea of the divine and its relation to the rational*, tr. John W. Harvey (Oxford: Oxford University Press, 1958), p. 6 (emphasis added).

8. Charles Williams, *Descent into Hell: A Novel* (Grand Rapids: William B. Eerdmans Company, 2002), pp. 16–17.

9. See Murphy, *Divine Holiness*, p. 25ff.

10. See Murphy, *Divine Holiness*, p. 29.

11. Murphy, *Divine Holiness*, p. 31.

12. Otto, *The Idea of the Holy*, p. 31.

13. Murphy, *Divine Holiness*, p. 31.

14. I note in passing that God's personhood is accepted, but not argued for, in Murphy's study, "As the God of Abrahamic theism is, at least analogously, personal, the relationships of unity that we can have with other personal beings are those that seem most relevant to giving an account of holiness," Murphy, *Divine Holiness*, p. 31.

15. Eleonore Stump, *Wandering in Darkness: Narrative and the Problem of Suffering* (Oxford: Clarendon Press, 2010) and *Atonement*, Oxford Studies in Analytic Theology (Oxford: Oxford University Press, 2018).

16. Stump, *Wandering*, p. 91. For another recent study of God's love, see Jordan Wessling, *Love Divine: A Systematic Account of God's Love for Humanity*, Oxford Studies in Analytic Theology (Oxford: Oxford University Press, 2020).

17. N.B. I make no claim here as to the relation between love and holiness. Clearly, traditional Christianity holds both *that God is love* (1 John 4:8) and *that God is holy* (Isaiah 6:3). But whether those predications entail something on the order of *that love is holy* or *that the holiest one is the most loving/lovable one*, is an idea I only gesture at here.

18. Stump, *Wandering*, p. 110.

19. For my view on how an immaterial God can be present at all locations see Arcadi, *An Incarnational Model of the Eucharist*, pp. 85–100.

20. Stump, *Atonement*, pp. 123–24.

21. Stump, *Atonement*, p. 127.

22. Stump, *Wandering*, p. 123.

23. Mittleman, *Does Judaism Condone Violence?*, p. 49.

24. Mittleman, *Does Judaism Condone Violence?*, p. 137.

25. Mittleman, *Does Judaism Condone Violence?*, p. 135.

26. Mittleman, *Does Judaism Condone Violence?*, p. 108.

27. Mittleman, *Does Judaism Condone Violence?*, p. 109.

28. Mittleman, *Does Judaism Condone Violence?*, p. 103.

29. Lev 19:2.

*Chapter 5*

# Homo adorans
## Giving Back to God
## What Is God's Own

We reach something of a hinge in this book. The previous chapters have focused largely on God and God's holiness. We pivot here to focus on humans and human holiness. As should be clear by this point, this bifurcation is somewhat artificial. Human holiness is derivative of and dependent on divine holiness. As a holy entity is that which is owned by God, then any discussion of human holiness will relate to the manner in which humans are owned by God. This chapter explores human holiness by thinking through the starting point for almost all treatments of theological anthropology, the image of God or *imago Dei* as found in Genesis 1:26–27. In this regard, we touch upon the doctrine of creation as well. For this chapter attempts to find the human location within the cosmos that God has created, which thereby provides a sense of what humans are supposed to do in this cosmos. The theory here offered is that humans are to render to God what is God's. And as everything is God's, we humans are to offer all things to God in gratitude, thereby recognizing the creation's holiness and contributing to our own.

## INTRODUCTION

Alexander Schmemann's mid-twentieth-century monograph, *For the Life of the World*, was a call to re-enchant the Christian conception of the cosmos in response to the secularizing program of modernism. In this and other works, Schmemann encouraged the Orthodox to retrieve a theological interpretation of their liturgical worship and encouraged all Christians to retrieve an ontologically thicker picture of reality than was presently on offer. These two themes converge in his pithy statement on theological anthropology from whence I draw the title of this chapter, "'*Homo sapiens,*' '*homo faber*' . . . yes, but, first of all, '*homo adorans.*' The first and basic definition of man [*sic*] is that he is *the priest.*"[1] Schmemann holds that the fundamental feature of humanity is that humans are worshippers—specifically priestly worshippers—of the one God from whence the cosmos came. What follows in this chapter is not an exercise in exegesis of the Orthodox theologian's corpus; rather it is a constructive probing of the suggestive framework Schmemann sketches. I will here argue for a theological anthropology that conceives of humans as priests at the center of the cosmos.

This chapter will progress—like many a sermon—with three points and a practical application. First, I will sketch a cosmological framework utilizing the neoplatonic schema of *exitus et reditus*, procession and return. I do not argue that this is precisely the framework that Schmemann has in mind, although I suspect it is not entirely foreign to Schmemann's thought. Second, I will pivot from neoplatonic cosmology to biblical theology, appropriating some recent work explicating a functional interpretation of the *imago Dei*. However, rather than emphasize the royal-functional aspect of the *imago Dei* that has been popular in the recent literature, I probe a priestly-functional motif for understanding the image of God in humans. I then fuse these two conceptions into a third point that describes the fundamental priestly role of the human being as one who stands as the hinge of the cosmos, gratefully offering the creation back to the creator. Finally, I conclude with some reflections concerning the practical application of this perspective on the areas of liturgical worship and the relation between faith and work.

## THE *EXITUS ET REDITUS* COSMOLOGICAL FRAMEWORK

I turn to the first plank in the model, the *exitus et reditus* cosmological framework as it is found within the broadly neoplatonic tradition.[2] Neoplatonic thought has as a central concern the perennial philosophical problem of the one and the many. Typically understood, neoplatonists prefer to prioritize the one over the many. One area this prioritization is manifest is in a cosmology that emphasizes the overall unity of reality. This unity of reality is primarily derived from the cosmos' origin in singularity, that is, all of reality owes its origin to the One (or the Good, those terms are largely interchangeable in most of the Neoplatonic tradition[3]). Since all of reality starts in unity, then all of reality retains the vestiges of this unity. This, of course, is despite the apparent diversity perceivable in our present experience of this reality. One vestige of this unity of reality becomes evident when we attend to the nature of causality, to which I turn with the help of Proclus.

## Proclus on Causality

In Proclus' *The Elements of Theology* the fabric of *exitus et reditus* is apparent throughout. This theme is evident not just with respect to ultimate causes like the One; rather in any and all causality does Proclus see this dynamic. For instance, he writes, "All things proceed in a circuit, from their causes to their causes again."[4] Yet, what applies in mundane causality, applies to all causality. "For out of the beginning all things are, and towards it all revert."[5] Now, "beginning" here is *arche*, which can mean "principle" as well, a helpful nuance when it applies to the cosmic sphere so as not to necessarily include chronological connotations. As Rorem comments, "For Proclus, procession and return were simultaneous and complementary aspects of the relationship between cause and effect, and between the various levels of causes and effects which constitute the interlocking 'chain of being.'"[6] This would be required if one is to preserve divine atemporality. Hence, the flow of all things out of the One need not be seen as a temporal ordering, but a logical one.

When the logical relations of cause and effect are teased out, Proclus shows the return as being a necessary feature of the procession. Proposition 31 states that, "All that proceeds from any principle reverts in respect of its being upon that from which it proceeds."[7] That is, effects revert or return to their cause because effects are brought about in order to satisfy their causes. If this were not the case, so says Proclus, then nothing would move toward any end. "But," he goes on "all things desire the Good, and each attains it through the mediation of its own proximate cause: therefore each has appetition of its own cause also."[8] This is to say that every cause is a move for and toward the Good, and the effects are a return to their cause, which caused them to move in the first place.

Moreover, Proclus says that, "Every effect remains in its cause, proceeds from it, and reverts upon it."[9] This is true, so he argues, because if an effect were only to remain in its cause, it would not be an effect because it would be impossible to distinguish it from the cause. However, if the effect "should proceed without reversion or immanence," that is, without returning and also remaining, then "it will be without conjunction or sympathy with its cause, since it will have no communication with it."[10] This is to say that the effect cannot be completely disconnected from its cause, otherwise it would cease to be, for effects are dependent on their causes. He then proceeds to eliminate all the combinations of remaining, proceeding, and reverting aside from the headlining combination of an effect remaining, proceeding, and returning to its cause.

## Ps-Dionysius on the Beginning and the End

Proclus' discussion of the procession and return motif applies to mundane causality as much as it does the dynamics of the cosmos. His emphasis on the beginning of the cause and the return to the *arche* (beginning/principle) can be a thread we pick up in Pseudo-Dionysius' work. Given the neoplatonic framework within which Pseudo-Dionysius expresses his ruminations on the structure of the heavens, it is not surprising to see the *exitus et reditus* motif at the very beginning of his *Celestial Hierarchy*.

The Areopagite opens his treaties with a famously provocative excerpt from the first chapter of the epistle of James, "Every good gift and every perfect gift is from above, coming down from the Father of lights."[11] For Pseudo-Dionysius, this passage is an impetus to seek epistemic assistance from the Father of lights in his effort to understand the fabric of the heavens:

> The Dionysian thought-world [. . .] is thoroughly oriented around the motif of procession and return, above all in the interpretation of Christian symbolism. The biblical and liturgical symbols are God's condescending revelation in our lower sphere for the uplifting purpose of returning us to the higher and divine realm.[12]

Hence, the light of divine revelation exits from the divine to return the minds of humans back to the contemplation of these heavenly realities.

While this might be taken as merely an epistemic project, this verse from James' letter fits snugly in a neoplatonic cosmological framework. What is true regarding one's cognitive efforts is also true on an ontological and cosmic level within the procession and return framework. All things process from the Father, constantly flowing in a bounteous outpouring from God. This, then, fills humans "anew as through a unifying power [. . .] leading us to the unity of the Shepherding Father and to the Divine One."[13] Ps-Dionysius then alludes to Paul's statement in Rom 11:36, "For from him and through him and to him are all things."[14] Hence, not only knowledge of God runs along an *exitus et reditus* pathway, but even the framework of reality can be seen to do as much.

## Thomas Aquinas on the End of Creation

I can here take Pseudo-Dionysius' appropriation of Paul's "from him and . . . to him" schema and fuse it with the ruminations on causality from Proclus above. This I do by way of identifying the *exitus et reditus* motif in Thomas Aquinas' discussion of God's motive for creation.

In his discussion of creation in the *Summa Theologiae*, Thomas titles the question on the nature of God as first cause of the cosmos, "The procession of creatures from God, and of the first cause of all things." However, Thomas is keen to show, not only is God the first cause—the first agent—God is also the final cause. He writes in the *responsio*:

> Every agent acts for an end . . . Now the end of the agent and of the patient considered as such is the same, but in a different way respectively . . . [I]t does not belong to the First Agent, Who is agent only, to act for the acquisition of some end; He intends only to communicate His perfection, which is His goodness; while every creature intends to acquire its own perfection, which is the likeness of the divine perfection and goodness. Therefore the divine goodness is the end of all things.[15]

Except for the first cause, all agents—all causes—act or cause for some end. This is the appetition in Proclus' thought or the fourth and final cause in Aristotelian ideology. Within the latter schema, the act/potency combination is a conceptual constituent of all causes subsequent to the first. However, the first cause is a special case in the Thomistic worldview. It is not fitting that the first cause be an act/potency mix; the first cause is *actus purus*. As such, it does not act for some end, rather the effects that come from this act are simply overflow of goodness, and the implicit or analogous intention of this overflow is the communication of its perfection. Or we might say in more personalistic terms, the overflow is God both creating and inviting the creation to participate in God's own goodness. But, given the conjunction of the cluster of concepts around the "Good" in the neoplatonist framework, this invitation is an invitation to participate in God's goodness / perfection / unity, for the Good, the Perfect, and the One are all ultimately identical.

For Thomas, the first cause is also identical to the final cause. As he states in the reply to objection 3 in this question, "All things desire God as their end."[16] Hence, in Thomas' conception of God as first and final cause, we have an ontological grounding for ascribing to God the status of Alpha and Omega. Rev 22:13, "I am the Alpha and the Omega, the first and the last, the beginning (*arche*) and the end (*telos*)."[17] Therefore, to round out this *exitus et reditus* section, all things come from God and all things are returning to God. What starts in unity, and is now manifested in diversity, will eventually—though not necessarily temporally—return to unity.

# A PRIESTLY-FUNCTIONAL EXPLICATION OF THE *IMAGO DEI*

What is the case according to neoplatonic cosmology regarding the One as the first cause can be layered over the Genesis narrative that is the Judeo-Christian account of the origin of all things. Regardless of how one understands the genre of the prologue to Genesis, the procession motif can be easily utilized to describe God's act of creation *ex nihilo*. Beginning with only God in the beginning (1:1), God speaks forth the entire created realm with each day adding greater diversity and multiplicity arising out of God's unity. Moreover, in an *exitus* vein, each day brings about entities that are dependent in some sense on the entities of previous days. Plants (1:11) are dependent on the distinction between land and water (1.9), sea and land animals (1:20, 24) are dependent on plants and the distinction between land and water for their life, and finally humans utilize both. Yet, the dependence relation of the entities created on subsequent days on the entities created on earlier days also has a teleological trajectory. The land is *for* the plants, the plants are *for* the animals, both are *for* the humans. As the last entity created in the creation week, the *exitus* of creation culminates in the creation of the humans, who—unique among the creation—are created in the "image" and "likeness" of God.[18]

## The Royal *imago Dei*

Interpretations of the image of God ascription to humanity abound in the history of theological and exegetical reflection. Largely, these interpretations have tended to fall into one of four categories—although the categories are not mutually exclusive—interpreting the image of God either: (i) structurally, as some feature or characteristic of humans; (ii) relationally, such that humans attain their quiddity vis-à-vis God or one another; (iii) functionally, as some sort of commission uniquely given to humans; or (/and) (iv) Christologically, as such that the Incarnate Christ is the paradigm image of God.[19]

Some in the biblical studies guild have pointed out that systematic theological reflection on the meaning of the *imago Dei* has not often taken into consideration the illumination that linguistic and cultural studies have shed on the concept. For instance, Bernard Batto claims that the examination of ancient Near Eastern literature and iconography yields an interpretation of the *imago Dei* such, "that God created humans to serve as his regents in administering the world. If God is the divine sovereign, then humankind is his viceroy on earth."[20] Likewise, Catherine McDowell takes a novel route to a similar conclusion in holding that the creation narrative is an attempt to "identify Yahweh as the father of Israel and the Israelite king."[21] In light of being the offspring of God, then, "humanity is king ruling at God's behest as his representative [. . .] the image of God carries with it the responsibility to represent God and his standards in the realm of law and justice."[22] These realms of "law and justice" clearly indicate royal connotations to this interpretation of the term *tselem* in the pericope.

Richard Middleton has done much to propagate the royal-functional interpretation of the *imago Dei*. He writes concerning this concept, "Although its semantic range is broader than this single meaning, we need to account for *selem* in many contexts clearly referring to a cult image, which in the common theology of the ancient Near East is precisely a localized, visible, corporeal representation of the divine."[23] This does not eliminate structural or relational explications of humanity in a full-orbed anthropology, but it does call into question the grounding of those perspectives in the text of Gen 1–2 itself. However, rather than exploring the ambiguity surrounding the use of idols in the religio-political milieu of ANE societies, Middleton emphasizes the political implications of this conceptual scheme by attending to the terms surrounding *tselem* in the pericope, "Such exegesis notes the predominantly royal flavor of the text, beginning with the close linkage of image with the mandate to rule and subdue the earth and its creatures in 1:26 and 1:28 (typically royal functions)."[24] Despite the association with *cultus* and the temple/ritualistic locales of idols, Middleton pivots to the royal connotations of this term. He goes on to summarize, "Humanity is created *like* God, with the special role of representing or imaging God's rule in the world."[25] Consequently, Middleton and others have averred that the image of God in humanity is a royal image, and humans live into their function as images when they properly exercise dominion or authority over the rest of creation as the royal representatives of God.

## The Sacerdotal *imago Dei*

I do not wish to argue that this is all false. Nevertheless, I do not think that it tells the whole story. While clearly the *adam* is charged in Genesis to "have dominion over" (1:26, 28) and "to subdue" (1:28) the creation, there are other aspects of the picture that indicate a priestly-functional motif undergirds or is more fundamental than this royal-functional implication of the *imago Dei*. For while I agree that the prologue to Genesis communicates God's authority or dominion over the created realm, this role is not immediately exercised by humans in the narrative. Rather, when we come to the first actions that the *adam* undertakes in Genesis—coming all the way in the 19th verse of chapter 2—we see that the *adam*'s first act is to name "every living creature." Is naming a royal task or a priestly task? I would suggest that naming is an instance of differentiating and the tasks of dividing, differentiating, and designating are centrally priestly jobs. For instance, Leviticus 10:10 includes God's delivering to Aaron fundamental aspects of his priestly vocation: "You are to distinguish (*badal*) between the holy and the profane, and between the unclean and the clean." Naming—especially in the sense Schmemann outlines (more on this anon)—is an act of distinguishing and differentiating, and hence is at the conceptual core of the priestly task.

Why do priests differentiate? Why do priest divide between clean and unclean or in fact bring about the designation of some object as holy by an act of consecration (i.e. the making clean)? They do so in order to offer the object back to God, as God has first done in the prologue of Genesis. In chapter 1, God has divided and differentiated the created realm into various kinds: celestial bodies, flora, and fauna. These are priestly functions. No doubt these functions show a measure of authority; priests are the authorized members of the community to do the differentiating. But then God undertakes another priestly activity. After the dividing and differentiating in the initial creative acts, God then offers all that God has created to the *adam*. By charging the humans to rule, to subdue, and to name, God offered creation to the human. Note that it is God in Gen 2:19 who brings the animals to the *adam* "to see what he would call them." The *adam* functions similarly by differentiating what God has offered to him and then, or so I argue, is to continue to image God by offering these back to God. In sum, God divides and distinguishes, then offers the creation to humans, humans respond in an imaging fashion by likewise dividing and distinguishing and then offering back to God.[26]

## HUMANS: THE HINGE OF THE UNIVERSE

In this next section, I fuse the neoplatonic cosmology outlined at the outset with the preceding conception of the *imago Dei* as a fundamentally sacerdotal vocation, keyed especially to human holiness and intensifying the holiness of the cosmos. What I suggest, then, is that humans in their priestly role can and ought to be seen as the hinges of the cosmos, the very turning point at which God completes the *exitus* of creation and begins the *reditus* of the cosmos back to God. We humans, then, function as the locus of the pivot from *exitus* to *reditus*, and our vocation is to join with God in the cosmic project of returning all things back to their source.

### Schmemann's Human

In order to join these two conceptual schemes, I turn back to Schmemann. Recall the passage that forms the basis for my chapter title, "'*Homo sapiens*,' '*homo faber*' . . . yes, but, first of all, '*homo adorans*.' The first and basic definition of man [*sic*] is that he is *the priest*."[27] But Schmemann goes on to specify just what is entailed in this "first and basic definition" of humans. For Schmemann, the human:

> stands in the center of the world and unifies it in his act of blessing God, of both receiving the world from God and offering it to God—and by filling the world with this eucharist, he transforms his life, the one that he receives from the world, into life in God, into communion with Him. The world was created as the "matter," the material of one all-embracing eucharist, and man was created as the priest of this cosmic sacrament.[28]

First, Schmemann specifies that humans stand at the center of the cosmos. We could imagine this center to be the center of a circle or sphere, and perhaps an interpretation like this is warranted. However, in light of the *exitus et reditus* cosmological framework, I think we ought to imagine humans as the center of the *exitus et reditus* circuit. Indeed, humans are at the center because, as Schmemann intimates, their vocation is to be the hinge point in the creation that actively participates in the return. Humans receive from God, but are also able to image God in offering the world back to God.

Secondly, as Schmemann describes, humans stand at the center of the cosmos in order to unify it in their act of blessing God. Unification—bringing things back to the One—is at the heart of the neoplatonic project. Humans are "receiving the world from God" through the *exitus* and then are unifying the world by "offering it to God" through the *reditus*. At this point, the neoplatonic concern for the one over the many comes back to the fore. The charge to the human priests is to participate in the cosmic unification or, better, *re*unification project that God is already engaged in. God is returning all things to their source and humans join with this in their blessing God and offering the creation to God.

Moreover, in this selection "offering" to God and "blessing" God stand in apposition to one another. Elsewhere Schmemann defines blessing in this manner, "To bless [. . .] is to give thanks. In and through thanksgiving, man [*sic*] acknowledges the true nature of things he receives from God, and thus makes them to be what they are. We bless and sanctify things when we offer them to God in a Eucharistic movement of our whole being."[29] Blessing God, for Schmemann here, is giving thanks to God. This giving of thanks occurs when humans offer the creation back to God. Engaging in the priestly office of offering the creation back to God culminates in the priestly function of offering eucharist, that is, thanksgiving. This, then, is how humans participate in the *reditus*, through their grateful offering the cosmos back to God, the first cause from which the whole creation flows.

## Naming

In this vein, we can bring back the naming task that is the first task the *adam* undertakes in Gen 2:19–20. Schmemann offers this theological interpretation of the phenomenon of naming:

> Now, in the Bible a name is infinitely more than a means to distinguish one thing from another. It reveals the very essence of a thing, or rather its essence as God's gift. To name a thing is to manifest the meaning and value God gave it, to know it as coming from God and to know its place and function within the cosmos created by God. To name a thing, in other words, is to bless God for it and in it.[30]

Naming is differentiating, but it also "reveals the very essence of a thing." This is just as in blessing God one "acknowledges the true nature of things," which then unifies the things as "coming from God."[31] Hence, the naming that is the blessing that is the thanksgiving is the swinging of the hinge wherein the *reditus* is achieved. When the humans recognize that the creation—the many—comes from God and is God's gift to humanity, they return it—unify it—by offering it back to God in thanks. In this circuit, not only do humans achieve their *telos* by being priests, all of creation reaches its *telos* by being offered back to its source.

## Imaging

In fact, at this juncture we can reappropriate the lessons of the other functional interpretation of the *imago Dei*, the royal-functional explication. Commentators in this stream of interpretation point to key terms in the Gen 1 pericope such as *radah* "to rule" or "to have dominion" or *kabash* "to subdue." These terms cannot be ignored for they are as intimately connected to *tselem elohim* as any. However, the question certainly has to be raised as to the *telos* of the subjection or dominion that God charges the *tselem* to execute. Are we to think that God set humans up as arbitrary rulers, simply ruling for ruling's sake? No, rather the priestly function provides a cosmological *telos* for the subduing mandate within the royal function. That is, the naming of Gen 2:19–20—a dividing and distinguishing priestly function—is a pre-requisite, and hence more fundamental, to the ruling or subduing mandates of the royal connotations of the *imago*.

The priestly function of the *imago Dei* is an imaging relation of God's priestly function because God is offering the whole cosmos and returning it to Godself. Humans image God by joining with what God is doing. God offers—what is God's own—the cosmos to humans, yes, but God is offering the cosmos to Godself by means of the human. God's ownership of the cosmos is always a conceptual component of the dynamic. Because of the radical contingency of the cosmos and the nature of God's aseity, God is in no need of the cosmos, much less does God need to offer the cosmos back to Godself, and even much less does God need humans to do the offering. However, in the gracious overflow of his goodness and perfection, God invites humans to participate in the holiness dynamic, which God could do without humans. Therefore, when humans participate in the *reditus*, they participate in God's bringing all things back to Godself. Or, in Thomist language, human priests participate in the process by which all things are being united with the perfection and goodness that is their first and final cause.[32] To participate in the *reditus* is to participate with God in God's holy-making of the cosmos.

## PRACTICAL APPLICATION

The foregoing lays a rather abstract conception of the place of humans in the cosmos. Here, I want to connect this perspective to some areas of practical expression.[33] The first area of practical application is our worship—specifically our communal liturgical worship—and the second area of application is our conception of the nature of work. First, I turn to worship.

### Worship

*Homo adorans* means humans as worshippers. What it means to worship can take diverse and varied interpretations.[34] Yet, one aspect of worship—in an especially priestly motif—is the manner in which worshippers offer thanks to God. I have already mentioned the Eucharist as an act of thanksgiving, and there are clear trajectories of practical application to that practice. However, here I want to focus on an act that is, in liturgical worship, a component of the Eucharist, although it comes before the *sursum corda*. I think some features of the offertory manifest the hinge nature of humanity particularly clearly.

Attention to aspects of the script of this portion of the liturgy can be interpreted with an *exitus et reditus* overlay.[35] When the minister invites the congregation to come to the Eucharist in the transition from the liturgy of the word to the liturgy of the sacrament, the minister will typically offer an offertory sentence, some of which are drawn directly from Scripture. One such is a quotation from Ps 50:14, "Offer to God a sacrifice of thanksgiving, and make good your vows to the Most High."[36] Here, then, the people are invited to these twin, or nested, actions of offering to God—specifically offering thanks to God—as they fulfil their vows to God. The people typically follow this mandate by offering gifts of money placed in the offering plates. These gifts are then brought to the altar with The Gifts, that is the bread and wine that will be used for the Eucharist.

At this point in the service, in some liturgical traditions, these offerings then participate in a particularly hinge-worthy action. This is manifested in a reference to 1 Chron 29 prior to the *sursum corda*. With the gifts placed on the altar before the minister, the minister recites portions of this chapter starting with verse 11, "Yours, O Lord, is the greatness and the power and the glory and the victory and the majesty, for all that is in the heavens and in the earth is yours. Yours is the kingdom, O Lord, and you are exalted as head above all," and then continuing with verse 14, "For all things come from you, and of your own have we given you." The inclusion of these words from Scripture reinforces this moment as a hinge moment. God is here worshipped in gratitude. God's greatness is here acknowledged as well as God's ultimate ownership of the cosmos. Then in light of this, those things that God has offered to humans—the creation to rule and subdue—are offered back to God in thanks. Worshippers here acknowledge that all things proceed from God along the pathway of the *exitus*, and then humans return them in a gift to God along the path of the *reditus*. Hence, liturgical worship can function as a locus for humans returning all things to God in their vocation as the priestly hinge in the cosmic procession and return.

## Work

Another way that liturgical worship functions is as a form of habituation to bring conceptual schemas to bear on other areas of life. I want to suggest that this cosmic priestly-functional theological anthropology, as manifested in our worship, can undergird a robust understanding of the relationship between faith and work. That is, the human exercise of our priestly vocation does not just occur in the liturgy, but has implications for our work Monday through Friday as well.[37]

If we recall back to the offertory sentences at the hinge of the Eucharistic liturgy, we see another sentence that functions in this archetypal manner of seeing our work as a cosmic offering. The minister can say, "Let us with gladness present the offerings and oblations of our life and labor to the Lord."[38] The money we might put into the offering plate is representative of the fruit of our life and labor. The work that we do on Monday through Friday is representatively transformed into the paycheck we receive. Then, in the liturgy, we gratefully offer a portion of this back to God. As Schmemann comments regarding this point in the liturgy, "the time has come now to offer to God the totality of all our lives, of ourselves, of the world in which we live."[39] The totality of our lives is here archetypally offered to God in thanksgiving.[40]

But what is manifested liturgically need not be just liturgical, for this conception of offering to God our life and labor can be brought to pervade our perspective on our work Monday through Friday. When we work in the world, we certainly follow the mandate to work and keep the creation as God charged the *adam* to do. Yet we also fulfil the priestly vocation of bringing into productive order the chaos of reality to offer it to God. Recall again the dividing and naming motif of the Genesis prologue. God brings order to the formless void by dividing, arranging, and organizing the chaos. Analogously—in an imaging fashion—the *adam* orders the animals by distinguishing, organizing, and naming them. So too, then, do humans subsequent to Adam bring order and arrangement to the creation through their acts of industry.

However, this work is not an end in itself. *Contra* a connotation of the royal-functional *imago Dei*, work is not merely ultimately for the obedience of a divine command. We do not have to work simply because God said so. Rather the *telos* of these productive acts of industry is to return the creation back to God in acts of grateful offering. The *telos* is to join with God in unifying the many by returning the cosmos back to the One, to God. Consequently, the practical conclusion in the realm of faith and work of applying the *exitus et reditus* motif in a priestly anthropology is to see all our work as an outflow of the human cosmic hinge vocation, whereby all things are united back to the first and final cause.

## CONCLUSION

In neoplatonic cosmology, the many of the cosmos begins in unity and returns to unity in the One. Christian neoplatonism can overlay this motif onto the creation narrative of the prologue to Genesis. When pursuing the meaning of the *imago Dei* of Gen 1:26–27, this cosmology adds credence to a minority report interpretation of a functional explication of the term. Humans function as priestly hinges in the cosmos, participating with God in God's grand reunification project. Humans unify creation by distinguishing and differentiating the creation, bringing order to that which has exited from God in multiplicity. Then in their blessing and giving thanks to God for the creation—rightly understood and rightly differentiated—humans offer the creation back to God and thereby fulfil their priestly function. What is more, liturgical practices surrounding the offertory of the Eucharistic liturgy reflect and teach this cosmological role. In this role, humans participate with God in unifying the cosmos as they offer to God a sacrifice of thanksgiving and acknowledge that all things come from God and of God's own do humans give back to God.

Humans, then, have a unique and vital role in participating in the holiness of the cosmos. As the source of all, God owns all. And as ownership by God is the key component of the holiness of holy things, all things are holy ... to some extent. In the *exitus* of creation, however, God sends out the cosmos from Godself into and out of nothing. Humans play a special role in the *reditus* of the cosmos back to God. When humans do this, they are participating with God in returning, and thereby recognizing, a higher degree of ownership of the world by God. Affixing this conception of the human task to the fundamental theological anthropological doctrinal concept of the *imago Dei* shows that the sacerdotal task of holy-making is at the very foundation of what it means to be human. In the next chapter, we continue focusing on the human side of holiness puzzling over not just how humans extend holiness into cosmos, but also themselves become holy.

## NOTES

1. Alexander Schmemann, *For the Life of the World* (Crestwood, NY: St. Vladimir's Seminary Press, 1988), p. 15.

2. I am here going to be using "neoplatonic" and "neoplatonism" in a lowercase sense to refer rather generally to forms and habits of thinking derived from Plato and those capital "N" Neoplatonists like Plotinus, Porphyry, and Proclus. Whether certain of my interlocutors like Pseudo-Dionysius or Thomas Aquinas are properly categorized as (capital "N") Neoplatonists is not of concern to me. I am simply interested in the broadly (lowercase "n") neoplatonic ideas discernible in their thought. In my examination of this motif, I am indebted to Paul Rorem's very helpful, "'Procession and Return' in Thomas Aquinas and His Predecessors," *The Princeton Seminary Bulletin* (1992): 147–163.

3. For example, Proclus writes that it belongs both to the Good to unify and to the One to unify, hence, "if unification is in itself good and all good tends to create unity, then the Good unqualified and the One unqualified merge in single principle . . . Goodness, then, is unification, and unification goodness; the Good is one, and the One is primal good." *The Elements of Theology*, ed. E.R. Dodds, 2nd ed. (Oxford: Clarendon, 1963), #13, 17.

4. Proclus, *Elements of Theology,* #33, 37.
5. Proclus, *Elements of Theology,* #33, 37.
6. Rorem, "'Procession and Return,'" p. 149.
7. Proclus, *Elements,* #31, 35.
8. Proclus, *Elements,* #31, 35.
9. Proclus, *Elements,* #35, 39.
10. Proclus, *Elements,* #35, 39.
11. Jam 1:17.
12. Rorem, "'Procession and Return,'" p. 152.
13. Pseudo-Dionysius, *The Celestial Hierarchy* [http://www.ccel.org/ccel/dionysius/celestial.ii.html], ch. 1.
14. Rom 11:36.
15. Thomas Aquinas, *Summa Theologia* Ia.44.4 resp [http://www.newadvent.org/summa/1044.htm#article4].
16. *ST* Ia.44.4 ad 3.

17. Rev 22:13. See also, Rev 1:8, 21:6.
18. One might think that the Sabbath is the last creation and hence is the terminus of the teleology of the creation week. However, Gen 2:2 does not say that God *created* the seventh day, just that *on* the seventh day God finished God's work and rested, and God blessed it (declaration, not creation) to bring about its status as the Sabbath.
19. A helpful survey can be found in Richard Middleton, *The Liberating Image: The* Imago Dei *in Genesis 1* (Grand Rapids, MI: Brazos Press, 2005), pp. 19–24. See also, Marc Cortez, *Theological Anthropology: A Guide for the Perplexed* (London: T&T Clark, 2010), pp. 18–27. For Christological interpretations, see, Marc Cortez, *Christological Anthropology in Historical Perspective: Ancient and Contemporary Approaches to Theological Anthropology* (Grand Rapids, MI: Zondervan Academic, 2016).
20. Bernard F. Batto, *In the Beginning: Essays on Creation Motifs in the Bible and the Ancient Near East* (Winona Lake, IN: Eisenbrauns, 2013), p. 97.
21. Catherine L. McDowell, *The Image of God in the Garden of Eden: The Creation of Humankind in Genesis 2:5–3:24 I Light mīs pî pīt pî and wpt-r Rituals of Mesopotamis and Ancient Egypt* (Winona Lake, IN: Eisenbrauns, 2015), p. 136.
22. McDowell, *The Image of God in the Garden of Eden,* p. 137.
23. Middleton, *Liberating Image,* p. 25.
24. Middleton, *Liberating Image,* p. 26.
25. Middleton, *Liberating Image,* p. 26.
26. A larger biblical-theological case for a priestly-functional interpretation of the *imago Dei* could be made from the conception of Eden as temple. For this move, see especially the work of G.K. Beale, in "Adam as the First Priest in Eden as the Garden Temple," *Southern Baptist Journal of Theology* 22 (2018): 9–24, "Eden, the Temple, and the Church's Mission in New Creation," *Journal of the Evangelical Theological Society* 48 (2005): 5–31, and *The Temple and the Church's Mission: A Biblical Theology of the Dwelling Place of God,* New Studies in Biblical Theology 17 (Downers Grove, IL: InverVarsity Press, 2004). Particularly instructive is Beale's discussion of Ezek 28 wherein, Beale argues, Adam is there portrayed as a priest in the Edenic temple (p. 75). One can also see these themes in Kenneth Mathews' commentary on Genesis, *New American Commentary: Genesis 1–11* (Nashville, TN: B&H, 1996), p. 210. A similar case for humanity's priestly vocation is made from Gen 1 and Ezek 16 by Crispin H.T. Fletcher-Louis in "God's Image, His Cosmic Temple and the High Priest: Towards an Historical and Theological Account of the Incarnation," in *Heaven on Earth: The Temple in Biblical Theology,* eds. T. Desmond Alexander & Simon Gathercole (Carlisle, UK: Paternoster, 2004), pp. 81–100. See also, Christopher Woznicki, *T. F. Torrance's Christological Anthropology: Discerning Humanity in Christ* (London: Routledge, 2022), pp. 124–128.
27. Schmemann, *For the Life of the World,* p. 15.
28. Schmemann, *For the Life of the World,* p. 15.
29. Schmemann, *For the Life of the World,* p. 73.
30. Schmemann, *For the Life of the World,* p. 15.
31. A similar line of thought from the ancient Near Eastern context of Genesis corroborates Schmemann's conception: "It was believed that the name of a living being

or an object was not just a simple or practical designation to facilitate the exchange of ideas between persons but that it was the very essence of what was defined," from J.M. Plumley, "The Cosmology of Ancient Egypt," in *Ancient Cosmologies*, eds. Carmen Backer and Michael Lowe (London: Allen & Unwin, 1975), p. 30 in John H. Walton, *Ancient Near Eastern Thought and the Old Testament: Introducing the Conceptual World of the Hebrew Bible* (Grand Rapids, MI: Baker Academic, 2006), p. 188.

32. A much larger project could, at this point, bring the Christological interpretation of the image of God into the conversation. Col 1 would be an apt place to start where Christ is referred to as "the image of the invisible God" (v. 15), in whom "all things hold together" (v. 17) and "the fullness of God was pleased to dwell" (v. 19), and through whom God works "to reconcile all things to himself" (v. 20). The latter clause would then be a jumping off point for a discussion of Christ's role as High Priest, a notion that pervades the Letter to the Hebrews. However, this essay more modestly attempts the probing of the priesthood of all humanity by attending to humanity's Edenic situation. For recent discussions of the nexus of Christology and theological anthropology see, among others, Stanley Grenz, *The Social God and the Relational Self: A Trinitarian Theology of the Imago Dei* (Louisville, KY: Westminster John Knox Press, 2001), especially ch. 5; Ian A. McFarland, *The Divine Image: Envisioning the Invisible God* (Minneapolis: Fortress, 2005), especially ch. 3; Kathryn Tanner, *Christ the Key*, Current Issues in Theology (Cambridge: Cambridge University Press, 2010), especially ch. 1; Oliver D. Crisp, *The Word Enfleshed: Exploring the Person and Work of Christ* (Grand Rapids, MI: Baker Academic, 2016), especially ch. 4; Marc Cortez, *ReSourcing Theological Anthropology: A Constructive Account of Humanity in the Light of Christ* (Grand Rapids, MI: Zondervan, 2017), especially ch. 3; and Haley Goranson Jacob, *Conformed to the Image of His Son: Reconsidering Paul's Theology of Glory in Romans* (Downers Grove, IL: IVP Academic, 2018). This Christological pivot would also benefit from Maximus the Confessor's "Abiguum 41," found in *On Difficulties in the Church Fathers: The Ambigua*, vol. II, ed. and trans. Nicholas Constas (Cambridge, MA: Harvard University Press, 2014), especially pp. 113ff.

33. This section could be taken either as an instance of *lex orandi, lex credendi*, whereby the liturgy corroborates my theological interpretation of the *imago Dei*, or as an instance of attempting to infuse already in place liturgical practices with further theological underpinning.

34. For a recent and provocative discussion, see Nicholas Wolterstorff, *The God We Worship: An Exploration of Liturgical Theology*, Kantzer Lectures in Revealed Theology (Grand Rapids, MI: Eerdmans, 2015).

35. "Script" is Wolterstorff's term in *The God We Worship*. In addition, I am speaking here from within the Anglican liturgical tradition, so my comments will reside most comfortably in that framework.

36. This is the first sentence listed in the 1979 Book of Common Prayer from The Episcopal Church, which arranges the sentences by canonical order.

37. I am not just here speaking as a professional theologian who thinks about God Monday through Friday. I am thinking of the small business owner, the corporate CEO, the janitor, lawyer, farmer, homemaker, etc.

38. Also from the 1979 Episcopal Book of Common Prayer.

39. Schmemann, *For the Life of the World*, p. 34.

40. I do not at all wish to suggest that the totality of our lives culminates in the money we put in the offering plate. Rather, the money is a symbolic representation of our life and labor. Moreover, the widow's mite reminds us that the totality of our lives can be symbolically represented by the smallest offering.

*Chapter 6*

# "You shall be holy, for I the Lord your God am holy"

Human holiness is derivative from divine holiness. As holiness indicates divine ownership, humans are holy insofar as they are owned by God and act in manners that reflect that ownership. The previous chapter explored how at the very beginning of the biblical conception of humans, joining with God in extending holiness in the world is a fundamental component of what it means to be human. Leviticus 19:2 (referred to also in 1 Peter 1:16) has God saying this: "You shall be holy, for I the Lord your God am holy." This utterance spoken by God is at the heart of Leviticus, a crucial hinge in the flow of rules and regulations that God enunciates in this book. Not only is it narratively central to the book, but it is also conceptually central as well. For God's holiness and the people's holiness are fundamental concerns of both this narrative and the religion of the Hebrew Scriptures. Yet, what does this sentence mean? What does God mean by it? Using speech act theory from the philosophy of language and continuing an engagement with the account of holiness proffered by Alan Mittleman, this chapter will argue that one's antecedent commitments to a particular conception of holiness have dramatic implications for one's categorization of the kind of speech act one takes God to perform with this utterance. If, on the one hand, one takes holiness to refer to an ethical category, then one will see the utterance in question as a command—God enjoining the people toward some ethical end. On the other hand, if one takes a metaphysical understanding of holiness—two species of which will be distinguished below—then one will read the utterance as the exact opposite of a command. Instead of placing obligations on the people, in this utterance God places obligations on Godself.

In what follows I will first discuss some methodological preliminaries with respect to (a) how I read this text, (b) how I will utilize speech act theory as an interpretive tool, and (c) the particular version of speech act theory that I will employ. Second, I will show how an interpretation of the sentence in question as a command requires that one make an antecedent commitment to the ethical explication of holiness. This interpretation is fair insofar as it goes, but when one pivots to consider a metaphysical explication of holiness, the command motif is found lacking. Thus, I turn to interpret this sentence under the rubric of a different speech act, that of covenanting. This speech act category better comports with a commitment to a metaphysical explication of holiness, but conversely falls short when holiness is considered under its ethical heading. I conclude by offering a synthesis of the ethical and metaphysical conceptions of holiness that thereby undergirds a synthesis of the twin speech acts performed by God in this utterance.

## METHODOLOGICAL PRELIMINARIES

### Canon and Narrative

First, in this chapter and elsewhere in this book I am taking a canonical and narrative approach to biblical interpretation. The main business of this chapter is to proffer an understanding of but one sentence in Tanakh—a sentence that has important theological implications with respect to our conception of the divine and the nature of holiness. However, I wish to avoid being bogged down in a myriad of exegetical issues that is the purview of much contemporary biblical studies. Thus, I simply accept the Hebrew Scriptures as a canonical whole, with this sentence and Leviticus as a whole featuring as component parts of it.

### Speech Acts and Biblical Studies

Second, the project here in this chapter and in chapter 10 draws heavily from speech act theory from the philosophy of language as a means of interpretation. I see speech act theory as a tool which can be utilized to probe the meanings of particular instances of any use of language. I will not anachronistically shoehorn the text into a contemporary mode, but rather use this tool to draw out some of the conceptual nuances embedded within the text. The simple premise of speech act theory is that all instances of language are instances of actions. There are no free-floating sentences the meaning of which we can grasp without any recourse to the agential intentions of speakers. Rather, speech is an action, and actions are performed by agents, and thus to understand the speech, we must understand what the agents are doing when they issue their utterances.

Two popular versions of speech act theory that have been utilized by biblical scholars have been those of the so-called founders of speech act theory,

J.L. Austin and John Searle. Austin's *How to do Things with Words*[1] is often credited for inaugurating the field of speech act theory. Austin's student John Searle provided a helpful advancement and specification of Austin's work in his *Speech Acts: An Essay in the Philosophy of Language*.[2] However, subsequent work in the field by Paul Grice,[3] Daniel Vanderveken,[4] Willliam Lycan,[5] and others has pushed speech act theory into a mainstay in contemporary philosophy of language.

The pioneering work of such biblical studies scholars as Anthony Thiselton,[6] Donald Evans,[7] Dietmar Neufeld,[8] and Richard Briggs,[9] among others, has shown that speech act analysis can be a boon to the task of biblical interpretation. Speech act theory focuses on the actions performed by speakers in the issuing of their utterances. In the utterance under examination here, the speaker is none other than God. However, I am not here concerned with projects, such as that of Nicholas Wolterstorff,[10] to use speech act theory as a means of showing Scripture as a whole as an instance of divine discourse. Rather, I am simply interested in how to understand this utterance spoken by God in this narrative in a manner that we might understand any other instance of speech by any other character in the narrative, be it Moses or David or Nebuchadnezzar. This is precisely the kind of biblical linguistic phenomenon that speech act theory is useful for analyzing.

## Alstonian Distinctives

William Alston offers a contemporary account of speech act theory in his *Illocutionary Acts and Sentence Meaning*. Here he presents a tripartite distinction within a speech act. Typically a speaker performs three conceptually different speech acts in any instance of uttering. These acts are, on Alston's terms: *sentential acts*, *illocutionary acts*, and *perlocutionary acts*. "These acts" says Alston, "constituted a hierarchy. One performs an illocutionary act by (in) performing a sentential act. And one (normally) performs a perlocutionary act by (in) performing an illocutionary act. A typical act of speech involves all three."[11]

The first speech act in Alston's categories is the *sentential act* (SA). This is simply what the speaker said, as in, what specific words or sounds were uttered.[12] For instance, take a sentence that I find myself uttering often: "Please pick up your toys." The sentential act can be made explicit by an *oratio recta* report of simply: "James said, 'Please pick up your toys.'" Alston includes as sentential acts instances such as (a) when utterances are given as elliptical for a sentence and (b) when actions are given as surrogates for a sentence. On (a), one might utter "Ouch" as being elliptical for something like, "I am currently feeling pain!" Or on (b), suppose, I give my colleague a high-five, which would serve as a surrogate for a sentence like, "You did a great job!" Both "Ouch" and a "high-five" can count as sentential acts in Alston's theory. Upon the foundation of sentential acts rests the two other speech acts, illocutionary acts (IA) and perlocutionary acts (PA).

PAs are the effect or effects an utterance has on an audience.[13] The PA is not a statement about a speaker but rather about the recipient of an utterance, the audience or addressees. For instance, suppose I utter the sentence "Please pick up your toys" to my son. Upon hearing this, my son might pick up his toys. Whatever is provoked in him by my IA bearing SA is the PA.

For Alston, IAs are the locus of utterance meaning. To describe an IA is to make explicit the content of the utterance. Suppose Tom, says, "Ouch!" The IA, as expressed in an *oratio obliqua* report, might be "Tom *expressed* that he was in pain." The pivotal feature of Alston's account of illocutionary acts is the normative element in which Alston observes speakers participating. For Alston, to accurately describe a speaker's performance of an illocutionary act is to accurately state that the speaker is "taking responsibility for the satisfaction of a condition"[14] or conditions. The questions interpreters need to ask of an illocutionary act is what sorts of things did a speaker take responsibility for in the utterance of her sentence? Answering this question helps interpreters understand what type of illocutionary act was performed and to understanding the content of the illocutionary act.

Alston distinguishes illocutionary acts into five types: Assertives, Directives, Commissives, Exercitives, and Expressives. These include:

ASSERTIVES: merely asserting, acknowledging, concluding, etc.

DIRECTIVES: ordering, requesting, suggesting, etc.

COMMISSIVES: promising, contracting, betting, etc.

EXERCITIVES: adjourning, appointing, nominating, etc.

EXPRESSIVES: thanking, congratulating, expressing delight, etc.[15]

This chapter will make use of Directive and Commissive type IAs in the analysis of Leviticus 19:2.

## Holiness

Recall that I have taken the concept of ownership to be the foundational issue in my account of holiness. Holy entities are those that are owned by God. Ownership is a relation between (at least) two entities. Holiness as ownership entails two related aspects of holiness, holy as property and holy as an ethical ideal. On my configuration, I refer to these as two poles to the concept of holiness as the ethical pole and the metaphysical pole, with the metaphysical pole being subdivided into the property and possession nuances. These ranges of meaning are not mutually exclusive and, indeed, coalesce within the ownership range of meaning. That being said, how these conceptual ranges coalesce, and what their relation to one another is, still seems puzzling. This puzzle comes to the fore when we attend to Leviticus 19:2 and attempt to discern just what kind of speech act God is performing with this utterance. Hence, with these procedural and preliminary conceptual frameworks in mind, I now move to employ Alston's account of illocutionary acts in order to glean insight into the meaning of Leviticus 19:2, "You shall be holy, for I the Lord your God am holy."

## THE DIRECTIVE INTERPRETATION

A *prima facie* interpretation of this utterance would take it to be a command.[16] On this score, God identifies one of God's own central attributes and directs the Israelites to act or be in accordance with this attribute. However, as will become clear further on, this interpretation is most at home with an antecedent commitment to the *ethical goodness* understanding of the concept of holiness. There is clearly some narrative support for such an interpretation. For in Leviticus, and Leviticus 19 especially, God commands the people of Israel numerous times. The conceptual symmetry of Leviticus 19 with Exodus 20—what we popularly call the Ten Commandments—has also not escaped the notice of commentators.[17] Rooker titles the section of his commentary wherein he considers this utterance as "Holiness Commanded."[18] He goes on, "In vv. 1 and 2 of Leviticus 19 the Lord tells Moses to address the entire assembly of Israel and *admonishes* them to be holy as God is holy . . . God is *commanding* them to be different from the nations around them. This call is no different from the *command* given to the Israelites upon their arrival at Mount Sinai when God *commanded* the Israelites to be a kingdom of priests and a holy nation."[19] On this interpretation, God commands God's people to be holy.

In Alstonian speech act theory, speech acts of commanding, ordering, or the like fall under the Directive category of illocutionary acts. This category is so called by Alston due to these acts being instances of speakers attempting to direct or influence the actions of their audiences.[20] Directives illocutionary acts are those whereby a speaker places on an audience obligations to perform certain actions. The act of placing these obligations can, however, come in a range of intensities. At its strongest, a Directive illocutionary act is a command (e.g., says the sheriff to the bandit, "Reach for the sky!"). In different social, relational, and linguistic contexts, the intensity of obligations can diminish greatly (e.g., while passing through the buffet line, "Try the quiche, it looks delightful!"). In fact, contextual elements govern how one understands one and the same sentential act uttered by different speakers in different situations. Within a military context, for example, when the commanding officer calls out "Attention!" an order is issued and all subordinates are obliged to stand up. When I call this out in my classroom, the force of the Directive is diminished. The intensity of the obligatory relationship between myself and my students is not the same as that which obtains in a military context. Thus, my utterance of "Attention!" might more be properly considered a request or a plea. Yet, despite the difference in intensity of obligation, both these instances of uttering "Attention!" are Directive illocutionary acts.

Alston provides a schema whereby we can analyze the manner in which a Directive illocutionary act obtains. This schema offers us the opportunity to draw out the implications or contextual features of a wide array of Directive instances, from strict commands to simple requests. I here present in full Alston's Directive schema followed by a few brief comments of exposition. This will be followed in the next section by an application of this schema to the utterance in question.

## Directive Illocutionary Act Schema

Alston uses a number of variable letters in his illocutionary act schema. These variables simply serve as placeholders for the variety of terms and entities that can play the same role in various illocutionary act instances. For Alston, "U" is the *speaker* or *utterer*; "S" is the specific *sentence* uttered, the sentential act; "H" is the placeholder for *hearers* or *addressees*; "R" (or past tense "R'd") is not a variable but is Alston's abbreviation for *taking responsibility* (or past tense *took responsibility*). With these in mind, the Directive illocutionary act schema is:

> U D'd in uttering S (where "D" is a term for some Directive illocutionary act type, a purporting to be producing a certain kind of obligation on H to do D) iff in uttering S, U R'd that:
>
> 1. Conceptually necessary conditions for the existence of the obligation are satisfied. (These includes such things as that it is possible for H to do D, that D has not already been done, etc.)
> 2. Circumstances of the utterance of S are appropriate for the production of the obligation in question. (This includes the appropriate authority for orders, the right kind of interpersonal relationship for request, etc.)

3. By uttering S, U lays on H a (stronger or weaker) obligation to do D.
4. U utters S in order to get H to do D.

Recall that the distinctive feature of Alston's account of speech acts is his focus on the normative responsibilities of speakers in issuing their utterances. A sentential act is categorized as a certain illocutionary act due to what speakers take responsibility for when they speak. In veridical Directive illocutionary acts we will be able to identify that an utterer took responsibility for the satisfaction of conditions 1–4. Instead of discussing each of these conditions at present, I will fill in the variables for the utterance under examination and exposit these conditions in this instance.

## Directive Interpretation

In order to employ the schema for our specific utterance in question, we need to fill in the variables in the schema with components of the Leviticus 19:2 passage. Thus, in this instance, U, the utterer, is *God*; D—a term for purporting to be placing obligations on the addressees—I construe as *commanded holiness*; the specific sentence is of course, *"You shall be holy, for I the Lord your God am holy"*; and finally the audience or H of the utterance is *the people of Israel*. We are now at a position to fill in the schema for this specific instance as an *ex hypothesi* occasion of a Directive illocutionary act. Hence,

*God commanded holiness* in uttering *"You shall be holy, for I the Lord your God am holy"* (where *"commanded"* is a term for some directive illocutionary act type, a purporting to be producing a certain kind of obligation on *the people of Israel* to *be* or *become holy*) iff in uttering *"You shall be holy, for I the Lord your God am holy,"* God R'd that:

1. Conceptually necessary conditions for the existence of the obligation are satisfied. (These includes such things as that it is possible for *the people of Israel* to *become holy*, that Israel has not already become holy, a certain conception of holiness is in place, etc.)
2. Circumstances of the utterance of *"You shall be holy, for I the Lord your God am holy"* are appropriate to produce the obligation in question. (This includes the appropriate authority for orders, the right kind of interpersonal relationship for request, etc.)
3. By uttering *"You shall be holy, for I the Lord your God am holy,"* God lays on *the people of Israel* a (stronger or weaker) obligation to *become holy*.
4. God utters *"You shall be holy, for I the Lord your God am holy"* in order to get *the people of Israel* to *become holy*.

Here I exposit each of these conditions with an eye toward elucidating the underlying concept of holiness requisite for the Directive analysis to go through.

I actually here want to walk backward through the Alstonian conditions as that will take them in increasing order of impact on our conceptual framework. The fourth condition merely specifies within the schema that we understand God to be undertaking the responsibility that God's utterance is in fact attempting to place the obligation on the people. Likewise, in terms of conceptual ease, condition three in the Alstonian schema merely specifies that it is the uttering of the sentence in question that brings about the obligation being placed on the addressee. In this instance, the uttering of "You shall be holy, for I the Lord your God am holy" brings about the state of affairs such that Israel has a stronger or weaker obligation to be or become holy.

The second condition can be construed as a contextual consideration: is the context appropriate for a command or order to be issued? This condition would govern such components as the chronological context, the interpersonal relations between utterer and hearer, the conventions in place in the culture in which the utterance was made. For instance, we can highlight the importance of this second condition by recourse to instances where orders or commands are not made because of an inappropriate relational context. Suppose a soldier walks into a meeting of the Joint Chiefs of Staff and calls out, "Drop and give me twenty push-ups!" Obviously, this order would not obtain due to the inappropriate interpersonal and conventional nature of a soldier giving orders to superiors. In order for a veridical Directive illocutionary act to obtain, it must be issued in an apt context.

Given the narrative portrayal of God in the Torah, it does not seem as though God can fail to perform God's speech acts in a context appropriate to them. And this clearly seems to be the case in this instance. Within the narratives of Scripture, God is nothing less than the supreme authority over the entire cosmos. Having this supreme authority, God can issue orders or commands at will. Furthermore, in these narratives God is not just the God of the cosmos, God is specifically the God of the people of Israel—the very addressees of this utterance. This in fact is the conceptual focus of the second half of the utterance in question, that the speaker is "the Lord your God." Moreover, in the surrounding narrative God repeatedly reminds God's addressees of this interpersonal relationship.[21] Clearly, then, God possesses the appropriate authority and interpersonal relationship with God's addressees to be able to issue a command at this time.

The first condition probes those elements that are conceptually necessary for a veridical Directive speech act of a certain kind to obtain. It is under this heading that I think we can most clearly see the distinction within the notion of holiness between the ethical goodness framework and either metaphysical conceptual framework. For, what would be conceptually necessary conditions for the existence of the obligation to be holy? As I plugged in the variable in Alston's schema, a first condition that naturally comes to mind would be that it is possible for the people of Israel to become holy. The implicit notion here is that if one orders the impossible, the order is null and void, and thus no obligations are placed on the addressees. Suppose I gave the order to "square a circle" or to "be red but not colored." Since none of these states of affairs are possible, no obligation accrues to my addressee. Depending on how one understands the term "order" we might say that in fact an order has not even been issued.[22] Now, the notion of possibility here—which is one that Alston himself uses—is going to be context-specific. For instance, standing in a buffet line I might issue to my colleague the Directive illocutionary act of recommending by saying "Try the quiche, it looks delightful!" Yet my colleague has an egg allergy such that if he were to try the quiche he would inevitably suffer a migraine. In this instance I would be trying to direct his activities—laying on him obligations to do something—but he would be unable to comply. There is nothing logically, metaphysically, or even physically impossible about my colleague's failure to be able to eat quiche, he is simply not able to eat it for the sake of his health. But, as with the previous examples, my illocutionary act fails in this instance in not being able to fulfill this condition.

With this notion in place, we can probe which conception of holiness best fits this type of illocutionary act. For it would seem that neither metaphysical explication of holiness fits the Directive notion of placing obligations on hearers to do something. The metaphysical-possession range of holiness holds holy entities to be owned by God. But it does not seem as though *being possessed by* is really an obligation that an entity can seek to fulfill. Rather, owners take possession of objects, objects do not foist themselves onto owners. Thus because Israel is not able to make themselves the possession of God, God cannot be seen here to be placing on them the obligation to become his. A similar sentiment is found when turning to the metaphysical-property range of holiness. If holiness were some property like *being red* or *being four-sided*, it would be odd for God to place on Israel the obligations to instantiate a property, especially a property that seems to be the purview only of God as the one who is holy.

That God alone is intrinsically holy emerges as a theme throughout Scripture. The corollary of this theme is that other entities are only derivatively holy—that is, holy in proximate relation to God. For instance, the first use of the term *qds* in Torah is in relation to the seventh day of the creation week, which God makes holy because it is a day separated for God's use of rest.[23] Similarly, in the Unburnt Bush vignette, the ground around the bush is "holy" (*qodesh*) because of its proximity to God's presence in the midst of the bush.[24] Or consider the "Holy Place" that is made as such by a concentration of God's presence.[25] Object are holy because they are related in some significant sense to God.

There are some instances where entities are referred to as being unequivocally holy in a manner of an intrinsic attribute, and these are most pointedly used in referring to God as holy. For instance, in the second clause of our passage in question, "I the Lord your God am holy" (Lev. 19:2). This is echoed in 20:26 and 21:8 when God says unequivocally "I the Lord am holy" (*qadosh 'aniy YHWH*) and "I, the Lord who sanctify you, am holy" (*qadosh 'aniy YHWH meqaddishkem*). Moving outside of Leviticus, in the context of Hannah's prayer of thanksgiving for Samuel she prays, "There is none holy like the Lord" (*'en-qadosh kaYHWH*). Of course there is the narratively and liturgically important acclamation by the angels of Isaiah 6:3, "Holy, holy, holy, is the Lord of hosts." Finally, there is the repeated construction of referring to God as "the Holy One," as if none other were as such intrinsically.[26] In fact, it appears from a bird's eye perspective that the entirety of Scripture is an effort to show that none but God are holy and it is only in proximity to God—whether physical or relational—that one is able to likewise become holy. Thus, it would indeed be strange for God to place on Israel the obligations to instantiate this metaphysical state of affairs.

Although it would be difficult to square a metaphysical understanding of holiness with a command to be holy, the conceptual range of holiness that does fit within this illocutionary act schema is the ethical goodness range. Ethics just is that rubric under which we evaluate human actions and obligations. God directing the people to be holy by placing on them the obligations to act in certain ways toward a telos of ethical goodness fits well with the other commands that God issues in the surrounding narrative. Whereas it seems odd to place metaphysical obligations on someone, it is perfectly intuitive for one to place ethical obligations on someone. Thus, I argue, if one is to interpret the utterance "You shall be holy, for I the Lord your God am holy" as a command—a Directive illocutionary act—then one must have an antecedent commitment to the ethical goodness range of meaning for the term "holy."

However, this is not the only illocutionary act option on offer. An alternative illocutionary act category would fit better not with an ethical understanding of holiness, but with the metaphysical one. And to this category I now turn.

## THE COMMISSIVE INTERPRETATION

Ephraim Rader comments on Leviticus 19:2, "Only God himself *makes holy*, in the sense that it is his own coming that brings close. This is why [God] says of [God's] law: 'Keep my statutes and do them; I am the Lord who sanctify you' (Lev. 20:8)."[27] The Directive illocutionary act interpretation is not able to countenance either metaphysical ranges of holiness, preferring to understand God as placing obligations on Israel toward some ethical end. But how, on that interpretation, does God make holy? It would seem as though the people were the ones fulfilling their obligations by making themselves holy. In order to understand what it would mean for God to "make holy" in this situation, we need to consider another kind of speech act that falls under the Alstonian category of a Commissive illocutionary act.

Commissive illocutionary acts are the flipside of Directive illocutionary acts. That is, whereas Directives are such that speakers purport to place obligations on addressees, Commissives are such that speakers purport to place obligations on themselves. The archetypal instance of the Commissive is the promise, but other in-kind instances are contracting, betting, or covenanting. When I promise to meet Sue for tea at 10 a.m. tomorrow morning in uttering, "I will meet you for tea tomorrow at 10," I place obligations on myself. Were I to utter to Sue, "Please, meet me at 10 tomorrow for tea," I would be attempting to place obligations on Sue (subject, of course, to the conditions and considerations of the Directive illocutionary act analysis). For the utterance under consideration, on this interpretation, God does not place obligations on Israel to be or become holy, God places obligations on Godself to make Israel holy. As with the previous section, I present here the Alstonian schema for Commissive illocutionary acts followed by an application of that schema to the Leviticus 19:2 utterance including a commentary and argument for this interpretation's superiority.

## Commissive Illocutionary Act Schema

U C'd in uttering [S] (where "C" is a term for a Commissive illocutionary act type, a purporting to produce an obligation on U to do D) iff in uttering S, U R'd that:

1. Conceptually necessary conditions for U's being obliged to do D are satisfied.
2. H has some interest in U's doing D.
3. U intends to do D.
4. By uttering S, U places herself under an obligation to do D.

As with all illocutionary act type on the Alstonian theory, interpreters attempt to get clear on what speakers take responsibility for in the issuing of their locutions. With Commissives it is important to get clear on what obligations speakers are responsible for placing on themselves. A *promise* to meet for tea is a simple illustration. *I*, the speaker, *promise*—place an obligation on myself to do some act—in uttering, "I will meet you for tea tomorrow at 10," if Sue and I have conventions in place that make sense of promising; Sue has some interest in meeting me for tea or in my doing what I say I will do; I intend to meet for tea; and my making my utterance I do in fact place the obligation to meet for tea on myself. Thus, in making a promise by means of an utterance, I take responsibility for the satisfaction of these conditions.

I take it that an illocutionary act that is related to promising is that of covenanting. They are related in both being instances of the more general category of Commissive illocutionary acts. However, I take it that a covenant is a more intense Commissive than a promise; just as a promise is a more intense Commissive than, say, a statement of intention ("I might stop by for tea"). Covenants also place more weight on the interrelational dynamics between the parties involved in the covenant. Since God is the speaker of this sentence we have already noted that God takes responsibility for the satisfaction of various conditions. Given the Commissive illocutionary act, we further have to discern what obligations God is purporting to place on Godself.

## The Commissive Interpretation

To begin to apply this type of illocutionary act to an interpretation of the utterance in question, we need to again fill in variables in the schema: once again, U is *God*; C—a term for a particular illocutionary act type—is *covenanted*; the S, sentence, is again *You shall be holy, for I the Lord your God am holy*; D is *the making of H holy*; and finally the H—*hearers*—of the sentence are the people of Israel. Thus, we arrive at a full version of the schema for the utterance in question:

*God covenanted* in uttering *"You shall be holy, for I the Lord your God am holy"* (where *"covenanted"* is a term for a Commissive illocutionary act type, a purporting to produce an obligation on *God* to *make people of Israel holy*) iff in uttering *"You shall be holy, for I the Lord your God am holy,"* God R'd that:

1. Conceptually necessary conditions for *God's* being obliged to *make people of Israel holy* are satisfied.
2. *The people of Israel* have some interest in God's *making them holy*.
3. *God* intends to *make the people of Israel holy*.
4. By uttering *"You shall be holy, for I the Lord your God am holy,"* God places Godself under an obligation to *make the people of Israel holy*.

Like with the Directive illocutionary act analysis let me instead take these conditions in reverse order.

Condition four, similar to condition four of the directive illocutionary act, merely states that the illocutionary act in question is executed by means of the sentential act under consideration. This condition specifies that it is the utterance in question that brings about this obligating. Conditions three and two are likely to be granted by the reader of Torah without argument. Why else would God go through an elaborate process of bringing the people out of Egypt, taking them to Mt. Sinai, giving them the Law, and telling them here and elsewhere that God is interested in the people's holiness? Whether one buys a Commissive interpretation of this specific utterance or not, it is clear to the reader of the narratives as a whole that God intends the people to be holy. Thus, if God intends the people to be holy, and God can make holy, then the conjunction of these two premises yields the third condition that God intends to make the people of Israel holy.

Regarding condition two, do the people of Israel have some interest in God's making them holy? We have few narrative clues as to the intentional states of the people at the time of their hearing this utterance. On a canonical approach, the narrative of Leviticus fits in with the action of Exodus, wherein, presumably, the people sit through receiving all these instructions. Does the narrative indicate that we are to suppose that the people know Leviticus to be an expression of God's intention to make them holy? Perhaps or perhaps not; it might be that this is why God has to continue to remind them of God's own holiness. But if the Israelites have been paying attention to God's liberating them from Egypt, the lightning, the thunder, and the horn blasts of Sinai, as well as God's revelation of Godself as being holy, then it stands to reason within the narrative that the people would in fact be interested in being or becoming holy, however that is to come about.

Condition one, however, is where the real rubber meets the road in this analysis. If the people of Israel are interested in being made holy, and God intends to make them holy,[28] and God utters a sentence that appears to place on Godself an obligation to make the people of Israel holy, what are the further conceptual conditions necessary for God to do this? First, there is an obvious candidate condition: *that God and Israel are entities that can enter into covenants*. Implicit in this conceptualization is the premise that both God and the people of Israel are agents. It seems conceptually impossible for non-agential entities to be parties to a covenant. This would violate the second and third conditions for a Commissive illocutionary act, for agency is required both for having "interest" (condition two) in something occurring and for one to "intend" (condition three) something. The narratives of Torah clearly portray God as an agent who creates, speaks, and covenants with other agents.

A key feature of Commissive illocutionary acts, and one that relates to the condition of the parties being agents, is the ability of the speaker to place obligations on themselves. One cannot place obligations on oneself that one does not have the authority or right or ability to undertake. I can promise to meet Sue for tea the next morning, but I cannot promise Sue that she will get the job she is interviewing for.[29] I can place obligations on myself to do things within my power, but I cannot oblige myself to do something it is not logically, metaphysically, or physically possible for me to do. Are the conditions of God's utterance of "You shall be holy" such that God can place on Godself the obligation to make holy? Given the unequivocal attribution of holiness to God, Radner is right in holding that only God can make holy, but only if we take holiness here to refer to the metaphysical range of meaning.

A conceptual condition that needs to be in place if this analysis is to go through is that holiness cannot be construed here as ethical goodness. God cannot make other agents ethically good, except perhaps instrumentally by enjoining them to follow the Law. But then, if this is the case, God cannot obligate Godself to make these other agents ethically good. Yet, God can certainly obligate Godself to bring about holiness in the people either *qua* metaphysical-property or *qua* metaphysical-possession. Thus, here is where it is clear that either metaphysical view of holiness fits as the conceptual antecedent to a Commissive interpretation. God can obligate Godself to bestow some property on the people, especially a property that is also one of God's attributes. Likewise, God can obligate Godself to take possession of the people in some sense more robust than the ownership relation God already enjoys. Hence, if one understands holiness within its ethical goodness range, one derives a Directive interpretation of our key utterance; if one understands holiness under either the metaphysical-property or metaphysical-possession heading, then one derives a Commissive speech act interpretation.

## SYNTHESIS

If all three conceptual ranges of holiness are legitimate, how is one to interpret the utterance under investigation? Does one's antecedent commitments to a particular emphasis of holiness entail excluding a plausible interpretation of this utterance? I suggest that Alstonian speech act theory can allow one to take an "all of the above" approach to this particular utterance. For Alston makes no requirement that one sentential act yields one and only one illocutionary act. That is, one can perform more than one illocutionary act with one sentential act, thus we can understand this single utterance by God to be an instance of *both* a Directive and a Commissive illocutionary act.

Perhaps two examples will serve to illustrate this point. Suppose Sue is a bit reluctant to meet me for tea tomorrow at 10 am, perhaps she has a lot of work to do and does not think that she can afford to take a break. By saying, "I will meet you for tea tomorrow at 10" I can both be placing obligations on myself to meet the next day—a Commissive illocutionary act—and I can place obligations on Sue to meet the next day—a Directive illocutionary act. Yet these two illocutionary acts are performed by way of the same sentential act. Or, suppose while at tea I were to utter so both the waiter and Sue can hear me, "I'll take the check." This single sentential act can be interpreted as a request—another instance of a Directive—of the waiter to bring the check and as well as another Commissive illocutionary act directed towards Sue wherein I obligate myself to pay for the tea.

With one and the same sentential act, "You shall be holy, for I the Lord your God am holy," God can both perform a Directive illocutionary act and place obligations on Israel to pursue ethical goodness and perform a Commissive illocutionary act whereby God places obligations on Godself to make Israel holy by way of a metaphysical property and God's possession of them. Mittleman does not take this approach without modification, but he refers to the work of Moshe Hayim Luzzatto who offers this description of holiness, "Holiness is two-fold. Its beginning is labor and its end reward; its beginning is exertion and its end, a gift. That is, it begins with one's sanctifying himself (*mikadesh 'atzmo*) and ends with his being sanctified (*mikadishim oto*)."[30] This dynamic, then, is reminiscent of the two-sidedness of covenants. Israel is to do its part, following the ethical and ceremonial guidelines outlined in the book of Leviticus, and God will do God's part, giving of Godself and taking the people to Godself. Mittleman glosses Luzzatto, "Human beings *can* persevere in thought and action, constantly directing their will toward the sanctification of action (*kedushat ha-ma'aseh*). After which, God may let his holiness descend and dwell upon them (*yashreh alav kedushato*)."[31]

As a corroboration of this interpretation, the two-sidedness of this state of affairs can be seen just a few chapters later in Leviticus 22, especially verses 31–33. Here God says, "You shall keep my commandments and do them, I am the LORD . . . I am the LORD who sanctifies you, who brought you out of the land of Egypt to be your God, I am the LORD." It would seem odd to interpret the first clause in this utterance as a Directive illocutionary act, for that would introduce unneeded redundancy. One does not need to command commandments; a command just is what a commandment is. Rather, this is an expression of the two-sidedness of holiness. Israel is to do her part, "keep my commandments," and God will do God's part, "I am the Lord who sanctifies you" (*'aniy YHWH meqaddishkem*). As God is holy in Godself, so too does God covenant to make the people of Israel holy from God's own self, if they do all that God commands.

## CONCLUSION

At the heart of the biblical narrative is the manner in which God and humans are related. According to Torah, God calls a certain people out of Egypt to have a particular, unique relationship with them. An important part of that relationship was the manner in which the people would align themselves with God, following God's commands and indeed becoming like their God. "You shall be holy, for I the Lord your God am holy" (Leviticus 19:2), presents a small encapsulation of who and what God is, and the implications for the people of God. Rather than seeing this divine utterance as simply a command, another command among longs lists of commands, seeing this utterance as an instance of both commanding and covenanting, whereby God places obligations both on the people to pursue ethical goodness and on Godself to bring about the people's metaphysical holiness, best comports with the narrative and conceptual milieu in which this utterance is made.

## NOTES

1. J.L. Austin, *How to Do Things with Words* (Cambridge, MA: Harvard University Press, 1962).
2. John Searle, *Speech Acts: An Essay in the Philosophy of Language* (London: Cambridge University Press, 1969).
3. See, for instance, Paul Grice, *Studies in the Way of Words* (Cambridge, MA: Harvard University Press, 1989).
4. Daniel Vanderveken, *Meaning and Speech Acts*, vol. 1 *Principles of Language Use*, vol. 2 *Formal Semantics of Success and Satisfaction* (Cambridge: Cambridge University Press, 1990–1991).
5. Willliam Lycan, *Philosophy of Language: a Contemporary Introduction*, 2nd ed. (New York: Routledge, 2008).
6. See especially Anthony Thiselton, *New Horizons in Hermeneutics* (Grand Rapids, MI: Zondervan Publishing House, 1992).
7. Donald Evans, *The Logic of Self-Involvement: A Philosophical Study of Everyday Language with Special Reference to the Christian Use of Language About God As Creator* (London: SCM Press, 1963).
8. Dietmar Neufeld, *Reconceiving Texts As Speech Acts: An Analysis of 1 John* (Leiden: Brill, 1994).
9. Richard Briggs, *Words in Action: Speech Act Theory and Biblical Interpretation: Toward a Hermeneutic of Self-Involvement* (Edinburgh: T & T Clark, 2001).
10. Nicholas Wolterstorff, *Divine Discourse: Philosophical Reflections on the Claim That God Speaks* (Cambridge: Cambridge University Press, 1995).
11. William Alston, *Illocutionary Acts and Sentence Meaning* (Ithaca, NY: Cornell University Press, 2000), p. 2, parenthetical insertions original.

12. Alston, *Illocutionary Acts and Sentence Meaning*, p. 28.

13. Alston, *Illocutionary Acts and Sentence Meaning*, p. 26. Cf. Austin's definition: "what we bring about or achieve *by* saying something, such as convincing, persuading, deterring, and even, say, surprising or misleading," *How to do Things with Words*, p. 109.

14. Or conditions. Alston, *Illocutionary Acts and Sentence Meaning*, p. 54.

15. Alston, *Illocutionary Acts and Sentence Meaning*, p. 3.

16. Translations of this passage into English tend to express this interpretation. ESV, NASB, NKJ, NRS, and RSV all render the first clause of the passage: "You shall be holy," with the English "shall" typically denoting an instruction with heightened intensity, such as an order or command; the NLT has, "You must be holy"; and the NIV has the imperative sounding "Be holy."

17. See, for instance, Mark Rooker, *Leviticus,* New American Commentary (Nashville: Broadman & Holman, 2000), p. 252; John Hartley, *Leviticus*, Word Biblical Commentary (Dallas: Word Books, 1992), p. 310.

18. Rooker, *Leviticus*, p. 252.

19. Rooker, *Leviticus*, p. 252, emphasis added. Also, Hartley, "Since Israel's holiness is learned and is derived from Yahweh, the *command* for Israel to become holy is expressed in a verbal sentence; the use of the verb 'be, become,' captures the maturing dimension of holiness on the human plane," p. 312.

20. Alston, *Illocutionary Acts and Sentence Meaning*, p. 97.

21. In Leviticus this formulation occurs in 11:44; 18:2, 4, 30; 19:2, 3, 4, 10, 25, 31, 34, 36; 20:7, 24; 23:22, 43; 24:22; 25:17, 38, 55; 26:1, 13.

22. Typically, we would refer to this as purporting or attempting to order, which Alston's schema accounts for. However, perhaps one is inclined to consider impossible "orders" as orders nonetheless, and then one might simply conceive of this as an empty order.

23. Gen 2:3.

24. Exod 3:5.

25. Reference to the Holy Place occurs throughout the Torah and the Prophets, but see especially Exod. 26:33, 34; 28:29, 35, 43; 29:30, 31; 31:11; 35:19; 39:1, 41; Lev. 6:16, 26, 27, 30; 7:6; 10:13; 16:2, 3, 16, 17, 20, 23, 24, 27; 24:9; Num. 18:10; 28:7; 1 Ki. 6:16; 7:50; 8:6, 8, 10; 1 Chr. 6:49; 2 Chr. 3:8, 10; 4:22; 5:7, 9, 11; 29:5, 7; 35:5; Ezr. 9:8; Ps. 24:3; 134:2; Eccl. 8:10; Isa. 57:15; Ezek. 41:4, 21, 23; 42:14; 44:27; 45:3, 4; 48:12; Dan. 9:24.

26. This term is sparsely used of persons who are not God such as in Num. 16:7; Ps. 16:10; 106:16; Dan. 4:23; 8:13. But for clear reference to God see, 2 Ki. 19:22; Job 6:10; Ps. 71:22; 78:41; 89:18; Prov. 9:10; 30:3; Isa. 1:4; 5:19, 24; 10:17, 20; 12:6; 17:7; 29:19, 23; 30:11, 12, 15; 31:1; 37:23; 40:25; 41:14, 16, 20; 43:3, 14, 15; 45:11; 47:4; 48:17; 49:7; 54:5; 55:5; 60:9, 14; Jer. 50:29; 51:5; Ezek. 39:7; Hos. 11:9, 12; Hab. 1:12; 3:3.

27. Ephraim Radner, *Leviticus*, Brazos Theological Commentary on the Bible (Grand Rapids, MI: Brazos Press, 2008), p. 207.

28. It might be observed that a perfect being, if the God of this narrative be considered such, cannot intend to do something impossible. If this is the case, then the satisfaction of condition three is dependent upon the first condition obtaining. But since it is already clear from the narrative that God does in fact intend the holiness of the people, then God's making the people holy is possible. Thus, the analysis of condition one might be more aptly considered an exploration of how it is the case that condition one is satisfied.

29. Assuming I am not the one doing the hiring.

30. Moshe Chayim Luzzatto, *The Path of the Just*, Shraga Silverstein, trans. (New York: Feldheim, 1990), p. 13 in Alan Mittleman, "The Problem of Holiness," *Journal of Analytic Theology* 3 (2015): 29–46, p. 40.

31. Mittleman, "The Problem of Holiness," p. 40, glossing Luzzatto, *The Path of the Just*, p. 328. Emphasis Mittleman's.

*Chapter 7*

# Redeeming Ownership

## *Transignification and Justification*

"You shall be holy" is an utterance God speaks to God's people. Whether these people are God's due to the old covenant or the new, this is a phrase that all followers of God wish to hear directed at them. Within the Christian theological framework, justification is that doctrinal locus under which theologians discuss the initial instance of God bringing about a particular kind of ownership relation between God and God's people. We might think of justification as the initial step in fulfilling a Commissive illocutionary act like was discussed in the previous chapter. God's people become holy when God fulfills God's covenantal word and makes them God's own. This chapter makes a connection between a conception of the Eucharist and a conception of the nature of justification. The hope is that by attending to a theory of the former, we might gain some clarity on the latter as it pertains to justification as a step in human holiness.

### INTRODUCTION

That Jesus calls a piece of bread and a measure of wine by the terms, respectively, "my body" and "my blood" is not in question. This much is clear from but a moment's glance at the relevant passages of the Synoptics and 1 Corinthians.[1] Furthermore, these locutions form the heart of nearly all celebrations of the Eucharist, irrespective of the denominational locale in which these liturgical utterances are made. What, however, is in question is just what these curious utterances mean and how the realities they denote relate to the salvific holiness of the humans who hear these words and consume the bread and wine—newly termed "body" and "blood." Transignification is one attempt to address the question of what these utterances mean. The term was initially coined in the mid-twentieth century by the Dominican Edward

Schillebeeckx as he proposed to explicate a Roman Catholic understanding of Christ's presence in the Eucharist, whilst avoiding the challenge of deploying an Aristotelian metaphysic in a day when that ontology no longer seemed tenable. Despite the fact that the metaphysical reflections of the Stagirite philosopher are no longer seen in contemporary metaphysical circles as untenable, there is much in this proposal that can be appropriated for an account of Christ's presence in the Eucharist regardless of one's penchant for—or aversion to—a substance ontology. Further, this Eucharistic proposal has much to offer sacramentally minded Christians not constrained by the dictates of the Roman Catholic Church. Moreover, so I will argue, there are conceptual resources within this Eucharistic proposal that can be brought to bear on soteriological issues.

The plan of this chapter is as follows. I first review Schillebeeckx's initial mid-twentieth century proposal. This is followed by discussions of similar proposals found in the analytic literature by Michael Dummett and Harriett Baber. I then pivot to consider the phenomenon of prosthesis use and some of the psychological-therapeutic perspectives offered by prosthesis users. This will do two things. First, it will provide us with an underpinning to a straightforward, first-order discourse analysis of the curious Eucharistic utterances. Second, it will provide a model for how it might be that human beings are incorporated into the body of Christ, thus constituting a soteriological model of justification. Finally, I show how slight nuances in one's perspective on the consecrated Eucharistic elements can have implications for how one understands the holiness of the redeemed human.

I should note from the outset that I do not think this model makes an explicit endorsement of a particular theory of the atonement. I think that a range of standard atonement models could be consistent with the motif proffered here. If one thought, along the lines of some in the Eastern Orthodox tradition, that all one needs is a theosis model of the atonement, then one might see the model presented here as telling the whole story. If, however, one were keen to include penal or satisfaction elements in one's theory of the atonement, then one could easily tell this story with these elements as the preamble and with this model becoming a story about sanctification. Furthermore, while I take the transignification theory of the Eucharistic presence as a serious and worthwhile one, it differs in important respects from what I have defended elsewhere. That said, because I make use of some of the conceptual infrastructure of my previous work in this one, the distinguishing features between the two views are subtle.

## SCHILLEBEECKXIAN TRANSIGNIFICATION

Christ said of a piece of bread, "This is my body" and of a measure of wine, "This is my blood." Ministers standing *in persona Christi* make the same utterance. Ministers might also, when distributing the consecrated elements, make the utterance, "This is the body of Christ" or "This is the blood of Christ." Schillebeeckx helpfully shows that discussions of the mechanics of the Eucharist prevalent in the medieval period through the Council of Trent were primarily concerned with presenting a metaphysical state of affairs wherein these statements came out as true. The primary motivation was a positive statement, that "This is the body of Christ" is true on the level of first-order discourse. As Schillebeeckx writes, "[W]e may say that the concept of 'transubstantiation' points to nothing more, but also to nothing less, than the Catholic feeling for the biblical and distinctively Eucharistic real presence of Christ within the medieval framework of thought."[2] This is to say that a doctrine of transubstantiation was not the end of Eucharistic ruminations, it was rather the means by which medieval Roman Catholics secured the notion of the real presence. The dispute, however, was two-fold. First, as the example of John Wycliffe shows, the question was raised as to whether the absence of the bread and wine was required to secure the real presence. Secondly, as the example of Schillebeeckx himself shows, the question was raised as to whether an Aristotelian substance ontology was a necessary philosophical framework for proper explications of the real presence.

The first component of the dispute, exemplified by the *doctor evangelicus* John Wycliffe, pertains to the Roman requirement to deny that the bread or the wine continues to be present after the consecratory utterances are made by the priest. Although Pope Innocent III had used the term "transubstantiation" at the Fourth Lateran Council (1215), no official proclamation as to the metaphysical implications of this term had been forthcoming. The Council of Constance (1418) was called in part to counter views on the Eucharist promulgated by Wycliffe and his followers, including Jan Hus. This council decreed Wycliffe and Hus to be heretics and the council gave these errors as the basis for their heresy. They were condemned for holding:

1. The material substance of bread, and similarly the material substance of wine, remain in the sacrament of the altar.[3]
2. The accidents of bread do not remain without their subject in the said sacrament.[4]
3. Christ is not identically and really present in the said sacrament in his own bodily person.[5]

Lateran IV and Constance required the belief that in the consecration of the bread and wine of the Eucharist, Christ became substantially present "under the form" of bread and wine. Constance further specified that this substantial change necessitate two further beliefs. First, one had to believe that after consecration the substances of the bread and wine were no longer present on the altar. Secondly, that what remained on the altar was the corporeal presence of the substance of the body and blood of Jesus Christ, which is identical with the body of Christ sitting at the right hand of the Father.

The second component of the dispute into which Schillebeeckx entered concerned whether an Aristotelian substance ontology is required for a canonical Roman explication of the real presence. To this, Schillebeeckx issued a resounding "no." Schillebeeckx concludes, "The dogma [of transubstantiation] was thought out and expressed in 'Aristotelian' categories, but the strictly Aristotelian content of these categories was not included in what the dogma intended to say. Christ's real presence in the Eucharist is therefore not tied to Aristotelian categories of thought."[6] This interpretation of the conciliar statements allowed Schillebeeckx the freedom to pursue an explication of the real presence within a different category of thought. For Schillebeeckx, this meant a turn to phenomenology, and specifically the phenomenology of experiencing the Eucharist within the ritual of the Roman Catholic Church.

In light of Schillebeeckx's determinations regarding what is required by the Roman canons and what is untenable about Aristotelian ontology, he turns to ground an account of the real presence in other terms. This is apparent when he asks the question, "What is the *reality* that we experience in our perception of the Eucharistic form?"[7] But reality, for the phenomenologist, is the significance of an object for the perceiver, from the perspective of the perceiver. For Schillebeeckx:

> *What* appears, in our experience, as bread and wine *is* the "body of the Lord" appearing to us (as sacramental nourishment). The significance of the phenomenal forms of bread and wine changes *because* by the power of the creative Spirit, the reality to which the phenomenal refers is changed—it *is* no longer bread and wine, but nothing less than the "body of the Lord," offered to me as spiritual nourishment.[8]

The objects that were formerly perceived as bread and wine have, for the perceiver, become phenomenally the body and blood of Christ. This would, it seems, secure both the real presence of the body of Christ and allow one to hold that the bread was no longer present, thus allowing one to maintain fidelity to the spirit of the Roman Catholic conciliar statements, even if not expressing that spirit in the idiom of Aristotelian categories. However, further specification of Schillebeeckx's suggestive theory is possible, and for this I now turn to consider some recent analytic treatments of the issue.

## RECENT EXPLICATIONS OF TRANSIGNIFICATION

The touchpoints between the ensuing analyses and Schillebeeckx's proposal will be apparent, but what follows makes use of not just phenomenology but a descendent of this philosophy attending to social ontology. A basic, and very rough, notion underlying the commitments of social ontology is that the nature(s) of items in the cosmos—the "what-it-is" of things—are determined, not discerned, by humans. In the context of our social interactions and in service to them, the items that are utilized in these interactions are given meaning and their natures. In application to the Eucharist, as bread and wine take their meaning from social interactivity—as do all objects—their natures can be changed from what they are normally taken to be.

Michael Dummett approaches the question of the doctrine of the Eucharistic presence by setting up a simple interrogation of a would-be participant in the Eucharist. He writes, "I propose to understand the doctrine as requiring no more than that the correct and unqualified answer to the question 'What is it?,' asked of either of the consecrated elements, is 'The Body of Christ' or 'The Blood of Christ.'"[9] This much is straightforward and many traditions have wished to analyze the curious phrases that ministers utter on this simple level. However, Dummett's social ontological model of the Eucharist puts a great deal of emphasis on the nature of, what he calls "deemings." I will focus on how these so-called deemings function pertaining to artifacts, such as those ordinary objects made by humans. It might be that a deeming model undergirds the ontology of natural kinds as well as artifactual kinds, but this could prove controversial and is not necessary to my project, since I take it that bread and wine are not natural kinds, but the product of human ingenuity and creativity (of course, bread and wine are made from natural kinds, such as grain, water, and grapes, but it takes human effort to bring from these natural objects the artifactual elements of bread and wine).[10] The basic idea behind Dummett's deemings is that artifacts are not anything until humans deem or declare them to be some specific entity. Moreover, artifacts exhibit a necessary plasticity such that whereas a particular object, O, at time t1, may be considered an X, yet at t2, O is deemed to be Y, and hence at t3, O is in fact a Y and no longer an X. How might this work? Dummett uses an instance of an ashtray as an illustration. Suppose we have in mind an ashtray and suppose we have a smoker in mind, call him "Matt." Suppose this ashtray is a shallow bowl with some notches taken out of the rim wherein cigarettes and cigars might rest comfortably when not finding a home in Matt's mouth. It does not seem as though an ashtray is a natural kind—ashtrays are not harvested from ash trees. Hence, when the glass smith forges the tray, Matt buys the tray, and then flicks his ashes into said tray, this artifact is deemed an ashtray.

Now imagine this situation. Suppose Matt accidentally knocks his ashtray off his coffee table and it smashes beyond use, he throws it in the bin, but the cigar in his mouth is growing dangerously in need of a flick of ash removal. Matt seeks a small bowl from his kitchen. Suppose this is a small cereal bowl having heretofore been used exclusively for breakfast foods. Matt could take this bowl, utter, "This is an ashtray" and flick his cigar ashes into the, now known as, ashtray. Matt would be at this point deeming the cereal bowl an ashtray. Although we might frown at Matt's use of the cereal bowl as an ashtray and although we might think twice if Matt in the future were to offer us a bowl of cereal, artifacts do not carve up reality at the joints. Humans carve parts of reality into artifacts, and in so doing, at times, change artifacts from one to another.[11]

One important component to Dummett's deemings, and this is especially highlighted in Baber's appropriation of transignification (more on this anon), is that in order for these deemings to stick, they must take place within a socio-linguistic community that adopts the new status of the object in question. That is, if the rest of the members of Matt's household continued to refer to the cereal bowl turned ashtray as a cereal bowl, kept cleaning out the cigar ashes, and kept eating cereal from it, it would not seem as though Matt's deeming took. Rather, the deeming (especially of one object to another) has to be ratified, at least in language, especially in practice, by the socio-linguistic community in order for a veridical deeming to have been said to occur.

The application of this story to the Eucharist is quite simple. Prior to the utterance of the curious words at the Last Supper, both the bread on the table and the wine in the cup were certain artefacts, standard ones known as "bread" and "wine." When, however, Christ took the bread in his hands, drew his fellow diners' attention to it, and uttered, "This is my body," on this analysis, Christ was deeming the bread to be his body. Because Christ is God, his deemings are to be taken as authoritative by any who believe him to be God. Dummett even states that taking the bread as Christ's body requires the antecedent belief in the Incarnation, and thus those who do not have the requisite antecedent belief cannot be expected to hold the deeming to have obtained.

Baber follows suit in the transignification motif in her two articles, explicitly invoking Dummett at one point. Baber avers that her transignification model grounds the aptness of the liturgical utterance, and does so in a much more metaphysically simple manner than previous attempts to secure the real presence in the history of theological reflection. She construes the change in the elements to be a matter of a change in the institutional conventions respecting the elements. According to her model, "the act of consecration is a conventionally generated action analogous to, for example, the act of writing out a cheque."[12] By all empirical counts, a rectangular piece of paper with numbers and letters on it is literally worth no more than a piece of paper. Yet, given certain conditions constituted by particular social and institutional conventions, a check one writes for $200 *is*, on Baber's view, $200. The meaning of the object goes beyond its empirical makeup. Following this analogy, given the conventionally generative actions of the Eucharistic liturgy, when a minister says of a piece of bread that it is the body of Christ, the bread in fact becomes the body of Christ. Might one allege that this view is simply subjective, being based on the psychological states of the participants in the liturgy? Baber argues that the presence of the body of Christ *qua* institutional fact is similar to other standard social conventions:

> But marriage, money, boundaries, and the like are not "subjective." They are the products of collective rather than individual intentionality and the institutions in which it is embodied. An individual cannot by his own initiative, through believing, wishing, or acting as if it were so, enter into or dissolve a marriage, acquire citizenship or increase the value of his portfolio. And, on the account proposed here, the presence of Christ in the Eucharist is likewise secured by the collective intentionality of an institution, viz. the Church.[13]

Employing a social ontological framework, Dummett and Baber show that while some things in our world are the result of institutional or social convention, they are no less real. Hence, the reality of the real presence of Christ in the Eucharist need not be construed by deploying a substance ontology, but can be explicated using well-worn social ontology. However, like Dummett's view, assenting to the truth of the metaphysical state of affairs that undergirds the liturgical utterance requires the antecedent participation in the relevant institution that sanctions the institutional fact of that object being the body of Christ.

But, one might aver, Christ presents us with a very odd situation indeed. For it is one thing to tell us that a cereal bowl has been deemed an ashtray, yet it seems perhaps a bit more extreme to hold that an object like a piece of bread has been deemed a natural kind like human body and that we are to now consider this bread to be the body of Christ. Might this not seem a step too far for a deeming socio-linguistic state of affairs? Here is where we now pivot to consider the testimony of prosthesis users to push on the intuition that this situation is in fact beyond the pale. For, what occurs in an instance of prosthesis use is that some artifact—the product of human ingenuity and creativity—is deemed to be part of a user's body and the user and her socio-linguistic community take it as such.

## PROSTHESIS USE

In the Eucharist, Christ denotes a piece of bread—an artifact—to be his body. Understood along the lines demarcated by Schillebeckx, Dummett, and Baber, this can be taken as an act of deeming whereby the object—the piece of bread—takes on a new social ontological status. Although this kind of a linguistic situation might be easy to understand in the "cereal bowl to ashtray" or "piece of paper to check" illustrations, some might balk at applying this state of affairs to the "piece of bread to the body of Christ" situation. I suspect that the main area of nervousness for the detractor would be the manner in which an artifact is supposed to be conceived of as becoming a human body—something that is thought to be entirely organic. However, while it is certainly the case that human bodies are by and large constituted by organic parts, in the case of prosthesis use non-organic objects—artifactual objects—come to be incorporated into the bodily systems of the prosthesis users such that these prosthetics become, through a process of deeming, parts of the prosthesis user's body. I will exposit this phenomenon here and then make an application of this to the Eucharist before taking all these themes to the sphere of justification.

The use for a prosthetic limb comes when a person desires to accommodate their body for a limb that is missing due to limb loss or congenital limb-deficiency. A prosthetic limb serves the purpose of providing a means for an amputee, for example, to engage in the world and with her body image in a manner similar to the manner she engaged in the world prior to amputation. "Incorporation" is a term referring to the manner in which the prosthetic device is integrated into the users' bodily system—in terms of her bodily awareness, perceptual ability, bodily self-identity, peripersonal space, and so on. Although a thorough survey of the relevant psychological literature is outside the scope of this present study, I here point to a few instances where incorporation appears to have occurred to a sufficient level that prosthesis users considered their prosthetic to be their body.

For instance, many prosthesis users report that their prosthesis is as much a component of their bodies as are their bodies' organic parts. One user writes, "Within my body schema, my prosthetic is as much a part of my body as my skin, blood, and organs."[14] Likewise, too, does another user report on the use of a new prosthetic device, "One of the major factors in my satisfaction with a new prosthesis is how little I feel it. That may sound strange, but to me, my prosthesis is an extension of my body."[15] For both of these prosthesis users, a non-organic and artifactual object has become part of the users' body. These other objects have been properly incorporated into the bodies of their users. Murray comments, "That prostheses can complete a body, i.e., that they can become 'part of' the body, is testified by both amputees and people with congenital limb absence."[16] The result of this incorporation is that some prosthesis users even attest to considering the incorporation sufficient to the point that the prosthesis completes the body. Another user attests, "Well, to me it's as if, though I've not got my lower arm, it's as though I've got it and it's (the prosthesis) part of me now. It's as though I've got two hands, two arms."[17] What these testimonies indicate is that one ought not balk at the notion that an artifact can, within a socio-ontological framework, become a veridical part of a person's body.

Now, it is not necessary for a prosthesis user to perform some explicit act of deeming. She does not need to look at her prosthetic leg and declare, "This is my body," although an act of this nature can certainly serve the incorporation process. What is sufficient for incorporation to have occurred is the kind of self-attestation and self-conceptualization demonstrated in the aforementioned testimonies. The lesson learned from these forays into the realm of prosthesis use, is that the kind of deeming that occurs in "cereal bowl to ashtray" can also occur in situations of "artifact to body part" and hence there is grounds for the application of this conception to the Eucharist to explicate a transignification explanation of "piece of bread to body of Christ."

## THIS IS MY PROSTHESIS

It seems to me that there are resources within this ontological framework for following the letter as well as the spirit of the Roman canons. But this means that the difference between adopting this framework while holding to a Roman conception and adopting this framework while holding to a non-Roman conception is subtle. The difference between a Roman transignification and a non-Roman transignification turns not on the answer to the question, "Is this the body of Christ?"—both will answer, "yes." The difference turns on the answer to the question, "Is this a piece of bread?" The Roman is required to answer this, "no." The non-Roman is free to answer in the affirmative.[18] One's intuitions on this score are revealed in how one approaches other instances of a change in signification or deeming. Is the cereal bowl turned ashtray still a cereal bowl? Is the small, rectangular piece of paper still a piece of paper in addition to being $200? Is the prosthetic leg still an artifact made by human hands of inorganic material as well as the amputee's leg? If one has the intuition that in the other instances of a change in signification the original item ceases to be—ceases to exist as what it once was—then it seems to be one can satisfy the desiderata of the Roman canons with a clear conscious. If, however, one has the intuition or commitment to the fact of the remaining original entity in addition to whatever other signification the object expresses by a veridical deeming, then when one applies this conception to the Eucharist one ends up with a non-Roman perspective on the consecrated bread and wine.

My concern here is not to resurrect outdated ways of maintaining fidelity to the letter or spirit of the Tridentine canons. Faithful adherents to the Roman Catholic teaching magisterium are certainly required to hold to the twin notions of the absence of the bread/wine and the substantial presence of Christ's body/blood. However, Catholics of a non-Roman variety are free to draw on these conceptual resources to exposit alternative means for securing a conception of the real presence of Christ in the Eucharist. But I note that there are Roman and non-Roman ways of applying the deeming motif to the Eucharist and this will carry over in the next section to Roman and non-Roman ways of applying this motif to justification.[19]

Regardless of what one says about the continued presence of the bread, the transignification model—with a social ontology infrastructure—can deliver on a straightforward understanding of Christ's utterance, "This is my body." What Christ means is that the object formerly known only as bread has, in an act of deeming, become in reality the body of Christ. I now turn to apply these reflections to the area of soteriology.

## DEEMED RIGHTEOUS

The Eucharist has certainly been a locus for much dispute in the history of theological reflection. The disputes over the doctrine of justification do not pale in comparison. My purpose here is not to settle the disputes in either of these doctrines, but merely to draw out some level of conceptual interrelationship between the two. The preceding reflections on transignification brought about a perspective on the Eucharist that holds the minister—in the context of the ecclesial community and standing *in persona Christi*—to deem the bread and the wine as the body and blood of Christ. I showed these linguistic deemings of these specific artifacts to be related to the kind of deeming that might occur when a prosthesis user deems her prosthesis to be properly a part of her body. As the testimony of these users indicate, a deeming of this nature makes it such that when one asks of an amputee if her prosthetic is her body, she answers in the affirmative. Likewise, when we ask if the consecrated bread is the body of Christ, we too can answer in the affirmative. In the realm of soteriology, a similar phenomenon can be seen to occur. Only, in this realm it is not bread or a prosthetic leg that is being deemed, it is we humans who are *re*-deemed as we are made holy.

The exegetical issues pertaining to the right interpretation of Paul's letter to the Romans are deep, and the variety of interpretive motifs vast. I do not pretend that what I say here settles any of these complex issues. However, I want to point out that there is a dovetail between the transignification deeming motif and one plausible interpretation of Paul's use of *dikaioō*.[20] One way of explicating Paul's notion of justification in the Christian tradition has been to hold that God declares a Christian righteous in the act of redemption. This is a forensic explication of justification. The Christian has not merited or earned justification due to any acts she has performed, rather the righteousness belongs to Christ, and this is then credited or awarded to or counted as the Christian's righteousness. But this notion of the declarative word of the righteousness of a Christian has clear resonances with the deeming motif of transignification. God performs some speech act that brings it about that the Christian—within God's socio-ontological world—is righteous.

The further implications of this distinction for soteriology should be clear. If the deeming motif is to be carried along from prosthetic use to the Eucharist to the individual Christian, then the distinction between a Roman and a non-Roman perspective carries through as well. Of course, note that I am not talking about Roman or non-Roman perspectives on soteriology. I am using the term "non-Roman" to refer to views wherein the original entity remains, and I am using the term "Roman" to refer to views wherein the original entity does not remain. Hence, a Roman take would have it that when God deems the human being to be part of the body of Christ or to be saved or to be regenerate, that human is no longer what it once was. Whereas a non-Roman perspective would aver that while being deemed a new entity, the human always retains, under some consideration, its original status. Let me unpack these implications in more detail.

A Roman-inspired soteriological motif would have it that Paul's description of the Christian as a "new creation" means a completely new entity. Paul writes in 2 Corinthians 5:17, "So if anyone is in Christ, there is a new creation: everything old has passed away; see, everything has become new." As on the Roman model of the Eucharist the bread ceases to be bread, and the wine ceases to be wine, after the deeming of the entities as the body and blood of Christ, so too would the human cease to be what it once was and instead become a new entity. A non-Roman perspective on this phenomenon might look like Luther's *simul justus et peccator* motif. Although from one angle the Christian is to be seen as righteous and a new creation—redeemed, it is also understood that the Christian is still a sinner and retains something of the Christian's original unrighteousness. Regardless of whether one opts for a Roman-inspired or non-Roman-inspired application of the transignification motif, it is easy to see how a similar socio-ontological phenomenon as occurs in the Eucharistic deeming can be seen to occur in the act of justification.

## CONCLUSION

When God says to God's people, "You shall be holy" we can take this to be an instance of God re-deeming the people that God takes to be God's own. When once people did not belong to God, God's speech act brings about God's ownership of the people. In Christian theology, this initial act of making the people to belong to God falls under the doctrinal heading of justification. This chapter has shown that we can explicate this phenomenon by means of a transignification theory of the Eucharist. In a parallel manner as Christ takes ownership of the bread and wine and deems them his body and blood, so too does God do this with humans in justification, and thereby make them holy.

The fact does not escape me that another Pauline motif applicable in this regard is to refer to the Church as the body of Christ.[21] Those Christians whom God has redeemed by deeming them righteous are thought by Paul to be incorporated into the body of Christ, an ownership relation of a very intimate sort. As I indicated before, it is not necessary for a veridical act of deeming to occur that the deemer actually utter some deeming sentence. Matt can deem his cereal bowl to be an ashtray just in virtue of his use of the object as an ashtray. Sue does not have to deem her prosthetic her body in order for it to be her body, she just has to sufficiently incorporate it into her bodily system in order for this deeming to go through. In the case of the Eucharist, we do have an explicit deeming utterance, both Christ and ministers say of a piece of bread, "This is my body" or "This is the body of Christ." On this analysis, then, Christ need not utter any explicit sentence in order for human redemption—human's being declared righteous—to occur. However, the conception of Christ uttering some form of a declarative word to the redeemed has been a part of the traditional Protestant reflection on this theological phenomenon. Hence, I might suggest that in addition to deeming a piece of bread as his body, we might see that the deeming word that Christ might speak to all the humans who are redeemed in the act of redemption could be understood to be—as in the Eucharist—"This is my body."

## NOTES

1. Matthew 26:26–28, Mark 14:22–25, Luke 22:14–20, 1 Corinthians 11:23–26.
2. Edward Schillebeeckx, *The Eucharist* (London: Sheed and Ward, 1968), p. 60.
3. Norman Tanner, *Decrees of the Ecumenical Councils: Vol. 1* (London: Sheed and Ward, 1990), p. 411: "*Sustantia panis materialis, et similiter substantia vini materialis, manet in sacramento altaris.*"
4. Tanner, p. 411, "*Accidentia panis non manent sine subiecto in eodem sacramento.*"

5. Tanner, p. 411, "*Christus non est in eodem sacramento identice et realiter in propria persona corporali.*"
6. Schillebeeckx, *The Eucharist*, p. 102.
7. Schillebeeckx, *The Eucharist*, p. 145, emphasis original.
8. Schillebeeckx, *The Eucharist*, p. 149.
9. Michael Dummett, "The Intelligibility of Eucharistic Doctrine" in William Abraham and Stephen Holtzer, (eds.), *The Rationality of Religious Belief: Essays in Honor of Basil Mitchell* (Oxford: Oxford University Press, 1987), p. 234.
10. For an engaging and fascinating study of these material components of the Eucharist, see David Grummett, *Material Eucharist* (Oxford: Oxford University Press, 2016).
11. I am not here arguing that one must think that the human to reality relationship is one of making not matching *in toto*. Rather it is simply the case that for non-natural kinds, artifactual kinds, humans make these. It might be that humans discover oak trees, tigers, and copper, but humans make cereal bowls, wooden tigers, and jewelry.
12. H.E. Baber, "The Real Presence," *Religious Studies* (2013b) 51.1, p. 21. See also her 2013a, "Eucharist: Metaphysical Miracle or Institutional Fact?" *International Journal for Philosophy of Religion* 74.3, pp. 333–52.
13. Baber, "The Real Presence," p. 26.
14. Elizabeth Wright, "My Prosthetic and I: Identity Representation in Bodily Extension," *Forum: University of Edinburgh Journal of Culture and the Arts* 8 (2009), p. 1.
15. C.D. Murray, "An interpretive phenomenological analysis of the embodiment of artificial limbs," *Disability and Rehabilitation* 26.16 (2004), p. 970.
16. Murray, "An interpretive phenomenological analysis," p. 970.
17. Murray, "An interpretive phenomenological analysis," p. 970.
18. This situation is akin to the manner in which one might find oneself faced with a Roman or non-Roman perspective on the Eucharist emerging out of the panentheistic-panpsychist framework discussed previously.
19. I remind the reader here that I mean "Roman" and "non-Roman" in this instance just to refer to the absence of the bread or the continued presence of the bread. I do not mean that this will necessarily align with official Roman Catholic teaching on the theology of justification.
20. In Romans, this term can be found in Rom. 2:13; 3:4, 20, 24, 26, 28, 30; 4:2, 5; 5:1, 9; 6:7; 8:30, 33. Other Pauline instances include 1 Cor. 4:4; 6:11; Gal. 2:16, 17; 3:8, 11, 24; 5:4; 1 Tim. 3:16; Tit. 3:7.
21. Clear examples are Romans 12:3, "we, though many, are one body in Christ"; 1 Cor 12:13, "For in one Spirit we were all baptized into one body"; 1 Cor 12:27, "Now you are the body of Christ and individually members of it"; Eph 1:22–3, God "put all things under his [Christ's] feet and gave him as head over all things to the church which is his body."

*Chapter 8*

# Unlimited Ownership

## *The Anglican Articles on the Means of God's Ownership of Humans*

If justification is that doctrinal loci concerned with investigating the manner that God takes ownership of the human, the doctrine of the atonement focuses on the means by which this justification can occur. Christian theories of salvation pull towards poles that represent universalizing extremes on one end and particularizing extremes on the other. One sees explications of salvation in the Christian tradition drawn all the way to the universalizing pole by arguing for full-blown universalism. Contrawise, there are explications that tend toward the particularizing by proffering that Christ's work is limited to some segment of humanity significantly less than the total amount of humans. The unlimited atonement theory, typically construed, attempts to find a *via media* of sorts between these poles. By, again typically construed, emphasizing the "sufficiency-efficiency" distinction, the unlimited atonement theorist attempts to hold together a universalizing proclivity regarding the sufficiency of Christ's work for all humans, together with a particularizing tendency regarding the efficiency of Christ's work for only some humans.

The Anglican tradition is often held up as the Christian tradition uniquely in pursuit of *via media* between a plethora of theological topics regarding doctrine, liturgy, and polity. Many of the early theological formularies of this tradition reflect an attempt to find a middle ground between competing extremes. One such formulary is the Thirty-Nine Articles of Religion, which offer the (or *an*) Anglican angle on a number of issues particularly controversial in that most theologically controversial of centuries in the Christian tradition: the sixteenth. Some of the Articles clearly attempt to find a middle path between, for instance, Roman Catholicism and Anabaptism, or Lutheranism and Reformed thought, or even intra-Anglican positions. The Articles' view of salvation—and specifically the scope of the work of Christ—likewise, as I will show, attempts to find a soteriological *via media* that might best be described as unlimited atonement. Hence, this chapter explores the early Anglican views on the scope of the atonement by probing the teaching of the Articles themselves and by surveying the tradition of commentating on these Articles. In the process, I will argue: (1) that unlimited atonement well-characterizes the teaching on the atonement from the Articles, (2) the manner that the Articles describe faith functioning in achieving the efficacy aspect of the sufficiency-efficiency model can be understood utilizing the conceptual framework of dispositional properties from contemporary metaphysics, and (3) contrary to a recent attempt to characterize unlimited atonement in the Anglican tradition, faith is the only stimulus condition for this efficacy for all humans who are saved.[1] All this sets a basis for the work of Christ being applied to the Christian, resulting in the Christian's derivative holiness.

## UNLIMITED ATONEMENT IN THE XXXIX ARTICLES

As noted, the Thirty-Nine Articles of Religion were the early Anglicans' attempt at staking out views on various theological positions that would come to be the hallmark of the Church of England. The Articles emerged over the course of a few decades in the mid-sixteenth century as the newly independent Church of England sought to articulate its positions on some of the more controversial theological topics of the day. They reached something of their final form in 1571 when they were included in the *Book of Common Prayer*. In no wise were the Articles as comprehensive or exhaustive as other Protestant formularies of the day—such as the Augsburg Confession—or subsequent ones—such as the Westminster Confession of Faith. However, they do address such theological, and specifically soteriological, issues as one might expect would arise from the sixteenth century. In what follows, I survey some of the locations wherein the Articles speak most clearly on the issue of the scope of the atonement, along with some engagement with the tradition of theological commentaries on these Articles.[2]

### Original and Actual Sin

In two locations in the Articles, a distinction is drawn between original sin and actual sin.[3] Both Article II and Article XXXI indicate that Christ's work is applicable to both categories of sin. Moreover, not only is Christ's work applicable to both categories—in support of the unlimited atonement position—Christ's work is applicable to *all* sins that fall into these categories, not just the sins of the elect.

This first place in the Articles where Christ's atoning work crops up comes in Article II, which deals specifically with the "Word, or Son of God, which was made very man." The focus of this Article is a simple expressing of Creedal Christology. Regarding this, the Article states that Christ is God "of one substance with the Father" and a human being, the nature of which the Word took "in the womb of the blessed Virgin, of her substance." A clearly Chalcedonian influence comes when the Article specifies that "the Godhead and the manhood were joined together in one person, never to be divided."

Then in explicating the work of Christ, the Article turns to outline that Christ suffered, was crucified, died, and was buried (alluding to the Apostles' Creed), "to reconcile His Father to us, and to be a sacrifice, not only for original guilt *but also for all actual sins of men*" (emphasis added). This latter clause is identical to the statement on the Son of God found in the Augsburg Confession. I take it that the primary objective of framers of the Articles for these clauses is to ensure that the faithful understood that no other means than Christ's work were required to cover the sins of humans. Many of the Articles ought to be read as responses to (popular, if not official) Roman Catholic theological positions. The worry the framers seem to have in mind is a perspective that would say, "well, Christ's work deals with original guilt, but we need something extra like penance or pardons or indulgences to deal with the ongoing problem of the execution of actual sins." W.H. Griffith Thomas comments, "The Article is thus intended to cover all forms of moral evil, whether those associated with the sin of Adam, or those due to man's personal action. The Bible clearly distinguishes between 'sin' and 'sins,' the root and the fruit, the principle and the practice, and the Article teaches that our Lord's Atonement covers both of these."[4] Hence, there is a universalizing pull in this Article: Christ's work is not just a solution for a particular aspect of the problem of sin (original guilt), but is the solution for the entirety of the sin problem—original and actual sin.

These comments reflect the Articles' teaching that all *classes* of sin are addressed in Christ's work, but the Articles'—and their commentators—also indicate that all *members* of all classes of sins are also covered. In fact, it is the case that at times in the history of the dissemination of the Articles the effort was made to particularize the universalizing tendency of the understanding of Christ's work by removing the universal quantifier in "for all actual sins of men." As E.T. Green comments:

> The omission of the word "all" in some modern copies is entirely without authority. The wording is important because strongly anti-Calvinistic, Calvinism teaching that Christ did not die for all sins, but for those of the elect only. That

the Calvinistic party considered the word "all" hostile to their doctrine is proved by the fact that in the text as revised by the Westminster divines it is wanting.[5]

By "Calvinist" here, I take it that Green means the five-point variety with its emphasis on limited atonement. Moreover, Edgar Gibson too makes note of the importance of the preservation of "all" in the Article. Gibson writes,

> Attention is drawn to this assertion of the universality of redemption, because in various editions of the Articles the important word "all" has been, without the slightest authority, omitted in order to force the article into agreement with the Calvinistic theory of "particular redemption," *i.e.*, the doctrine that Christ died not for *all* but only for "the elect."[6]

Clearly, much is made by these Anglican commentators on the Articles that Christ's work is for all sins is the proper interpretation of the Articles.

In fact, the commentators wish to go so far as to emphasize that the Articles specify that Christ's work is for *all* sins of *all* humans. As with many theological or Scriptural statements, the meaning of the statement turns significantly on the identification of the antecedent to a pronoun: Who is "us" in "to reconcile His Father to *us*"? Or the specific members included in a general term: Who are "men" in "for all actual sins of *men*"? A similar issue arises in Article III when it states, "Christ died for *us*." Again, Gibson writes, "For the *universal* character of redemption and the fact that it was for *all* men that Christ died, appeal may be made to S. John iii. 16 . . . The breadth of such language is quite inconsistent with narrower theories that would limit the saving work of Christ to 'the elect.'"[7] Hence, "all" ought to be understood in the simplest and most straightforward manner as indeed all humans, not just all the elect.

Whereas a particularization of the work of the atonement to only the elect is found in such places as the Westminster Confession of Faith, the term "the elect" is nowhere to be found in the Anglican Articles. Rather, as Griffith Thomas states, "the Atonement means that God in the Person of His Eternal Son took upon Himself in vicarious death the sin of the whole world. The offer of mercy is made to everyone, since there is no sinner for whom Christ did not die, and every sin, past, present, and future, is regarded as laid on and borne by Him."[8] Griffith Thomas here clearly expresses the position that the Articles teach that the scope of Christ's work is unlimited; all the sins of all humans are sufficiently atoned for by Christ's death.

## Sufficiency-Efficiency

As just alluded to, the Lombardian sufficiency-efficiency distinction—and related characterizations—is even noted by some of the commentators on the Articles. R.L. Cloquet juxtaposes the language found in Article II with that found in Article XXXI when he writes, "But if we compare the analogous and indeed almost synonymous words of the thirty-first Article [. . .] unless we adjust Scripture teaching to our own narrow theories, we must conclude that Christ's Death was an Atonement for the sins of all mankind—*sufficient* for all, *efficient* for some."[9] This is a hallmark phrase of the unlimited atonement position: Christ's work is sufficient for all humans, but only efficient for some segment less than the total number of humans. Cloquet further specifies the sufficiency-efficiency distinction by describing another contrast, this one between "objective universality" and "subjective individuality." Cloquet comments on 2 Cor 5:14–15,[10] "Here we have plainly set out the *objective universality* of Christ's death or atonement, in 'that he died for all'; and the *subjective individuality* of the living power of that death, in 'they which live unto him which died for them.'"[11] From an objective angle, Christ's work is sufficient for the redemption of all humans—this is a pull toward the universalizing pole. But from the subjective angle of the individual human, Christ's work is only efficiently applied to those who have faith, of which the tradition is clear that this is not all humans—and hence the pull toward the particularizing that results in a *via media* position.

The universal objective value of Christ's work is also an emphasis of Gibson's reflections on Article II. He states:

> Language such as that [of Article II] is surely incompatible with any theory that denies the objective value of the Atonement. To maintain that the *whole* value of the death of Christ lies in its effect upon the minds and hearts of men by the supreme revelation which it makes of the love of God is to evacuate the words of Scripture of their plain meaning, and to introduce a method of interpretation which, if permitted, will enable men to evade the force of the clearest declarations.[12]

For Gibson, denial of this universal objective scope of Christ's work is to distort the plain reading of Scripture, which he takes the Articles to reflect, and thus open the door to all manner of reinterpretations of doctrine. Rather, the *via media* position of unlimited atonement with limited application best characterizes the Scriptural position, as interpreted by these Anglicans.

This *via media* comes across when characterizing the Articles' position between five-point Calvinism and Arminianism. This is a particular concern of E.A. Litton's theological commentary on the Articles. His reflections on the manner that the sufficiency-efficiency distinction preserves the *via media* of Anglicanism is worth quoting at length:

> The death of Christ placed mankind as a whole in a new and favourable position as regards God, though by many this position may never be realised or made their own; it was a propitiation not for our sins only, but also for the sins of the whole world (1 John ii. 2). A public advantage was thereby secured, which however may become a savour of death unto death or of life unto life according as it is used (2 Cor. ii. 16). And is not this substantially the meaning of the assertors of particular redemption when they admit, as they do, the *sufficiency* of the Atonement for the sins of the world, or ten thousand worlds? And on that sufficiency ground the right and the duty of ministers or missionaries to proclaim to all men that if they repent and believe they will be saved? This proclamation could not be made if there had not been effected by the death of Christ a general expiation for our fallen race. And thus the combatants may not be in reality so much at variance as they had supposed. The most extreme Calvinist may grant that there is room for all if they will come in; the most extreme Arminian must grant that redemption, in its full Scriptural meaning, is not the privilege of all men.[13]

Litton holds that the *via media* of unlimited atonement best preserves the evangelistic mandates found in Scripture. All humans are potentially redeemed, but not all humans are ultimately actually redeemed. Yet, the honest proclamation of the Gospel, for Litton and others, is dependent on the conception of potentiality that unlimited atonement affords, and of which more will be said in this chapter anon.

Although the distinction between the sufficiency and efficiency of the work of Christ goes back to Peter Lombard, the Anglican Articles and the commentators on them put forth this perspective in order to articulate a middle way between the universalizing and particularizing pulls of Christian theories of salvation. Before we probe the thread regarding the potentiality of all to be saved, in the next subsection I turn to examine the Articles' concern for the *solus Christus* of Reformation theology.

## The Sufficient Sacrifice of Christ

The context for many of the Articles—and especially Article XXXI—is clearly a polemic against a certain interpretation of Roman Catholic sacramentalism pertaining to the notion of Eucharistic sacrifice. I say "a certain interpretation" because it is not clear to me that there is not great divergence between (a) an official Roman doctrine of Eucharistic sacrifice, (b) popular conceptions within Roman circles concerning Eucharistic sacrifice, (c) the early Anglicans understanding of the Roman position on this issue, or (d) early Anglican caricatures of either (a) or (b). What is at issue in Article XXXI is the attempt to secure the sole sufficiency of Christ's work on the cross for the remission of sins. This Article is as anti-Pelegian as it is anti-Roman, although likely in the minds of many early Anglicans, these two are one and the same.

Regarding Christ's "one oblation . . . finished upon the cross" Article XXXI states,

> The Offering of Christ once made is that perfect redemption, propitiation, and satisfaction, *for all the sins of the whole world*, both original and actual; and there is none other satisfaction for sin, but that alone. Wherefore the sacrifices of Masses, in the which it was commonly said, that the Priest did offer Christ for the quick and the dead, to have remission of pain or guilt, were blasphemous fables, and dangerous deceits. (Emphasis added)

As we have seen previously, the distinction between original and actual sin is not relevant to limit the scope of Christ's salvific work. But likewise does the inclusion of the universal quantifier regarding the sin of "the whole world" serve to push against the particularizing draw of the limited atonement theory. Griffith Thomas here comments on this Article and refers to the Latin version of the first line, "*Oblatio Christi semel facta*," "The force of 'once' should be particularly noted as meaning 'once for all' (*semel*), answering to the New Testament words ἅπαξ, and ἐφάπαξ (Rom 6:10, Heb 7:27; 9:12, 26, 27, 28; 10:10; 1 Pet 3:18)."[14] I take it that this phrase and his comments on it have an eye both to the chronological and the anthropological in their focus on the universal quantifier. Christ's sacrifice is "once for all" in that it occurred at one time and yet is sufficient for all times. Moreover, Christ's sacrifice occurred once by one individual and yet is sufficient for all humans and all sins committed by all humans. This is expounded in the next line where the Article specifies that all the sins of the whole world are addressed in the satisfying work of Christ's one sufficient sacrifice.

This theme also comes to the fore by means of some phrases in Article XV. Continuing with the theme of finding indirect atonement doctrine within expressions pertaining directly to Christology, Article XV likewise conveys a universal sufficiency of Christ's work. After reiterating the notion that Christ is of the same nature as other humans, and specifying in Chalcedonian fashion that Christ is "like unto us in all things, sin only except," the Article states that Christ, "came to be the lamb without spot, Who by sacrifice of Himself once made, should take away the sins of the world." The limited atonement position takes it that Christ's sacrifice is not sufficient to take away the sins of the whole world, but only the sins of the elect. On the contrary, these Articles stress the universal sufficiency of Christ's sacrifice to be "the propitiation for our sins, and not for ours only, but also for the sins of the whole world," as the quoting from 1 John 2 in the Comfortable Words expresses.

## Liturgical Corroboration

This liturgical note can briefly transition us away from the Articles to turn to the Anglican liturgy as a means of corroborating the unlimited atonement perspective in the Anglican formularies. The Anglican tradition has long been conceived of as a Protestant tradition influenced heavily by the maxim, *lex orandi, lex credendi*. It is sometimes quipped that when the Lutherans and Reformed were forging their identities in the sixteenth and seventeenth centuries they wrote confessions and catechisms, when the Anglican were forging theirs, they wrote a prayer book. This, of course, is not entirely fair for the Lutherans and Reformed also composed liturgies and, as this chapter shows, the Anglicans also attempted to express their theology in propositional form. Here I offer a brief foray into liturgical theology in order to corroborate the reading of the Articles of Religion presented. This specifically concerns the universalizing trend in the Articles' conception of the extent of the work of Christ.

I quote here from the Communion office from first Edwardian Prayer Book published in 1549. In this liturgy, the priest would say prior to the Eucharistic blessing:

> O God heavenly father, which of thy tender mercie diddest geve thine only sonne Jesu Christ to suffre death upon the crosse for our redempcion, who made there (*by his one oblacion once offered*) a full, perfect, and sufficient sacrifyce, oblacion, and satysfaccyon, *for the sinnes of the whole worlde*, and did institute, and in his holy Gospell commaund us, to celebrate a perpetuall memory of that his precious death, untyll his comming again.[15]

The phrase "by his one oblation once offered" is clearly connected to Article XXXI's language of "The Offering of Christ once made is that perfect redemption, propitiation, and satisfaction, for all the sins of the whole world." Again, while anti-Roman Catholic rhetoric regarding the sufficiency of Christ's sacrifice is likely primarily in sight, the universalizing pull of unlimited atonement is also characterized by the "perfect" and "sufficient" sacrifice of Christ. Moreover, this liturgical element includes the reminder that this work is for the "sins of the whole world" with no qualification or restriction.

The unqualified application of Christ's work on all the sins of all humans is brought again to the fore later in the same liturgy. Near the climax of the Eucharistic blessing the priest says:

Christ our Pascall lambe is offred up for us, once for al, when he bare our sinnes on hys body upon the crosse, for he is the very lambe of God, that taketh away the sines of the worlde: wherfore let us kepe a joyfull and holy feast with the Lorde.

The allusion to John the Forerunner's proclamation about Christ conveys the sufficiency of Christ's sacrifice that it is offered "once for all" whereby he "takes away the sins of the world." This conception is, of course, repeated just a bit later in the liturgy during the *Agnus Dei*: "O lambe of god, that takeste away the sinnes of the worlde: have mercie upon us."

One can find key expressions of Anglican theology in its early Articles and its liturgy. When one probes these formularies for their teaching on the scope of the atonement, it is clear that the unlimited atonement perspective best fits data. Moreover, this has been the interpretation of a number of commentators on the Articles in the Anglican tradition. The Articles' focus on the manner in which Christ's work addresses all sins—original and actual—of all humans expresses well the sufficiency-efficiency distinction that is the trademark of the unlimited atonement standpoint. Furthermore, the Articles and liturgy emphasize the sole and total sufficiency of the sacrifice of Christ for all these sins. Yet, these formularies do not teach a full-blown universalism. Rather, I argue, a *via media* can be plotted by attending to the role that faith plays in making actual the potentially universally effective work of Christ.

## SALVIFIC EFFICACY AS A DISPOSITIONAL PROPERTY

The picture painted by the Articles on the scope of Christ's work, I think, can be further probed by showing the application of this work to be akin to the manner in which dispositional properties function within the powers metaphysics conceptual scheme.[16] What I will argue here is that in the unlimited atonement model portrayed by the Articles, all humans are potentially save-able, for the scope of the atonement is sufficient for all. What is required for this potentiality to become actual is the presence of faith in the individual. I here first sketch the notion of dispositional properties and then apply this idea to the salvific context. The next section addresses a potential objection to the sole requirement of faith as the means for making effective the sufficient work of Christ.

Properties are features of objects. For instance, a porcelain teapot might have such properties as *being made from porcelain*, or *being 16 ounces in weight*, or, on some occasions, *being full of tea*. A dispositional property is certain kind of property or feature of an object that refers to the object's ability to change in ways that are specific to that kind of object. We might say an object has a disposition or capacity or tendency to change in certain ways in certain contexts. These contexts are sometimes referred to as stimulus conditions—as in, these conditions stimulate the change in an object. For example, we would typically think that a porcelain teapot has the property of *being fragile*. But *"being fragile"* just means that in a certain context—like being smashed with a mallet—the teapot would shatter. Hence, we can say that the teapot has the dispositional property of *being such that it would shatter when struck with a certain amount of force*. We can imagine a porcelain teapot on a counter, and this teapot has this dispositional property, even though the teapot is resting undisturbed. If, however, the stimulus condition noted in the conditional of the dispositional property is activated—say, I strike the teapot with a mallet—then the state of affairs noted in the first part of the property description (i.e., shattering) obtains (and I have a mess to clean up!).

Here is another example: think of simple table salt. Salt, as we learn in school, is *soluble*. Yet, this property is a dispositional property. It is more specifically stated that salt is *being such that were it immersed in liquid it would dissolve*. Hence, whilst in the salt shaker on the table, the salt is only potentially dissolved (it is *dissolvable*), once I catalyze the appropriate stimulus conditions—say, sprinkling it onto my soup—then this property comes to actualization. The point of both of these illustrations is to point out that noting dispositional properties helps us to specify where, when, and what changes occur that can so radically alter a particular object.

A similar analysis can be had for the actualization of salvation in an individual human on the unlimited atonement scheme. Because Christ's sacrifice is sufficient for "all the sins of the whole world" all that is needed for individual humans is that they are placed in the appropriate condition to receive the benefits of Christ's sacrifice. I quoted Litton earlier, and do so again, on just this point, "The death of Christ placed mankind as a whole in a new and favourable position as regards God, though by many this position may never be realised or made their own."[17] On the unlimited atonement theory according to the Anglican variety sketched above, faith is the stimulus condition requisite for "making their own" Christ's work in the lives of some segment less than the total number of humans. In this manner, one can hold to the universality of the objective work of Christ without being compelled to embrace universalism. Rather the subjective individuality of faith makes effective Christ's work for particular humans. Thus, in good Reformational *sola fide* fashion, faith is the only ingredient, so to speak, that differentiates the saved from the damned.

This dispositional analysis, I think, fits well with another Article of Religion, Article XI on justification. This Article states, "We are accounted righteous before God, *only* for the merit of our Lord and Saviour Jesus Christ by Faith [. . .] that we are justified by Faith *only* is a most wholesome

Doctrine." Note that these clauses state that it is *only* by faith that the merit of Christ's work applies to those individuals to whom it applies. Simply put, faith is *the* stimulus condition to make effectual the work of Christ for an individual. In the next section, I will argue that it is best to hold fast to the singularity of this conception, even in the face of a potential objection.

## SOLA FIDE NOT JUST NORMALLY, BUT ALWAYS

The view of the scope of Christ's work sketched in this chapter has been that Christ's sacrifice is sufficient to atone for all sins of all humans. However, it is also the teaching of the Christian tradition that not all humans receive the benefit of this sacrifice. In the previous section, I showed how one could think of faith as that stimulus condition within which the universal objectivity of Christ's work is made subjectively individual. Yet, might we not ask a question about those who potentially do not have faith? If faith is the sole ingredient needed to effect salvation for individuals, does that not mean that those who are unable to exercise faith due to cognitive limitations are also unable to tap into the benefits of Christ's work? Just such questions arise from a recent discussion of unlimited atonement in the English or Anglican tradition.

### Crispian English Hypothetical Universalism

In his *Deviant Calvinism: Broadening Reformed Theology*, Oliver Crisp attempts to show that there is more diversity of theological positions within the Reformed tradition than is often considered.[18] One such effort at broadening Crisp takes is to show that limited atonement is not the only perspective on the scope of Christ's work in the Reformed tradition. In order to show this, he probes the work of some English Reformed theologians in order to present a view he calls "English Hypothetical Universalism."[19] For this scheme, Crisp describes the following flow to the state of affairs of humans coming to be reconciled with God:
1. The atonement is sufficient for all of humanity, upon the condition of faith.
2. God intends the work of Christ to bring about the salvation of all those who have faith.
3. Faith is a divine gift.
4. *Normally*, fallen human beings obtain salvation through Christ by means of the interposition of divine grace logically prior to salvation, producing faith.
5. God provides faith for the elect.[20]

Regarding (1) we can understand this as the dispositional character of the atoning work of Christ. The work of Christ is *sufficient* for all, that is, all humans are potentially save-able. However, any human that is actually saved requires the condition of faith, that is, we might say, given the stimulus condition of the exercise of faith, making the atonement *efficient* for this class of humans. Now, what appears to be a universal statement in (1) is then shown, on Crisp's view, to be not universal in (4). Rather what is shown in this description is that (1) is the normal or typical state of affairs for salvation, but (4) admits of exceptions to this rule. In a footnote to proposition (4), Crisp writes, "The caveat 'normally' is inserted because there may be classes of fallen humans who are saved *without* faith, such as the severely mentally disabled and infants who die before the age of discernment."[21] Hence, for Crisp, *most* humans who are saved have the universally sufficient work of Christ applied to them by faith, but there "may" be some humans who are not saved in this standard manner.

To my mind, however, the atonement situation need not be so complicated, and we can Ockhamize this situation (to coin a verb) to make it simpler and more consistent. On the Crispian interpretation, God has to provide one means of stimulating atonement in one class of humans—faith—and another means of stimulating atonement in another class of humans, those who are "severely mentally disabled and infants who die before the age of discernment." Call the first class Ordinary Humans (OH) and the subsequent class Specific Humans (SH). OH are "saved by faith" and SH, presumably, are saved by some other means. However, an Ockhamized way to construe the situation is to hold that OH and SH are both saved by the same means, which is faith; *sola fide* always, not just normally.

The clue for advancing this simpler conceptual framework is in Crisp's own proposition (3), "Faith is a divine gift." I see no reason to hold that any divine gift is necessarily predicated upon a prior or natural quality, feature, or property of any individual human. According to the Scriptural witness, God has no problem making an ineloquent shepherd like Moses God's mouthpiece, enabling a man who was born blind to see, or bringing a dead person back to life. Rather, God gives God's gifts to whom God wishes and the exercise of those gifts is due to the—at times, cooperative—power of the human with God's fundamental empowerment. But how this looks, how the divine power is manifest, how the gift is exercised, is and will be as individually unique as the individual human is unique. Simply put, it does not seem to me required to say that God normally provides one way to apply the atonement to OH and another to apply the atonement to SH. Not only does this strain the *sola fide* principle of the theology of the Articles, it is a less simple situation as well.

## Infant Baptism as Test Case

One way to probe the consistency of the *sola fide* ingredient is through a test case of a standard Anglican and Reformed liturgical practice, infant baptism. Regarding this ancient practice the Article XXVII says:

> Baptism is not only a sign of profession, and mark of difference, whereby Christian men are discerned from others that be not christened, but it is also a sign of Regeneration or new Birth, whereby, as by an instrument, they that receive Baptism rightly are grafted into the Church; the promises of forgiveness of sin, and of our adoption to be the sons of God by the Holy Ghost, are visibly signed and sealed; Faith is confirmed, and Grace increased by virtue of prayer unto God. The Baptism of young Children is in any wise to be retained in the Church, as most agreeable with the institution of Christ.

One might wonder how it is that infants or those without the cognitive abilities of adult humans would be able to have their faith "confirmed." Would it not seem as though an individual is first to profess faith and then to have that faith confirmed in the waters of baptism? In fact, just such a scenario is envisioned by Crisp.

However, John Calvin is instructive on this point, wherein he argues that we do not know that infants—or any SH—do not have faith. In the *Institutes* Calvin argues against the Anabaptists who would require that those who are baptized be of a certain age. He writes, somewhat colorfully:

> Therefore, if it please him, why may the Lord not shine with a tiny spark at the present time on those whom he will illumine in the future with the full splendor of his light—especially if he has not removed their ignorance before taking them from the prison of the flesh? I would not rashly affirm that they are endowed with the same faith as we experience in ourselves, or have entirely the same knowledge of faith—this I prefer to leave undetermined—but I would somewhat restrain the obtuse arrogance of those who at the top of their lungs deny or assert whatever they please.[22]

Note that Calvin here is not so bold as to declare definitively that infants do have faith, as Luther before him had. Rather, Calvin takes the epistemically humble stance of asserting that we cannot know that those SH are without faith. Given the logic of unlimited atonement and attention to the Crispian (3), I would be inclined to argue that any member of SH has the work of Christ applied to them in the same manner as those in OH. Consequently, it seems to me, one can hold that the only stimulus condition necessary in order for the dispositional property of being saved by Christ is faith—for the members of OH and SH alike.

## CONCLUSION

Human holiness is about the ownership by God of humans. The atonement is that doctrinal locus where theologians explore how the work of Christ provides the means by which human justification can occur, which thereby brings about an intimate ownership relation between God and humans—resulting in the human's derivative holiness. This chapter has explored unlimited atonement in the Anglican tradition by attending to the Articles of Religion, an early Eucharistic liturgy from this tradition, and some historical commentaries on both. What these formularies teach regarding the scope of the atonement is that every individual human is potentially a human that could be saved. In this regard, humans have the dispositional property of *being saved* if they are found to be in the proper stimulus condition. Hearkening to the Reformation staple of *sola fide*, I averred that faith is that only missing ingredient that need be added to the human condition in order to make Christ's sufficient work efficient for a particular individual. Despite Crisp's suggestion that some segments of the human population might be saved in another manner, I argued that it is simpler and more consistent with other Christian practices—namely, infant baptism—to hold that all humans who are saved possess the divine gift of faith, albeit in manner that are as individually unique as there are unique individuals. Hence, while Christ's work is universally sufficient for salvation, it is efficient by only faith for some particular humans who are made holy by it.

## NOTES

1. My purpose in this chapter is not to legislate for Anglicans which view on the scope of the atonement Anglicans *ought* to have or which is *the* authentic Anglican position. There are, have been, and will be Anglicans who favor limited atonement, just as there are, have been, and will be Arminian Anglicans. I do contend that the unlimited atonement position is most harmonious with a straightforward read of the Articles, but Anglicans have long been comfortable with less straightforward readings of these Articles on nearly every topic they discuss.

2. For further specific discussion of other figures in the English unlimited atonement tradition, see especially: Michael J. Lynch, *John Davenant's Hypothetical Universalism: A Defense of Catholic and Reformed Orthodoxy* (New York: Oxford University Press, 2021); Alan Ford, *James Ussher: Theology, History, and Politics in Early-Modern Ireland and England* (New York: Oxford University Press, 2007); and Jonathan D. Moore, *English Hypothetical Universalism: John Preston and the Softening of Reformed Theology* (Grand Rapids, MI: Eerdmans Publishing Co., 2007). Many editions of the Articles of Religion are available. For this chapter, I have used the version found on the Church of England's website at https://www.churchofengland

.org/prayer-and-worship/worship-texts-and-resources/book-common-prayer/articles-religion, accessed June 4, 2021.

3. Original sin is in Article II referred to as "original guilt." Although principled distinctions are made in theological discourse between original sin and original guilt, in this context these terms appear to be synonymous.

4. W. H. Griffith Thomas, *The Principles of Theology: An Introduction to the Thirty-Nine Articles* (London: Longmans, Green and Co., 1930), p. 50.

5. E. Tyrrell Green, *The Thirty-Nine Articles and the Age of the Reformation: An Historical and doctrinal Exposition in the Light of Contemporary Documents* (London: Wells Gardner, Darton, & Co., 1896), p. 34.

6. Edgar C.S. Gibson, *The Thirty-Nine Articles of the Church of England* (London: Methuen & Co., 1898), p. 149.

7. Gibson, *Thirty-Nine Articles*, p. 151, emphasis original.

8. Griffith Thomas, *Principles of Theology*, pp. 58–59.

9. Robert Louis Cloquet, *An Exposition of the Thirty-Nine Articles of the Church of England* (London: James Nisbet & Co., 1885), p. 26, emphasis original.

10. "For the love of Christ urges us on, because we are convinced that one has died for all; therefore all have died. And he died for all, so that those who live might live no longer for themselves, but for him who died and was raised for them" (NRSV).

11. Cloquet, *Exposition*, p. 26, emphasis original.

12. Gibson, *Thirty-Nine Articles*, p. 152.

13. E.A. Litton, *Introduction to Dogmatic Theology on the Basis of the XXXIX Articles of the Church of England* (London: Elliot Stock, 1882), pp. 285–286, emphasis original.

14. Griffith Thomas, *Principles of Theology*, p. 414.

15. Emphasis added. Many editions of the Book of Common Prayer can be found here: http://justus.anglican.org/resources/bcp/england.htm. For the Communion service in uses here, see http://justus.anglican.org/resources/bcp/1549/Communion_1549.htm, accessed June 4, 2021.

16. A very helpful encyclopedia entry is Sungho Choi and Michael Fara, "Dispositions," *The Stanford Encyclopedia of Philosophy* (Spring 2021 Edition), Edward N. Zalta (ed.), https://plato.stanford.edu/archives/spr2021/entries/dispositions.

17. Litton, *Dogmatic Theology*, p. 285.

18. Oliver Crisp, *Deviant Calvinism: Broadening Reformed Theology* (Minneapolis: Fortress Press, 2014), chap. 7.

19. I intend "unlimited atonement" to denote the same phenomenon as the phrase "hypothetical universalism." I also note that whereas in *Deviant Calvinism* Crisp refers to this position as "English Hypothetical Universalism," more recently he has taken to calling the view "Anglican Hypothetical Universalism." In both instances, Crisp is largely expositing and expanding upon the thought of John Davenant. For Crisp's more recent work on this topic, see *Freedom, Redemption and Communion: Studies in Christian Doctrine* (London: Bloomsbury, 2021), chap. 5.

20. Crisp, *Deviant Calvinism*, p. 201 (emphasis added).

21. Crisp, *Deviant Calvinism*, p. 201 (emphasis added).
22. John Calvin, *Institutes of the Christian Religion*, vol. 2, trans. Ford Lewis Battles, ed. John McNeill (Philadelphia: The Westminster Press, 1960), p. 1342.

*Chapter 9*

# Sanctification as Joint Ownership and the Indwelling of the Holy Spirit

As I have characterized it, holiness is an inherently relational phenomenon. Entities possess the attribute of holiness when they are owned by God. The only entity that possesses this attribute from the entity's self is God. Humans, then, are aptly termed holy when they stand in a particular kind of ownership relation to God—the kind of ownership relation whereby they are owned by God. As we progress through glancing at these doctrinal loci through the lens of holiness we move from the commencement of the Christian life—initial ownership of humans by God—to the continuation of the Christian life. Although the theological doctrines of justification and atonement are foundational to thinking about human holiness, the doctrine of sanctification is that doctrinal area that is most closely associated with human holiness. Hoping to avoid the etymological fallacy, the term itself derives from the notion of simply "making holy." We have seen previously in chapter 6 that when one leans toward the more metaphysical and possession connotations of holiness it is clear that "making holy" is the sole purview of God. God takes ownership of God's people and thus makes them holy as God is holy. But what of the ethical side of holiness? Here the Directive illocutionary act to be holy enjoins God's people toward actions befitting one who is owned by God. In response to the Directive of "be holy," humans "do something about it" in the act of being and becoming holy. This human response is what the doctrine of sanctification attempts to characterize. At the same time, one might wonder whether humans can actually do something about it on or of their own. This chapter sketches a vision of sanctification as a process of ethically responding to being owned by God by means of the indwelling of the Holy Spirit construed as a joint ownership of the human mind.

## ALSTON ON THE INDWELLING

It is commonplace in recent analytic discussions of the indwelling of the Holy Spirit to hearken back to a programmatic essay by William Alston—one of my recurring conversation partners. I will do likewise in this chapter. For Alston sets a scheme for categorizing various ways of understanding the phenomenon of the indwelling. His categories are (a) the "fiat" model,[1] (b) the "interpersonal" (or relational) model,[2] and (c) the "sharing" model.[3] I will discuss these in further detail anon. By and large the fiat model has been rejected outright in the contemporary discussion. Many theorists home in on models related to the interpersonal model. Alston himself advocated for the sharing model. Despite its falling out of favor recently, my hope in this chapter is to reinvigorate the sharing model of the indwelling. This conception fits neatly with the ownership holiness motif that I am pursuing in this book. For sharing is a kind of ownership, a kind of joint ownership. Thus, we can see sanctification as the process by which the joint ownership of a human is increasingly manifest in the human's actions, beliefs, and motivational structures.

As noted, William Alston has written a programmatic essay that has shaped the analytic conversation about the indwelling of the Holy Spirit. Alston himself locates this discussion as falling within the doctrinal locus of sanctification.[4] As such he too, then, sees the indwelling as integrally related to the holiness of the human. Alston notes, "an essential part of the work of the Holy Spirit in building up the Christian community is the regeneration and sanctification of its members."[5] Within this doctrinal area, Alston raises two fundamental questions that are central to investigations into this domain, first regarding the balance between divine activity and human activity in the moral transformation that the redeemed Christian undergoes, second, "how intimately is God involved in the individual in this process? How internal is he to these proceedings?"[6] By these two questions Alston investigates the three proposed models of the indwelling.

The first model, the fiat model, might seem to do well on the second question, but perhaps falters on the first. For as the name suggests, on the fiat model God immediately—as in, without mediator—alters the thoughts or motivational structures of a human. I might liken this to a "zapping" model. God simply zaps the human to give that human a new thought. Where at t1 Matt did not think about helping Sue, at t2 God zaps Matt with the idea to help Sue, and at t3 Matt acts on Matt's belief to help Sue. This model certainly has the air of interiority to it. By fiat, God directly acts on the mind of an individual to give that person new thoughts, feelings, or motivational attitudes. But this hardly seems to be the sort of thing that brings about the kind of cooperative effort that seems to be requisite to avoid turning the sanctified human into a puppet or automaton. To my mind, it also raises a rather intractable problem of evil or problem of sin question. If God is able to zap me with a new virtuous thought or new virtuous disposition, it would seem that God could be doing that all the time, or at least more frequently. Yet, God seems not to, for I—and other redeemed humans—still entertain vicious actions, still sin. Does this not, then, make God responsible for human failures? It might seem so and thus the fiat model seems to founder on the rocks of continuing to attribute actions to individual humans such that they may properly be termed the action of that particular human.

Secondly, Alston discusses what he calls the interpersonal model.[7] It is obvious that humans influence other humans and at times do so very profoundly. Beyond the influence that, say, parents have on children or teachers on students, we can think of the manner that humans easily pick up habits of thought, feeling, or even language from those around them. It seems part of our fundamental intellectual make up that we humans adopt the—vaguely put—ways of life of those around us. There is nothing particularly metaphysically rich about the fact that a teenager picks up the linguistic habits of the teenager's peers. We humans are influenced by those around us with whom we are in relationships.

This model of the indwelling then amounts to the Spirit engaging with the redeemed in just the manner as occurs in human-to-human interactions. For Scriptural support, Alston points to such passages as those in the Fourth Gospels' Upper Room discourses where the Spirit is indicated as teaching the followers of Jesus and bearing witness to the work of Christ. As Alston puts it, "the Holy Spirit is represented as one who will engage in such distinctly interpersonal activities as teaching, witnessing, loving, and uniting others into fellowship."[8] As we are in relationship with the Holy Spirit, we adopt some of the Spirit's ways of life and thus act in similarity to them.

I think the interpersonal model seems to preserve the cooperative nature of the indwelling well, but falters on the interiority component. When we think of human-to-human relations, we can talk a lot about the influences that we have on our actions or thoughts. We rightly credit (or discredit) others with helping us to act virtuously (or viciously) without thinking that their influence takes away our own responsibility for the thoughts or actions executed. However, it is my intuition that the relation of indwelling as accomplished by the Holy Spirit is more—perhaps much more—internal than even that of the most intimate human-to-human relationships. The Spirit is said to "dwell" in the redeemed (Rom 8:11, 1 Cor 3:16, 2 Tim 1:14, among others) in a location that allows the Spirit to groan for the human from a depth beyond words (Rom 8:26). No matter how much, say, a child acts, thinks, or speaks like the child's parent, this is very different from the kind of interiority Scripture envisions for the human-to-Spirit relationship as occurs in the indwelling.

Finally, Alston comes to his own preferred model, the sharing model of the indwelling of the Holy Spirit. Alston characterizes his view as such:

> all the talk of being filled, permeated, pervaded by the Spirit, of the Spirit's being poured out into our hearts strong suggests that there is a literal merging or mutual interpenetration of the life of the individual and the divine life, a breaking down of the barriers that normally separate one life from another.[9]

Alston is clear to note that the sharing model does not preclude aspects of the other two models. Perhaps it is the case that at times God can zap human minds. Perhaps it is the case that at times the manner in which humans learn to think, feel, and act more like Christ is through an interpersonal encounter with the divine. But neither of these other models are able to account for the interiority and cooperative nature of the desiderata Alston sets for himself regarding the indwelling. This permeation or perhaps even saturation of the mind of the human by the Spirit is able to put the Spirit's own thoughts or dispositions at an interior location of apprehension by the human. I quote Alston at length here:

> If God has permitted me to be aware (to some extent) of his loving tendencies in the same direct way that I am aware of my own, that means that they are "available" to me as models in a maximally direct and vivid fashion. I now have a sense of what it is, what it feels like, to love others in this fashion. I can model my attitudes, not just on external manifestations of love, but on the inner springs of those manifestations.[10]

It is from these inner springs of manifestations that the borders are permeated between what is solely the human's and what is shared by the human and the Spirit, which affords this model a level of intimacy that plumbs to the depths of indwelling.[11]

Alston attempts to characterize the joint nature of the sanctification process. On the sharing model, the Holy Spirit's sharing with the individual Christian creates contexts in which influential tendencies can move from Spirit to the mind of the redeemed. But, as Alston notes, "Tendencies can enjoy all degrees of integration into the dominant motivational structure."[12] This seems intuitive. I can have inclinations or tendencies toward two—even contradictory—ends and largely it will be the stronger one that I end up acting on. As I see it, the Spirit cannot so strongly influence the mind of the human so as to override the individual's ownership of the action, lest the action become solely owned by the Spirit and the agent is not able to say, "I did that." Indwelling is not possession like in some Hollywood movie demonic sense. Alston again, "unless I take active steps to encourage them and to dismantle the opposition there is no significant chance that they will influence my behavior."[13] In this manner does the cooperative component of this helpful model of the indwelling come to the fore.

## KROLL ON THE INDWELLING

Kimberly Kroll has offered the most detailed treatment of the indwelling of the Holy Spirit in the analytic theological tradition to date.[14] Her work not only offers a clear delineation of the various aspects of the indwelling, she also offers her own constructive model that appropriates the biblical image of the vine and the branches (what she calls the "Grafting Model"). Her study of this doctrine includes six desiderata (D1–6) for an apt characterization of the indwelling of the Holy Spirit. I find her specification a helpful framework for evaluating this phenomenon and present it here. For Kroll:

D1. the indwelling relation is a unique relation
D2. the indwelling relation is unitive
D3. the indwelling relation is personal
D4. the indwelling relation is transformative for the nondivine person in some way
D5. the indwelling relation is internal in a way that no other relation between persons and beings can be, and
D6. the indwelling relation is evidence of the eternal conditioned new covenant relationship.[15]

To my mind, D1 is one of the most apposite desiderata and helps to sift some of the recent models of the indwelling. Scripture seems to indicate that the relationship the redeemed human has with the Holy Spirit is unique and very much unlike any other relation a human might enter into. This is, to my mind, what makes interpersonal models less than desirable, for the manner that they appear so derivative of those relations humans enter into with one another on a regular basis. Union with God is not the sole purview of neoplatonic thinkers; this seems to come from the pages of Scripture itself.[16] D2 captures this as an aspect of the indwelling. For D3 we are reminded that although the indwelling is unique (D1), it is also somewhat familiar in being the union of two persons: a divine and a human. Accepting D3 is also a further plank in the argument of chapter 4 that God as holy entails God as person. D4 captures a bit of the ethical component to holiness that is the subject of this chapter. For humans, being indwelled by the Holy Spirit does not leave one unchanged, but rather serves as a catalyst toward the end of being (ethically) holy as the Lord their God is holy. One feature of the uniqueness of the indwelling relation (D1) is that it is (D5) more internal, more intimate, than any other relation that a human could enter into. Finally, D6 preserves the feature of the indwelling that it is a divinely initiated state of affairs. As we have seen in chapters 6 and 7, humans do not foist themselves upon God, rather God takes ownership of humans as and when and how God sees fit. After sketching my constructive model in the next sections, I will return to interrogate that model using Kroll's desiderata.

## SHARING THE MIND OF CHRIST

In 1 Corinthians 2:16 Paul states, "But we have the mind of Christ." What does it mean to have the mind of Christ? First, I think it is worth noting the ownership—indeed, joint ownership—language that pervades Paul's locution here. Whose mind is it that we are talking about here? Clearly one ought to think that Christ has his own mind. I do not suppose anyone would think that because others have "the mind of Christ" that this entails that Christ no longer has his mind. But, in fact, given the context of this passage in Paul's letter to the Corinthians, the mind most in question is not Christ's, but the "we" in the sentence—with the "we" being Paul and his audience. I take it that Paul here means that, individually, he and his readers each have a mind that is also jointly owned—in some sense—by Christ.

This joint ownership situation is what the doctrine indwelling of the Holy Spirit attempts to characterize. The Holy Spirit is "the Spirit of Christ," the one from the Father through the Son who leads humans back to the Father through the Son. As such, the Holy Spirit helps to conform our minds to the shape of Christ's. However, as we saw from Kroll's desiderata for an indwelling, we are not just talking about some fleeting, external relation. This relation, I will be offering, can be described as a joint ownership of the human mind by the human and the Holy Spirit—something that results in a state of affairs of the human indeed having the mind of Christ.

Now, perhaps the response could be, "Paul doesn't mean this *literally* or *physically* or something. He means 'mind' here like 'habits of thought, feeling, or actions.' So when Paul says that Paul has the mind of Christ he means that he has similar pattern of thoughts, feelings, or actions as Christ has. This is a 'What Would Jesus Do?' kind of thing." Certainly, this makes a lot of sense as a natural explanation. Think of the coach who has been instilling in her players a certain strategy, approach, philosophy to playing a particular sport. When match time comes and the coach is on the sideline, the coach hopes the players think and act in the match the way the coach would. The coach hopes the players have "the mind of the coach" as they engage in the sport. But this in no way requires a shared mind or joint ownership of a common mind. This state of affairs characterizes behavioral influence, albeit in a very specific domain of human activity.

I do not doubt for a moment that we humans can indeed "share a mind" in this looser or more colloquial sense. The coach/players analogy is apt, to my mind. However, then, in part in virtue of its *prima facie* mundaneness, this explanation does not aptly characterize the intimacy required for an account of the indwelling. This is just a standard objection to the relational model of the indwelling. The objection is not that this kind of external behavioral influence does not occur, it clearly does on a human-to-human level, and I see no reason to suppose it does not occur on a divine-to-human level. The objection is that this dynamic is simply too external to be considered an indwelling. Rather, what we are looking for is something more, something more internal, more intimate, more *in* to characterize the relation between the mind of Christ and the mind of the redeemed Christian than can be found in the relation between the mind of the coach and the mind of the players.

As St. Paul teaches us, the human can live even as Christ lives in that one. In fact, Christian theology has long taught that—far contrary to competition between God and the human—as the human is owned more and more by God, the human becomes more and more what they are to be and more and more properly themselves. For the human responding to God's speech act to "be holy," a process of sanctification involves developing the consistent habit of saying to the Spirit, "not my will, but thine be done." I think this can be well described by a state of affairs of the joint ownership of the human mind.

## Joint Ownership

We have seen that ownership is a particular kind of relation that obtains between entities. On its simplest form, ownership is a two-part relation where someone, A, owns some object, O, thus $ArO$. Yet, at times, individuals can enter into joint ownership of some object, decision, or action. Barcelona Football Club, for instance, is owned by the members of the club, totaling nearly 150,000. Members of the Club elect representatives—itself a collective action—to make decisions and manage affairs on a day-to-day level. Yet, all the while, we say it is the Club that has hired or fired managers, won or lost a match, or raised or lost revenue. These actions are owned by the club. The Supreme Court of the United States at present has 9 members. If the Court makes a decision on some ruling, we acknowledge this as an action the Court has executed. It does not matter for the purposes of American jurisprudence whether the decision was made with a 9–0 majority, 7–2, 5–4, or what have you, a majority decision is all that is needed for the Court to act and for the Court as a whole to own that action. What is clear from these illustrations is that individuals enter into joint ownership relations with one another in order to take actions with or by means of the owned entity.

Joint ownership is not as simple as sole ownership. On the simplest configuration of joint ownership, sharing is a three-place relation. There is individual A, individual B, and object O.[17] A and B share O, or AB$r$O. A and B share O if A and B both have claims to the ownership of O where A or B's individual relation of ownership of O is incomplete. Hence, both A and B own O.

But this can be understood in a few ways. First, it might be the case that the ownership that A and B enjoy of O is independent of one another. This would be a relation on the order of:

$$\text{JOINT OWNERSHIP} = (A r O) \wedge (B r O)$$

A scenario of this nature might admit of sole ownership should one of the sides of the conjunction cease to apply. That is, one might think that A's ownership of O is independent of B's ownership of O, such that were B to cease to exist, the relation between A and O would persist. Note, however, that JOINT OWNERSHIP is not the same state of affairs as might occur if we frontload the relationship between A and B in the ownership situation. This would be on the order of:

$$(\text{JOINT}) \text{ OWNERSHIP} = (AB)rO.$$

Here the state of affairs is such that it is A and B in relationship that constitutes the owner of O. Both JOINT OWNERSHIP and (JOINT) OWNERSHIP can be illustrated by the situation of when a married couple owns a house, for instance (at least in the American real estate world that I am somewhat familiar with). Both spouses enter into a joint ownership of the house. Should one of the spouses die, then the house becomes the possession solely of the surviving spouse and hence we learn this is an instance of JOINT OWNERSHIP. If, however, the couple were to divorce, then we come to learn that this was an instance of (JOINT) OWNERSHIP.

However, we might construe the conjunction in JOINT OWNERSHIP as entailing something like a necessity relation, whereby the ownership relation that A or B enjoys of O is dependent on the other party remaining in existence or continuing to own O.

$$\text{JOINT OWNERSHIP*} \ (A r O \text{ iff } B r O) \wedge (B r O \text{ iff } A r O)$$

I suppose we can think here of a situation in which A and B come into joint ownership of O, but one or other does not wish to own O. Perhaps two siblings inherit a restaurant from their newly deceased widowed mother. The restaurant requires some amount of initial investment in order for it to be maintained. Neither sibling has the means on their own for this investment, but they would if they pooled their resources. If one sibling, however, does not wish to invest in this manner, then both siblings would be forced (not, say of metaphysical necessity, simply a pragmatic "forcing") to give up their ownership in the restaurant.

All three ownership situations, JOINT OWNERSHIP, (JOINT) OWNERSHIP, and JOINT OWNERSHIP*, all can admit of varying degrees of ownership within the ownership $r$. It is a rough analogy but imagine it takes a 100% ownership stake in O for O to reach the stats "owned." In a sole ownership situation, 100% of O is owned by A. In any of the JOINT OWNERSHIP situations with two owners, it could be that 50% of O is owned by A and 50% by B (this is a situation less typical in marriages, but more so in the ownership of, say, corporations). In the case of Barcelona FC, the ownership stakes get smaller and smaller due to the great number of owners. But in order for an object to be owned, there must be some amount of ownership stakes totaling 100%.

It is somewhat more efficient for one owner to determine the ends for O. As might be imagined, it gets more complicated for O to have ends determined by it when there are multiple owners. What can happen, however, is that a joint owner can release other owners to take actions in the name of the owned entity. Take, again, a football club. For instance, at the time of writing, Liverpool FC is owned by the Fenway Sports Group (FSG). The principal owner of FSG is an individual, John W. Henry, but there are many partners or joint owners of FSG. In virtue of their joint ownership of FSG, they along with Henry own various sports entities such as Liverpool FC, the Boston Red Sox, and the Pittsburgh Penguins. One notable joint owner of FSG is the basketball star and current Los Angeles Laker, LeBron James. James, however, is likely not very engaged in the day-to-day operations of, say, Liverpool FC. As a joint owner, but one with a relatively small stake in FSG, James can rightfully say that he performed some action that FSG executed, say, paying the salary of Liverpool FC's goalkeeper, even if James himself did not explicitly perform a speech act like, "Let's give our goalkeeper a salary." Rather, he presumably released some control over FSG's actions even as he is considered a joint owner of FSG. All the while, even one with a relatively small ownership stake can be said to take meaningful part in the actions of the owned entity.

We see this in lawsuits frequently. An owner can be held liable for the actions an agent acting in the name of the owned entity takes, even if the owner did not specifically execute the action or even sanction it. An owner of, say, an oil shipping company can say, "it wasn't me who spilled all that oil in the ocean, it was the captain of the ship!" And although the latter clause of this sentence is apt, the owner is still held liable for the action in question. Of course, these liabilities need not just be for vicious actions. LeBron James as part owner of FSG can meaningfully be said to have paid the Liverpool FC goalkeeper. What is needed, however, is an instance of LeBron James saying (by means of reams of legal paper, no doubt), as a joint owner of FSG, I release John Henry (or Tom Werner or whomever) to execute actions regarding the salaries of Liverpool FC players. It might be as though James says concerning player salaries, "Not my will, but Henry's be done."

## The Joint Ownership of a Shared Mind

The theory I am proffering here is that we can think of the state of affairs of a human being indwelled by the Holy Spirit along the lines of the joint ownership of the human mind at particular times, for particular actions. In application to the holiness of the human as indwelt by the Holy Spirit, this is ultimately what I think is going on in that provocative line in the Lord's Prayer when the petitioner asks, "Not my will, but thine be done." This is an act or request of release of some control over the jointly owned entity, the human itself.

But which of our joint ownership models seems most apt to characterize this indwelling relation? Recall our three models of joint ownership:

$$\text{JOINT OWNERSHIP} = (ArO) \land (BrO)$$
$$(\text{JOINT}) \text{ OWNERSHIP} = (AB)rO.$$
$$\text{JOINT OWNERSHIP*} \ (ArO \text{ iff } BrO) \land (BrO \text{ iff } ArO)$$

I think for a jointly owned action to be properly characterized as an instance of an indwelt human, we ought to think that it occurs along the lines of JOINT OWNERSHIP*. Recall that in this situation the ownership relation obtaining between either A or B and O was dependent on the co-ownership by the other entity also owning O. Hence, for an indwelt action, so to speak, it must be the case that the mind that executed said action was of necessity jointly owned by the human and the Holy Spirit. What does this look like? Suppose some human, Sue, executes some action. If, Sue and the Holy Spirit shared the ownership of that mind as the action was executed, then it would be a result of the indwelling. Some might say that there are some actions that can *only* be executed by an instance of JOINT OWNERSHIP*. That is, only and all actions of virtue or goodness or love must be done by means of a supernatural empowering of the human agent.[18] If this picture is apt, then an attempted virtuous action would fail without the joint ownership of the Holy Spirit.

I think we ought to think of the joint ownership that is the indwelling to be an instance of JOINT OWNERSHIP* because it best fits the Krollian desiderata. Recall, Kroll's D1-6, that the indwelling is:

D1. a unique relation
D2. unitive
D3. personal
D4. transformative for the nondivine person in some way
D5. internal in a way that no other relation between persons and beings can be, and
D6. evidence of the eternal conditioned new covenant relationship.[19]

First, JOINT OWNERSHIP* is not necessarily a unique relation insofar as relations go, but it is unique when the object owned is a human mind. This seems to require the kind of supernatural ability that goes beyond anything but God could possess. Second, a JOINT OWNERSHIP* state of affairs is unitive for the entities involved. When an action is taken by a corporate entity,[20] it unifies the parts of the corporation. A level of subsidiary attribution can certainly occur. In a university, for instance, a faculty member of a graduate school can certainly say, "the college football team won the game," but can likewise say, "we won the game." The aptness of the "we" coming from the joint participation or affiliation with the larger body, the college.[21] Third, this characterization of the indwelling is certainly personal in that both owners, A and B, are persons. Fourth, the JOINT OWNERSHIP* ownership indwelling should indeed be transformative for the human in the relation. As Alston characterized his own sharing model, the indwelling "would be a foothold, a beachhead from which the progressive conquest of the individual's motivational system could get a start."[22] I think the JOINT OWNERSHIP* relation provides the context for how the transformation might occur, even if that transformation is not all at once. Fifthly, how are we to think about the internality of this instance of joint ownership? Recall that this also was a key question that Alston raised in his discussion of the indwelling. My own thought is that the internality of the indwelling arises because of the internality of the human mind. The human mind is internal to the human in a way no other component of the human is. If that innermost part of the human is jointly owned by the human and the Holy Spirit, in this strong JOINT OWNERSHIP* sense, then it would seem to satisfy this desideratum. The locus of ownership is as internal to the human as one can be. Finally, Kroll wishes the indwelling to be evidence of a new covenant relationship. I do think that indwelling by JOINT OWNERSHIP* achieves this, although not perhaps as the only evidence for a new covenant relationship. If we think of the old covenant as a suzerain-vassal treaty,[23] then this entails that the old covenant brought about a certain kind of ownership relation between God and God's people. Likewise, then, might we think that the new covenant continues in this ownership motif. Hence, sharing joint ownership of a human mind is evidence of a suzerain-vassal new covenant relationship.

Chapter 9

## DELEGATING ONE'S SHARE

Supposing that JOINT OWNERSHIP* is an apt way to characterize the indwelling relationship, we turn to think more specifically about how this aids in our understanding of sanctification, being made holy. Here we might think of the joint ownership of the mind of the redeemed human in the act of sanctification again along the lines of the analogy of degreed ownership stakes in the ownership of a football club. That is, the human can release some ownership over the human's own actions, delegating responsibility, and handing over some measure of control or responsibility to the Holy Spirit.

We might think that there is some percentage threshold requisite for being properly said to own an action. If I was only responsible for 10% of a group's action, I should only be credited with 10% of the results of that group's action. Suppose I own a 10% share of a stand at the beach that sells frozen bananas. If that stand makes a profit, I am only entitled to a 10% share of those proceeds. The actions of the franchise are only "mine" at the level of 10%, whether those actions result in losses or gains, regardless of whether those losses or gains are the result of the sale of frozen bananas, a fire insurance settlement, or the value of the lining of the walls of the stand.

However, this seems to me to confuse profit-making with action-taking. Actions are not executed by means of some percentage of force, so to speak, being contributed by various entities the result of which can be keyed up to the players in the action. If three individuals are pushing a broken-down Mazda MPV up a freeway off-ramp, we do not easily divide the percentages of force requisite for bringing said mini-van to the top of the ramp. Moreover, in our corporate illustrations we saw that it is quite legitimate to delegate decision-making responsibilities to certain of the joint owners, even while the entity as a whole owns the actions brought about by these decisions. We might think that some actions a human does only require a minuscule amount of Holy Spirit "force," perhaps sipping a cup of tea or breathing, whereas other actions might require a great deal of Holy Spirit force, say, loving one's enemies and blessing those who curse one. However, given the delegated ownership model in place here, there is nothing that prevents what we might think of as mundane actions from being delegated by the human to the Holy Spirit to a high percentage. In this regard, one can become more holy by a greater delegation of the percentage of volitional ownership that one gives to the Holy Spirit in any and all actions. The more actions one participates in to which the Holy Spirit is a contributing factor, the more that human is ethically able to execute holy actions. Contrary to the corporate world, where it seems that the increase of one's share in a corporation (or football club) is the goal, in sanctification the redeemed human hopes to release more and more of an ownership stake in their own mind and actions.

To my mind, this is a satisfactory picture to convey what Alston wished to find in the balance between divine and human activity in the indwelling relation. Delegated responsibility is not a hostile takeover. We ought not think of the Holy Spirit forcing the sale of shares of the human mind by the human. Rather, in an act of cooperation and release, the human merely delegates responsibility for decision-making and action-taking to one who knows quite a bit more about it. Presumably, LeBron James thinks that the directors of Liverpool FC know a great deal more about how much to pay a goalkeeper than he does. It is quite prudent for James to delegate responsibility for compensating players to other members of the joint ownership group, FSG. So too ought we to think (although our thoughts here are often clouded by sin, ignorance, and finitude) that the Holy Spirit knows quite a bit more about things like loving neighbors and acting virtuously. Taking the step to delegate responsibility to the Spirit in joint ownership preserves a balance of activity between divine and human where the divine does not overwhelm or override the human.

It is God who makes us metaphysically holy, but it is also God who makes us ethically holy. Yet whereas metaphysical holiness is the sole purview of God, ethical holiness does require a cooperation or participation by the human agent. However, this cooperation should not be seen as somehow wresting control from God, but more along the lines of ceding control to God. What, indeed, would it look like for a human mind to be taken over to nearly 100% by the Holy Spirit? It might look like something like a human who has said to the Holy Spirit, "not my will, but thine be done." As this occurs, a human grows in holiness, not because of one's own actions, but because that Spirit who is Holy works more and more in and through the human, making that one holy as the Spirit is holy.

## NOTES

1. William Alston, "The Indwelling of the Holy Spirit," in *Philosophy and the Christian Faith* ed. Thomas V. Morris (Notre Dame, IN: University of Notre Dame Press, 1988), p. 130.
2. Alston, "Indwelling," p. 132.
3. Alston, "Indwelling," p. 139.
4. Alston, "Indwelling," p. 121.
5. Alston, "Indwelling," p. 122.
6. Alston, "Indwelling," p. 124.

7. For other helpful interpretations of the interpersonal or relational model, see Steven L. Porter and Brandon Rickabaugh, "The Sanctifying Work of the Holy Spirit: Revisiting Alston's Interpersonal Model," *Journal of Analytic Theology* 6 (2018): 112–130, and Marilyn McCord Adams, "The Indwelling of the Holy Spirit: Some Alternative Models," in *The Philosophy of Human Nature in Christian Perspective* ed. Peter J. Weigel and Joseph G. Prud'homme (New York, NY: Peter Lang, 2016), pp. 84–99.

8. Alston, "Indwelling," p. 131.

9. Alston, "Indwelling," p. 141.

10. Alston, "Indwelling," p. 145.

11. For a similar approach that does not appeal to Alston's model see Christopher Woznicki, "Dancing Around the Theological Black Box: The Problem and Metaphysics of Perichoresis," *Philosophia Christi* 22.1 (2020): 103–121.

12. Alston, "Indwelling," p. 146.

13. Alston, "Indwelling," p. 146.

14. Kimberly Kroll, "The Condescension of the Spirit: the nature of the relation of the indwelling Holy Spirit," (doctoral thesis, University of St. Andrews, 2020).

15. Kroll, "Condescension of the Spirit," first stated on p. 4, this listing from p. 48.

16. See, for instance, Constantine Campbell, *Paul and Union with Christ: An Exegetical and Theological Study* (Grand Rapids, MI: Zondervan Academic, 2012).

17. I say "object" but I mean this in a loose sense, more like the direct object of a sentence. The object could be some physical item, an action, a state of affairs, etc.

18. For an account of the indwelling of the Holy Spirit by means of love, see Adonis Vidu, "The Indwelling of the Holy Spirit as Love," in *Love, Divine and Human: Contemporary Essays in Systematic and Philosophical Theology* ed. Oliver D. Crisp, James M. Arcadi, and Jordan Wessling (New York, NY: T&T Clark, 2020), pp. 165–186.

19. Kroll, "Condescension of the Spirit," p. 48.

20. By "corporate" I just mean individuals joined together in one body, not necessarily for economic purposes.

21. This is, of course, assuming that the graduate school faculty member is not also on the football team.

22. Alston, "Indwelling," p. 146

23. See, for instance, Jeffrey Niehaus, *God at Sinai: Covenant and Theophany in the Bible and Ancient Near East* (Grand Rapids, MI: Zondervan, 1995).

*Chapter 10*

# Pledging Allegiance to God and God's Holy Kingdom

In concluding this study of holiness, I think it apropos to end with a perspective on how we humans might show forth our holiness *qua* ownership. This chapter is an exercise in constructive liturgical theology that attempts to show how we humans liturgically demonstrate or catalyze our ownership by God, thus bringing about our holiness—perhaps even in some small fashion. Within an ownership relationship, the onus of the dynamic is certainly on the owner. As I have indicated, I do not think that objects can foist themselves onto owners. Initial ownership begins with the owner. For humans and their ownership by God that amounts to their holiness, this arises first from creation and the God-given human vocation to function as priests in God's cosmos. Secondly, humans are owned in a more intimate fashion by the redeeming justification that God declares when God deems humans as God's own. But humans also take their own step to agree with this declaration, Christians corroborate or affirm this work by their acceptance of it and—in sanctification—their cooperation with God. The human also may offer their own word, their own speech act, in this situation. Their agreement with God's taking ownership of them may take the form of aligning themselves with God and God's purposes. In this chapter, I call this pledging allegiance to God and God's kingdom.

Eucharistic liturgies in the Anglican and Orthodox tradition begin with a blessing of God and God's kingdom.[1]

<u>Anglican Church in North America</u>
**Celebrant**: +Blessed be God, the Father, the Son, and the Holy Spirit.
**People:** And blessed be his kingdom, now and forever. Amen.

<u>St. Basil & St. John Chrysostom</u>[2]
**Priest:** +Blessed is the kingdom of the Father and the Son and the Holy Spirit, now and forever and to the Ages of Ages.

**People:** Amen.

What is the meaning of this blessing? What are the minister and the people attempting to communicate to God? As we have done elsewhere in this book, from a speech act theoretic perspective, what actions are the minister and the people performing? In this chapter, I exposit several interpretations of the actions that are being executed when the minister and people make these opening utterances. I will analyze options proffered by Nicholas Wolterstorff and Alexander Schmemann, before developing one of Schmemann's suggestions to greater specificity. All along, I will be using a speech act theoretic infrastructure to argue that these opening utterances can be understood as the minister and the people pledging their allegiance to God and God's kingdom, thereby demonstrating their ownership by God. Before I turn to the constructive portion, I first here offer a recap of the speech act theoretic infrastructure.

## Speech Act Theory

Recall from chapter 6 that speech act theorists hold that utterances do more than just convey propositional content. Consider the sentences "Ouch!" or "Please pick up your toys." Rather than describing some state of affairs or stating some fact, speakers who utter these sentences are performing some action by way of their utterances. The speaker of the sentence, "Ouch!" performs the action of *expressing*, expressing some feeling of pain. The speaker of the sentence "Please pick up your toys" performs the action of *issuing* a request. Through and by these linguistic utterances speakers perform actions.

I am in this chapter continuing to use the account proffered by William Alston. For Alston, the illocutionary act is that which endows a sentence with meaning. Illocutionary acts can typically be made explicit by recourse to an *oratio obliqua* report that includes some characterizing verb. Recall that Alston delineates five categories of illocutionary acts: Assertives—acts like remarking, acknowledging, asserting; Directives—instances where a speaker attempts to influence the behavior of an addressee, like ordering or suggesting; Commissives—wherein a speaker places an obligation on themselves, such as a promise; Exercitives—the bringing into being of a conventional state of affairs like naming a ship or adjourning a meeting; finally, Expressives—the expressing by a speaker of some psychological state the speaker is in.

## FURTHER PRELIMINARIES

I take it that the liturgical utterance under examination is an instance of prayer. Yet, defining prayer is no small task.[3] I take a commonsense definition of prayer to be simply illocutionary acts directed toward God. However, some might point to instances of contemplative or meditative prayer which do not seem properly to be acts of communication, yet are also categorized as prayer. That may be all well and good, then what I want to focus on here is, what might simply be called, "communicative prayer." This may not be the only kind of prayer, but it certainly seems to be the species of prayer that is in play in liturgies where utterers seem to be addressing God. If God is not the target of an utterance in the liturgy, then that utterance is not a prayer. There are many instances in the liturgy where the minister speaks to the people, and even the people speak back to the minister.

Further, I will group the minister and the people together such that one can say they are both performing the same IA, even though verbally they say different words (they utter different SAs). In the Anglican liturgy, the people's words clearly complete the thought initiated by the celebrant's words. In both the Orthodox and Anglican liturgies, the people say "Amen," which I take to be an endorsement or ratification of what immediately precedes. Hence, I am going to tend to speak of the "minister," but I intend that to mean the minister and the people performing the one IA. Secondly, on this point, I hope "minister" might be a neutral description of the leader of the liturgy for the benefit of those who do not have "celebrants" or "priests" leading their liturgies. Next, I want to take these two utterances, the Anglican and Orthodox versions, here as functionally equivalent. That is we simply have two similar but different SAs that perform the same IA. This is easy to account for with Alstonian speech act theory. If Matt walks into the room and Tom says, "Hi!" and Sue says, "Hello," we can easily see that both Tom and Sue performed the same IA (say of *greeting* Matt, or of *welcoming* Matt) even though both speakers performed different SAs. Another preliminary point, I will tend to just write "Blessed be God . . ." by which I mean to include the entire utterance, this is just for the sake of brevity.

Finally for preliminaries, one must realize that these utterances are not just words on a page, but are enacted events that take place in the course of the Eucharistic liturgies. One will need to imagine the minister in the front of the worship space, leading the worship service. In Orthodox contexts and in Anglican *ad orientem* services, this involves the minister facing the altar with the minister's back to the assembled people. With these preliminary considerations in place, I turn now to a first possible interpretation of the opening blessing.

## THE OPENING BLESSING AS AN EXPRESSIVE IA

Nicholas Wolterstorff's book *The God We Worship: An Exploration of Liturgical Theology* is indeed an exploration of the theological ramifications of the liturgy. In the course of his reflections on the liturgy, he offers some potential guidance for an interpretation of the opening blessing. Wolterstorff writes, "One possibility is that blessing God and God's kingdom is no different from praising God and God's kingdom, or declaring them worthy of praise. That seems to me the natural interpretation when the blessing is spoken in the declarative mood."[4] I pause here to note that, in fact, "*praising* God and God's kingdom" and "*declaring* them worthy of praise" are two different illocutionary acts, and the second involves some ambiguity. I take "praising" to be an Expressive IA. When one praises, one expresses a particular psychological state of affairs. "Declaring" is a trickier term to unpack. It could mean something along the lines of what Alston calls an Exercitive: those acts that bring about a change in the world (say, for instance, in a marriage ceremony, "I now pronounce you . . ." or, in a job interview, "You're hired!").[5] Yet, we also have, in English, the *declarative mood* wherein a sentence represents some objective fact ("The fire hydrant is red."). I think Wolterstorff intends the latter given his reference to that mood, but if so, a declaration of the praiseworthiness of God is an Assertive IA, not an Expressive. Hence, I here pursue this first route of interpretation suggested by Wolterstorff, that of an expression. This will be followed by an examination of the second possible route of interpretation, that of an assertion.

### The Opening Blessing as an Expressive IA of Awe

A first possible route of interpretation is to take the utterance "Blessed be God . . ." as, says Wolterstorff, "no different from praising God and God's kingdom."[6] On the Alstonian speech act theoretic infrastructure, this is an Expressive IA. According to Alston, Expressive IAs are such that an utterer expresses an attitude or psychological state. Alston states, "the illocutionary act of expressing an attitude simply consists in linguistically purporting to have that attitude. It is a matter of making it public, getting it out into the open."[7] An act of praising makes explicit or public one's attitudinal stance toward God. I think this conception of the act of praising is helpfully informed by Wolterstorff's own discussion of worship in his book, which we discussed in detail in chapter two of this work. Recall that on this topic Wolterstorff writes, "I suggest that worship of God is a particular mode of Godward acknowledgment of God's unsurpassable greatness. Specifically it is that mode of such acknowledgment whose attitudinal stance toward God is awed, reverential, and grateful adoration."[8] Combining these two insights from Wolterstorff, as an Expressive IA, the utterance "Blessed be God . . ." would be construed as praise because it is an instance of the utterer linguistically purporting to have an attitude of awe about God (and/or God's kingdom).

In order to present clearly a variety of instances of specific IAs, Alston devises schema for each IA. Alston offers the following schema for interpreting Expressive IAs. As with my discussion in chapter 6, let me first decode his variable abbreviations before presenting the full schema for Expressives:

- U—an utterer or speaker
- P—some psychological state
- S—a sentence or sentence surrogate
- R—take responsibility (R'd—past tense)

**E-IA:** U expressed a P in uttering S iff in uttering S, U R'd that U has a P.

This can be articulated in smoother prose:

> An utterer expressed a psychological state in uttering a sentence if and only if in uttering that sentence, the utterer took responsibility for the fact that the utter was in said psychological state.

This is a general schema for all instances of Expressive IAs. I highlight the "R" of the schema for the normative notion that is a key factor of Alston's explication of IAs. An utterer has to own up to or intend to be performing a particular action in order for her utterance to count as that kind of action.

In order to employ it for our use in this particular interpretation of the opening blessing, we can plug in variables in the following manner:

**E-IAa1:** The minister expressed awe of God in uttering "Blessed be God . . ." iff in uttering "Blessed be God . . . ," the minister took responsibility that the minister was in awe of God.

Filling in the variables of the Expressive IA schema with the components of this interpretation of the opening blessing allows us to evaluate more thoroughly the adequacy of this interpretation.

Regarding this interpretation in its current form, perhaps it ought to be understood as a prayer, perhaps not. Attention to the form of the Expressive shows that there need not be an audience in veridical instances of expression. If I say, "Ouch" and thereby perform the IA of *expressing* pain, it need not be the case that anyone hears for this to be an instance of expression. Of course, this is not the case for all Expressives. For instance, suppose in response to Sheldon Vanauken bringing his wife, Davy, a cup of water in the night,[9] Davy utters, "Thanks." This can be analyzed using the schema above with a few slight modifications. In order to give a full account of this state of affairs we have to include variables for the hearer (H) and the impetus for the psychological state (X):

**E-IA:** U expressed a P to H for X in uttering S iff in uttering S, U R'd that U has a P to H for X.

And hence, with the variable filled in for this instance:

> Davy expressed gratitude to Sheldon for bringing a cup of water in the night in uttering "Thanks" iff in uttering "Thanks" Davy took responsibility that Davy was grateful to Sheldon for bringing a cup of water in the night.

We could also include an H and an X in the Opening Blessing analysis like so:

**E-IAa2:** The minister expressed awe of God to God for God's kingdom in uttering "Blessed be God . . ." iff in uttering "Blessed be God . . ." the minister took responsibility that the minister was in awe of God for God's kingdom.

Is this really best understood this way? To me it seems a little bit odd to express something to someone by referring to them in the third person. Furthermore, even Wolterstorff himself does not think this is the best interpretation of the opening blessing, but he offers another potentially better interpretation.

## The Opening Blessing as an Expressive IA of "the Optative"

Wolterstorff in fact decides to interpret this utterance in, as he refers to it, "the optative mood." Wolterstorff writes:

> A blessing spoken in the optative mood, whether over human beings or God, seems to me to call for a different interpretation, however. When God blesses God's newly-created human creatures, God is speaking in the optative mood and saying, *May you flourish. May you be fruitful and multiply and fill the earth.* So too when the priest in the Orthodox liturgy says, "Blessed be the kingdom of the Father, and of the Son, and of the Holy Spirit," he is speaking in the optative mood and saying, *May the kingdom of the Triune God flourish.*[10]

I take optative mood utterances to be also instances of Expressive IAs. I am not sure that when God says to Adam and Eve "Be fruitful and multiply. Fill the earth and govern it,"[11] God was expressing a hope or desire that humans do these things, rather than the command to do so, but I will leave that for another day. For the opening blessing we can analyze the utterance as an Expressive, but this is a different instance than the expression of praise I termed E-IAa. Optative mood sentences express the attitudes of hope, or desire or wish of the utterer for some future state of affairs. Thus, recall E-IA:

U expressed a P in uttering S iff in uttering S, U R'd that U has a P.

We can account for the Expressive as optative in the following manner:

**E-IAo:** The minister expressed the hope/desire/wish that the kingdom of the Triune God would flourish in uttering "Blessed be God . . ." iff in uttering "Blessed be God . . ." the minister took responsibility that the minister had the hope/desire/wish that the kingdom of the Triune God would flourish.

On this construal, the minister has a certain attitude of desiring the kingdom of God to flourish, and this is what the minister makes public in uttering, "Blessed be God . . ." Wolterstorff goes on in his book to explain how the "already/not yet" status of God's kingdom makes sense of the hope/desire/wish that God's kingdom would flourish. Let us leave this option open and turn to the other suggestion Wolterstorff made, that of seeing this utterance as a declaration.

## THE OPENING BLESSING AS AN ASSERTIVE IA

Wolterstorff suggests that we might interpret the utterance "Blessed be God . . ." as a declaration, by which he means a simple acknowledgment of fact, an indicative sentence in the declarative mood. There are two species of this genus of interpretation to explore. The first interpretation—from Wolterstorff—states that, "Blessed be God . . ." is equivalent to "Praiseworthy are you . . ."[12] God and God's kingdom are in a state of blessedness, and thus a sentence on the order of "Blessed be God . . ." or "Blessed is the kingdom . . ." merely acknowledges this fact. A second interpretation takes its cue from suggestive comments made by Alexander Schmemann.

## Acknowledging that God and God's Kingdom Are Blessed

What would it look like to perform the act of acknowledging the blessedness of God and God's kingdom? Acknowledgments fall into the Assertive IA category. Here is how Alston understands the act of asserting some proposition (where *p* is some proposition):

**A-IA:** U asserted that *p* in uttering S iff:

1. U R'd that *p*.
2. S explicitly presents the proposition that *p*, or S is uttered as elliptical for a sentence that explicitly presents the proposition that *p*.

Recall that, for Alston, utterance meaning is tied to that for which utterers take responsibility. For Assertives, the focus of this responsibility is the truth of the proposition that is being asserted. If we were to distill the utterance under analysis to its propositional core, on the Assertive interpretation, this core is: *God and God's kingdom are blessed*. Therefore, we can fill in our variables and proposition in this manner:

**A-IAb:** The minister asserted that *God and God's kingdom are blessed* in uttering "Blessed be God . . ." iff

1. The minister took responsibility that *God and God's kingdom are blessed*.
2. Blessed be God . . ." explicitly presents the proposition that *God and God's kingdom are blessed*.

Thus, we could follow Wolterstorff's suggestion and understand the utterance "Blessed be God . . ." as the minister and the people performing the act of acknowledging that God and God's kingdom are blessed. However, this is not the only possible Assertive IA explication.

## Acknowledging that God and God's Kingdom Are the Minister's Highest Value

Alexander Schmemann, whose magisterial treatment of the Orthodox Eucharistic liturgy we have already encountered, makes similar observations regarding the nature of the IA performed by the opening blessing. He initially categorizes this opening blessing—like Wolterstorff—as as an acknowledgment or a statement of fact. Although as we will see in the following quotation, the proposition that is acknowledged by way of the utterance has more to do with the utterer than the kingdom of God. Schmemann writes of the opening blessing:

> What does it mean to *bless* the kingdom? It means that we *acknowledge* and *confess* it to be our highest and ultimate value, proclaim it to be the goal of the sacrament—of pilgrimage, ascension, entrance—that now begins. It means that we must focus our attention, our mind, heart, and soul, i.e., our whole life, upon that which is truly the "one thing needful."[13]

On this interpretation, what is acknowledged is not the blessedness of God or God's kingdom, but the proposition that *God and God's kingdom are the highest value of the utterer*. Here is how this act would look as an Assertive IA:

**A-IAv:** The minister asserted that *God and God's kingdom are the minister's highest value* in uttering "Blessed be God . . ." iff

1. The minister took responsibility that *God and God's kingdom are the minister's highest value*.
2. "Blessed be God . . ." explicitly presents the proposition that *God and God's kingdom are the minister's highest value*, or
3. "Blessed be God" is uttered as elliptical for a sentence that explicitly presents the proposition that *God and God's kingdom are the minister's highest value*.

An explicit presentation of the proposition *God and God's kingdom are the minister's highest value* would probably look like the minister uttering, "God and God's kingdom are my highest value," which, of course, the minister does not here do. Rather this interpretation would hold that it is by means of uttering "Blessed be God . . ." that the minister presents the proposition *God and God's kingdom are the minister's highest value*. Certainly, Alston's schema can account for this, for condition two includes the provision that occasionally some SAs are issued as elliptical for explicit presentations of propositions. For example, I could give a "thumbs-up" sign as elliptical for a proposition like, "I agree with what you say." On this analysis, when the minister makes the opening blessing, the minister takes responsibility for the fact that God and God's kingdom are the minister's highest value, and the minister then presents that proposition by means of the opening blessing SA.

To this point in the analysis, we have four options for understanding what the minister and the people are doing in uttering "Blessed be God . . ."

1. *Expressing* awe of God (**E-IAa1/2**)

2. *Expressing* the hope/desire/wish that God's kingdom would flourish (**E-IAo**)
3. *Asserting* that *God and God's kingdom are blessed* (**A-IAb**)
4. *Asserting* that *God and God's kingdom are the utterer's highest value* (**A-IAv**)

Although I think each of these possible actions are plausible, I want to proffer that another route of interpretation suggested by Schmemann gets closer to the heart of the act being performed and, thus, is more nearly an act of prayer, understood as communication with God.

## THE OPENING BLESSING AS A COMMISSIVE IA OF PLEDGING ALLEGIANCE

An interpretation that harmonizes better with seeing this utterance as an instance of prayer and as one more directly related to the project of holiness is one that holds the opening blessing to be an instance of the minister and the people aligning themselves with or—perhaps better—pledging allegiance to God and God's kingdom. As the opening act of the liturgy, the minister and the people proclaim that they are God's and thereby are participants in God's kingdom. Schmemann writes that this utterance:

> [M]eans that now, already in "this world," we confirm the possibility of communion with the kingdom, of entrance into its radiance, truth, and joy. Each time that Christians "assemble as the Church" they witness before the whole world that Christ is King and Lord, that his kingdom has already been revealed and given to man and that a new and immortal life has begun.[14]

Rather than a simple act of confirming "the possibility of communion with the kingdom" or entering "into its radiance, truth, and joy," this utterance is an act of pledging or vowing or committing oneself to being in and continuing in God's kingdom.

This act too can be exposited with a speech act schema. Acts of this nature fall into the Commissive type IA. In chapter 6 we saw that Commissives are those IAs wherein one places some stronger or weaker obligation on oneself, for example a promise. If I say, "I'll meet you for tea tomorrow at 10am," in issuing that utterance I am placing certain obligations on myself and my future actions. Recall Alston's form for Commissives are as follows:[15]

**C-IA:** U C'd in uttering S (where "C" is a term for a commissive illocutionary act type, a purporting to produce an obligation on U to do D) iff in uttering S, U R'd for the states of affairs such that:

1. Conceptually necessary conditions for U's being obligated to do D are satisfied.
2. H has some interest in U's doing D.
3. U intends to do D.
4. By uttering S, U places herself under an obligation to do D.

I here first fill in variables for the instance of a Commissive that we are investigating, then I will exposit this schema for this instance. For the opening blessing as Commissive IA, the variables are filled in:

U (utterer)—Minister (and by extension the people)
C (a certain kind of commissive such as promising, contracting)—pledging allegiance
S (the sentence uttered)—"Blessed be God . . ."
D (some act)—participation in God's kingdom[16]
H (hearer)—God

This would render the schema in this instance as such:

**C-IAp:** The minister and the people *pledged allegiance to God and God's kingdom* (where this places on the minister and the people an obligation to participate in God's kingdom) iff in uttering "Blessed be God . . . ," the minister and the people took responsibility for the states of affairs such that

1. Conceptually necessary conditions for the minister and the people's being obligated to participate in God's kingdom are satisfied.
2. God has some interest in the minister and the people's participating in God's kingdom.
3. The minister and the people intend to participate in God's kingdom.
4. By uttering "Blessed be God . . . ," the minister and the people place themselves under an obligation to participate in God's kingdom.

In what follows, I walk through these conditions, making some general comments about the nature of Commissives while also expositing the notion of the opening blessing as a specific Commissive IA.

1. Conceptually necessary conditions for the minister's being obligated to participate in God's kingdom are satisfied.

This component of the Commissive IA schema generally preserves the rationality of the IA. Admittedly, "conceptually necessary" is a bit vague. However, this condition merely tries to make explicit that there have to be certain notions and conventions in place in order to explain just what it is to do some C. Just as in order to promise there necessarily must be some such thing as a promise, in order to bet there must be some sort of phenomenon as betting, in order to pledge allegiance to something there must be some entity to which one could pledge. What could the conceptually necessary conditions be for a minister and the people placing obligations on themselves to participate in God's kingdom? One obviously necessary item would be the existence of God and God's kingdom. One would have a hard time participating in a non-existent kingdom. But it seems that indeed a good deal of Jesus' teaching related to the kingdom of God being "at hand."[17] It would seem to be necessary that God's kingdom is the sort of entity that one could pledge allegiance to and thereby join. Further, a sufficient level of agency is required for individuals to place obligations on themselves. Perhaps also at least a rudimentary understanding of what it means to be a participant in God's kingdom would be required. We might also think that there are certain activities, or values, or beliefs that being a participant in God's kingdom would do or hold: for instance, loving God and neighbor, meeting together to hear Scripture, pray, fellowship, and celebrate the Eucharist, believing that Jesus is God and that God is Trinity, etc.

2. God has some interests in the minister's participating in God's kingdom.

A promise, the paradigmatic Commissive example, is an easy illustration in which one can see this condition satisfied. If Matt promises Tom $1000, Tom has some interest in Matt's doing D, giving $1000. However, suppose Matt said to Tom, "I'm going to beat you up and take your lunch money tomorrow." This also is a Commissive IA, specifically even a promise. Matt has placed upon himself certain obligations of future action in making this utterance. However, Tom has no "interest" in Matt fulfilling these obligations; in fact, Tom has interest in Matt's failing to do D. Thus, "interests" ought to be understood as "it concerns H that U do D" or "H is related to U's execution of D." Hence, even though Tom is not desiring Matt's beating him up, we can say that Matt's obligating himself to beat up Tom concerns Tom. Does God have interest in or does it concern God that the minister and the people participate in God's kingdom? Even the passive reader of the New Testament and the Christian tradition would see that God has some interest in people participating in God's kingdom.

This condition is one area of the Commissive IA that is especially helpful if we are to understand the opening blessing as an instance of prayer; for Alston's schema includes an "H" (hearer) as an integral component of a veridical Commissive act (see C-IA above). An Expressive need not necessarily have an audience when it is performed by an utterer. The same is true for an Assertive. There is nothing in the Alstonian schema that requires there to be an audience for the Assertive to obtain. It might be odd to comment or acknowledge or assert something to be the case without any interlocutors, but really all that is required is that the utterer take responsibility that $p$ in those instances.[18] However, the Alstonian scheme for Commissives includes the condition that there is some H who has an interest or concern in U's executing what U is obligating herself to perform. Again, promising would seem to be a helpful paradigmatic instance of a Commissive. When Matt performs the action of *promising* Tom that Matt will meet Tom for tea at 10 a.m. tomorrow, Tom is the hearer of that utterance and has interests in Matt executing what Matt has obligated himself to do. If Tom had not heard this, say, he was not even in the room, then we would not say that Matt had promised Tom anything.

In the instance under analysis here, the Commissive we are talking about here, the pledging of allegiance to God and God's kingdom, has God as the H and thus concerns God as the entity to which allegiance is being pledged. Yet, it is also the case that the H in this instance are the other participants in the liturgy. This further serves the interpretation of this IA as a *pledging allegiance*. I do not think that God needs us to speak audibly in order for him to know our communicative acts. Presumably the minister could just go to the front of the church, think "Blessed be God . . ." and the people could then think "and blessed be his kingdom . . ." and, ta-da! Commissive IA performed, prayer offered, allegiance pledged, end of story. But this is not what happens, the minister and the people all speak this stuff out loud. They get it out there, make it public, proclaim it audibly, both for the God who does not need to hear it and for their fellow participants in the liturgy who must hear it in order to receive it. The participants in the liturgy have interests in the other participants' pledging allegiance to the kingdom of God. If we view the Eucharist as the people of God joining together for the worship of God, to hear corporately the reading of Scripture, to offer prayers and supplications, to confess sin, and to receive the body and blood of Christ, then it seems very fitting that there be an act at the commencement of the liturgy whereby everyone professes to God and to one another their allegiance to the kingdom of God.

3. The minister intends to participate in God's kingdom.

One could utter "Blessed be God . . ." and not intend to participate in God's kingdom. One could be lying, one could be practicing diction, one could utter this phrase due to peer or social pressure. Neither Alston nor I think that speech acts are magic spells or occur *ex opere operato*. One has to intend to do something and take responsibility for the fact that you are so intending in order for the IA to obtain. In order for this to be a Commissive IA of pledging allegiance to the kingdom of God, and to thereby be a participant in God's kingdom, the utterer must indeed intend to participate in God's kingdom.

This third condition is helpfully illustrated by the promise example once again. Suppose Matt says to Tom, "I promise to meet you for tea at 10 am tomorrow," but Matt has no intention whatsoever of meeting Tom for tea. I take it that in this instance a Commissive IA has not occurred; Matt has not promised Tom anything. Now, this might strike someone as counterintuitive (and I am not sure the account rises or falls on this point), but in the illustration with Matt not intending to meet Tom for tea, but saying he would, is more accurately an instance of a lie than a broken promise. Neither are acts one ought to perform, and I am not sure which is worse, both ought to be avoided. One of the central features of Alston's account of speech acts is that speakers perform speech *acts* and acts are performed by agents and acts performed by agents need to have a certain level of intentionality to them to be considered the act of that agent.

Old examples from action theory are relevant in this instance. If Matt walks into a dark room and flips the light switch, but unbeknownst to him Sue has rigged the light switch so that when it is flipped it causes a chain reaction that results in Tom taking a fatal gunshot to the head, we do not thereby say that Matt killed Tom. Intention has a great bearing on the execution of an action. If one does not intend to promise, one does not promise.[19] In this instance, in order for a *pledge of allegiance* to take place, the utterer has to intend to participate in God's kingdom.

4. By uttering "Blessed be God . . . ," the minister places herself under an obligation to participate in God's kingdom.

Not only must the utterers intend to participate in God's kingdom, they must intend that uttering "Blessed be God . . ." places them under an obligation to participate in God's kingdom. This condition is an attempt by Alston to link up the utterance with the intention more tightly. Perhaps one could take responsibility for all that conditions 1–3 entail, but if one does not come out and say it, actually perform the SA, then one does not have the obligation placed onto them. Now, this condition is the route by which I would pursue a practical ministry application. For if this analysis is accurate, then I would suggest it ought to be part of the catechetical work of the minister to help the people realize that this pledge of allegiance is going on. Instruction on the liturgy should include something like, "When we say the opening blessing, this is your opportunity to pledge allegiance to God and God's kingdom. But that is not going to happen by a magic spell; you have to do it, you have to pledge allegiance, you have to join with me the minister in using this utterance as a means by which you pledge allegiance to God and God's kingdom."

## CONCLUSION

In conclusion let me just offer one bit of corroborating evidence for the "pledge of allegiance" interpretation of the opening blessing. In typical Anglican and Orthodox parishes, when this opening blessing is made, the manual gesture of the sign of the cross accompanies it. "Blessed be God, + the Father, the Son, and the Holy Spirit." Certainly, it occurs that just about every time the Trinitarian formula is uttered people will cross themselves. However, one of the purposes of the sign of the cross, and this is one of the earliest uses of it, is to demonstrate that you are a Christian, you place yourself under the cross, you are a person of the cross. In fact, making the sign of the cross bodily demonstrates that you are a member of the kingdom of God. Thus, it seems beautifully fitting that while verbally pledging allegiance to God and God's kingdom, one also bodily proclaims this same allegiance.

Pledging allegiance to God and God's kingdom entails a recognition of or submission to ownership by God. We can take a pledge of allegiance to the modern state as illustrative of—but certainly not identical to—this. When one pledges allegiance to a particular country one indicates that one intends to live in accordance with the laws and regulations of the country. I do not intend to take anything but the most generic stance on politics here. But this phenomenon is simply illustrated by, say, an instance of immigration. Suppose one were a citizen of the United States of America who immigrated to the United Kingdom. As long as one remained a citizen of the United States, one has certain obligations to (and, I suppose, opportunities afforded by) the USA. One needs to pay taxes on income, one is subject to certain laws of conduct, etc., and in general submit to the laws and regulations of the USA. But were one to forfeit citizenship in the USA and instead go through the process of naturalization into the United Kingdom, one would then pledge allegiance to the UK and its governing authorities, thereby submitting to that nation's laws and regulations. Now, I do not at all want to say that nation states *own* their citizens, this is only an analogous illustration, but even in a derivative sense we might metaphorically say that, at present, the USA *has* my allegiance as I submit to it in various respects.

Application of the illustration to the divine should produce less nervousness. When one pledges allegiance to God and God's kingdom, one does submit to God and indeed wish to communicate one's ownership by God. As we have seen this is one of the hallmarks of the Christian life, that I am not my own, but *belong* to God. As being owned by God, the Christian then participates in God's holiness, which is constituted by and is reflective of divine ownership.

## NOTES

1. In the Anglican tradition this opening is more likely to be found in the American context, both in the 1979 liturgy of The Episcopal Church (TEC) and the Anglican Church in North America (ACNA). For discussion of the TEC opening acclamation see Marion J. Hatchett, *Commentary on the American Prayer Book* (New York: HarperCollins, 1995), p. 318. I note in passing that neither the Tridentine Rite nor the *Novus Ordo* of the Roman Catholic Eucharistic liturgy includes this opening. Rather they both begin with, "In the name of the Father, and of the Son, and of the Holy Spirit. Amen."

2. http://www.goarch.org/chapel/liturgical_texts/liturgy_hchc.

3. For treatments of prayer in the analytic tradition see James M. Arcadi, "Prayer in Analytic Theology," in *The T&T Clark Handbook of Christian Prayer*, eds. John C. McDowell & Ashley Cocksworth (London: T&T Clark, 2021); Scott Davison, "Prayer," in *The T&T Clark Handbook of Analytic Theology*, eds. James M. Arcadi & James T. Turner, Jr (London: T&T Clark, 2021); Christopher Woznicki, "What Are We Doing When We Pray? Rekindling a Reformation Theology of Petitionary Prayer" *Calvin Theological Journal* 53.2 (2018): 319–343 and "Peter Martyr Vermigli's Account of Petitionary Prayer: A Reformation Alternative to Contemporary Two-Way Contingency Accounts" *Philosophia Christi* 20.1 (2018): 119–137; and Oliver D. Crisp, James M. Arcadi, and Jordan Wessling, *Analyzing Prayer* (Oxford: Oxford University Press, 2022).

4. Wolterstorff, *The God We Worship*, p. 50.

5. Austin and Searle actually call these *Declarative* IAs.

6. Wolterstorff, *The God We Worship*, p. 50.

7. Alston, *Illocutionary Acts and Sentence Meaning*, p. 104.

8. Wolterstorff, *The God We Worship,* p. 26.

9. To borrow an example from Vanauken's *A Severe Mercy*.

10. Wolterstorff, *The God We Worship*, p. 51 (emphasis original).

11. Genesis 1:28.

12. Wolterstorff, *The God We Worship*, p. 51.

13. Alexander Schmemann, *For the Life of the World*, reprint ed. (Crestwood, NY: St. Vladimir's Seminary Press, 2000), p. 47 (emphasis added).

14. Schmemann, *For the Life of the World,* p. 48.

15. Alston, *Illocutionary Acts and Sentence Meaning,* p. 97. The original text has "T" instead of "S" in the first part of the scheme. This, to me, appears to be a typographical error since T is nowhere else used by Alston as a variable and all the other instances of his descriptions of IAs he uses S to indicates SAs.

16. This might not be the most apt way of describing the obligation that one is under as a member of God's kingdom, so I just offer this as a suggestive way of describing what it means to D in this instance.

17. Even if, as Wolterstorff describes, there is a sense in which the kingdom is "not yet" awaiting the full inauguration of the eschatological kingdom of God.

18. However, here are two clarifications. First, it seems that it would be hard to enter into a normative position with no one available to hold the utterer accountable for what she took responsibility for. Second, some forms of Assertives are such that they fit into the flow of a conversation in a manner that seems to require another participant in the conversation; one cannot *reply* or *answer* if there had been no external impetus to perform these Assertives.

19. That being said, again, the person who utters a sentence in the form of a standard promise but has no intention of fulfilling the obligations is a liar and should not be trusted.

# Bibliography

Adams, Marilyn McCord. "The Indwelling of the Holy Spirit: Some Alternative Models." In *The Philosophy of Human Nature in Christian Perspective*, edited by Peter J. Weigel and Joseph G. Prud'homme, 84–99. New York, NY: Peter Lang, 2016.

Adams, Marilyn McCord. *Some Later Medieval Theories of the Eucharist: Thomas Aquinas, Giles of Rome, Duns Scotus, and William Ockham.* Oxford: Oxford University Press, 2010.

Alston, William. "The Indwelling of the Holy Spirit." In *Philosophy and the Christian Faith*, edited by Thomas V. Morris, 130. Notre Dame, IN: University of Notre Dame Press, 1988.

Alston, William. *Illocutionary Acts and Sentence Meaning*. Ithaca, NY: Cornell University Press, 2000.

Arcadi, James M. "'You Shall be Holy': a Speech Act Theoretic Theological Interpretation." *Journal of Theological Interpretation* 12, no. 2 (2018): 223–240.

Arcadi, James M. "A panpsychist panentheistic incarnational model of the Eucharist." In *Panentheism and Panpsychism: Philosophy of Religion Meets Philosophy of Mind*, edited by Godehard Brüntrup, Benedikt Göecke, and Ludwig Jaskolla, 189–206. Leiden: Brill, 2020.

Arcadi, James M. "Blessing God as Pledge of Allegiance: a Speech Act Theoretic Approach." In *Analyzing Prayer: Theological and Philosophical Essays*, edited by James M. Arcadi, Oliver D. Crisp, and Jordan Wessling, 65–85. Oxford University Press, 2022.

Arcadi, James M. "God is where God acts: Reconceiving divine omnipresence." *Topoi* 36, no. 4 (2017): 631–639.

Arcadi, James M. "Homo adorans: exitus et reditus in theological anthropology." *Scottish Journal of Theology* 73, no. 1 (2020): 53–66.

Arcadi, James M. "Idealism and participating in the body of Christ." In *Idealism and Christian Theology*, edited by James Spiegel, Joshua R. Farris, and S. Mark Hamilton, 197–215. New York: Bloomsbury Academic, 2016.

Arcadi, James M. "Idealism and participating in the body of Christ." In *Idealism and Christian Theology*, edited by James Spiegel, Joshua R. Farris, and S. Mark Hamilton, 197–215. New York: Bloomsbury Academic, 2016.

# Bibliography

Arcadi, James M. "Impanation, incarnation, and enabling externalism." *Religious Studies* 51, no. 1 (2015): 75–90.

Arcadi, James M. "Prayer in Analytic Theology." In *The T&T Clark Handbook of Christian Prayer*, edited by John C. McDowell and Ashley Cocksworth. London: T&T Clark, 2021.

Arcadi, James M. "Recent developments in analytic Christology." *Philosophy Compass* 13, no. 4 (2018): 1–12.

Arcadi, James M. "Recent philosophical work on the Eucharist." *Philosophy Compass* 11, no. 7 (2016): 402–412.

Arcadi, James M. "Redeeming the Eucharist: Transignification and Justification." In *Being Saved: Explorations in Soteriology and Human Ontology*, edited by Marc Cortez, Joshua R. Farris, and S. Mark Hamilton, 209–227. London: SCM Press, 2018.

Arcadi, James M. "Unlimited Atonement: Anglican Articles and an Analytic Approach." In *Unlimited Atonement: Amyraldism and Reformed Theology*, edited by Scott Harrower and Michael Bird, 123–145. Grand Rapids: Kregel Academic, 2023.

Arcadi, James M. *An Incarnational Model of the Eucharist*. Cambridge University Press, 2018.

Austin, J.L. *How to Do Things with Words*. Cambridge, MA: Harvard University Press, 1962.

Baber, H.E. "Eucharist: Metaphysical Miracle or Institutional Fact?" *International Journal for Philosophy of Religion* 74.3 (2013a), 333–52.

Baber, H.E. "The Real Presence," *Religious Studies* (2013b) 51.1, 21.

Batto, Bernard F. *In the Beginning: Essays on Creation Motifs in the Bible and the Ancient Near East*. Winona Lake, IN: Eisenbrauns, 2013.

Beale, G. K. "Adam as the First Priest in Eden as the Garden Temple." *Southern Baptist Journal of Theology* 22 (2018): 9–24.

Beale, G.K. "Eden, the Temple, and the Church's Mission in New Creation." *Journal of the Evangelical Theological Society* 48 (2005): 5–31.

Beale, G.K. *The Temple and the Church's Mission: A Biblical Theology of the Dwelling Place of God*. New Studies in Biblical Theology 17. Downers Grove, IL: InverVarsity Press, 2004.

Brüntrup, Godehard and Ludwig Jaskolla, eds. *Panpsychism: Contemporary Perspectives*. New York: Oxford University Press, 2017.

Calvin, John. *Institutes of the Christian Religion*. Vol. 2. Translated by Ford Lewis Battles. Edited by John McNeill. Philadelphia: The Westminster Press, 1960.

Campbell, Constantine. *Paul and Union with Christ: An Exegetical and Theological Study*. Grand Rapids, MI: Zondervan Academic, 2012.

Case-Winters, Anne. "Rethinking Divine Presence and Activity in World Process." In *Creation Made Free: Open Theology Engaging Science*, edited by Thomas Jay Oord, 77–89. Eugene, OR: Pickwick Publications, 2009.

Choi, Sungho and Michael Fara. "Dispositions." In *The Stanford Encyclopedia of Philosophy*, edited by Edward N. Zalta, Spring 2021 edition. Accessed June 10, 2021. https://plato.stanford.edu/archives/spr2021/entries/dispositions/.

Cloquet, Robert Louis. *An Exposition of the Thirty-Nine Articles of the Church of England*. London: James Nisbet & Co., 1885.

Coakley, Sarah. "What Does Chalcedon Solve and What Does It Not? Some Reflections on the Status and Meaning of the Chalcedonian 'Definition.'" In *The Incarnation: An Interdisciplinary Symposium on the Incarnation of the Son of God*, edited by Stephen T. Davis, Daniel Kendall, and Gerald O'Collins, 50–66. Oxford: Oxford University Press, 2002.

Cortez, Marc. *Christological Anthropology in Historical Perspective: Ancient and Contemporary Approaches to Theological Anthropology*. Grand Rapids, MI: Zondervan Academic, 2016.

Cortez, Marc. *ReSourcing Theological Anthropology: A Constructive Account of Humanity in the Light of Christ*. Grand Rapids, MI: Zondervan, 2017.

Cortez, Marc. *Theological Anthropology: A Guide for the Perplexed*. London: T&T Clark, 2010.

Craig, William Lane. *God Over All: Divine Aseity and the Challenge of Platonism*. Oxford: Oxford University Press, 2016.

Crisp, Oliver D. *The Word Enfleshed: Exploring the Person and Work of Christ*. Grand Rapids, MI: Baker Academic, 2016.

Crisp, Oliver D., James M. Arcadi, and Jordan Wessling. *Analyzing Prayer: Theological and Philosophical Essays*. Oxford: Oxford University Press, 2022.

Crisp, Oliver D., James M. Arcadi, and Jordan Wessling. *The Nature and Promise of Analytic Theology*. Leiden: Brill, 2019.

Crisp, Oliver. *Deviant Calvinism: Broadening Reformed Theology*. Minneapolis: Fortress Press, 2014.

Crisp, Oliver. *Freedom, Redemption and Communion: Studies in Christian Doctrine*. London: Bloomsbury, 2021.

Davison, Scott. "Prayer." In *The T&T Clark Handbook of Analytic Theology*, edited by James M. Arcadi and James T. Turner, Jr. London: T&T Clark, 2021.

Dummett, Michael. "The Intelligibility of Eucharistic Doctrine" in William Abraham and Stephen Holtzer, (eds.), *The Rationality of Religious Belief: Essays in Honor of Basil Mitchell*. Oxford: Oxford University Press, 1987, 234.

Fletcher-Louis, Crispin H.T. "God's Image, His Cosmic Temple and the High Priest: Towards an Historical and Theological Account of the Incarnation." In *Heaven on Earth: The Temple in Biblical Theology*, edited by T. Desmond Alexander and Simon Gathercole, 81–100. Carlisle, UK: Paternoster, 2004.

Ford, Alan. *James Ussher: Theology, History, and Politics in Early-Modern Ireland and England*. New York: Oxford University Press, 2007.

Forrest, Peter. "The Personal Pantheist Conception of God." In *Alternative Concepts of God: Essays on the Metaphysics of the Divine*, edited by Andrew A. Buckareff and Yujin Nagasawa, 101–116. Oxford: Oxford University Press, 2016.

Gasser, Georg. "God's omnipresence in the world: on possible meanings of 'en' in panentheism." *International Journal for Philosophy of Religion* 85 (2019): 43–62.

Gibson, Edgar C.S. *The Thirty-Nine Articles of the Church of England*. London: Methuen & Co., 1898.

Göcke, Benedikt Paul. "Concepts of God and models of the God-world relation." *Philosophy Compass* 12 (2017): 1–15.

Göeke, Benedikt Paul. "Panentheism and Classical Theism." *Sophia* 52 (2012): 61–75.

Goodman, Lenn E. *Love Thy Neighbor as Thyself*. New York: Oxford University Press, 2008.

Goodman, Lenn E. *The Holy One of Israel*. Oxford: Oxford University Press, 2019.

Green, E. Tyrrell. *The Thirty-Nine Articles and the Age of the Reformation: An Historical and Doctrinal Exposition in the Light of Contemporary Documents*. London: Wells Gardner, Darton, & Co., 1896.

Grenz, Stanley. *The Social God and the Relational Self: A Trinitarian Theology of the Imago Dei*. Louisville, KY: Westminster John Knox Press, 2001.

Grice, Paul. *Studies in the Way of Words*. Cambridge, MA: Harvard University Press, 1989.

Griffith Thomas, W. H. *The Principles of Theology: An Introduction to the Thirty-Nine Articles*. London: Longmans, Green and Co., 1930.

Grummett, David. *Material Eucharist*. Oxford: Oxford University Press, 2016.

Hartley, John. *Leviticus*. Word Biblical Commentary. Dallas: Word Books, 1992.

Hatchett, Marion J. *Commentary on the American Prayer Book*. New York: HarperCollins, 1995.

Hill, Jonathan. "Introduction." In *The Metaphysics of the Incarnation*, edited by Jonathan Hill and Anna Marmodoro, 1–8. Oxford: Oxford University Press, 2011.

Jacob, Haley Goranson. *Conformed to the Image of His Son: Reconsidering Paul's Theology of Glory in Romans*. Downers Grove, IL: IVP Academic, 2018.

Jenson, Philip. "Holiness in the Priestly Writings." In *Holiness: Past & Present*, edited by Stephen C. Barton, 23–38. London: T&T Clark, 2003.

Jenson, Philip. *Graded Holiness: A Key to the Priestly Conception of the World*. JSOT 106. Sheffield: Sheffield Academic Press, 1992.

Kroll, Kimberly. "The Condescension of the Spirit: the nature of the relation of the indwelling Holy Spirit." Doctoral thesis, University of St. Andrews, 2020.

Litton, E.A. *Introduction to Dogmatic Theology on the Basis of the XXXIX Articles of the Church of England*. London: Elliot Stock, 1882.

Loke, Andrew Ter Ern. "*Creatio Ex Nihilo*" In *The T&T Clark Handbook of Analytic Theology*, edited by James M. Arcadi and James T. Turner Jr., 85–99. London: T&T Clark, 2021.

Luzzatto, Moshe Chayim. *The Path of the Just*. Translated by Shraga Silverstein. New York: Feldheim, 1990.

Lycan, William. *Philosophy of Language: a Contemporary Introduction*, 2nd ed. New York: Routledge, 2008.

Lynch, Michael J. *John Davenant's Hypothetical Universalism: A Defense of Catholic and Reformed Orthodoxy*. New York: Oxford University Press, 2021.

Mathews, Kenneth. *New American Commentary: Genesis 1–11*. Nashville, TN: B&H, 1996.

Maximus the Confessor. "Abiguum 41." In *On Difficulties in the Church Fathers: The Ambigua*, vol. II, edited and translated by Nicholas Constas, 113–149. Cambridge, MA: Harvard University Press, 2014.

McDowell, Catherine L. *The Image of God in the Garden of Eden: The Creation of Humankind in Genesis 2:5–3:24 I Light mīs pî pīt pî and wpt-r Rituals of Mesopotamis and Ancient Egypt*. Winona Lake, IN: Eisenbrauns, 2015.

McFarland, Ian A. *The Divine Image: Envisioning the Invisible God*. Minneapolis: Fortress, 2005.

McGinnis, Andrew M. *The Son of God Beyond the Flesh: A Historical and Theological Study of the* extra Calvinisticum. T&T Clark Studies in Systematic Theology vol. 29. London & New York: T&T Clark, 2014.

Middleton, Richard. *The Liberating Image: The Imago Dei in Genesis 1*. Grand Rapids, MI: Brazos Press, 2005.

Mittleman, Alan L. *Does Judaism Condone Violence? Holiness and Ethics in the Jewish Tradition*. Princeton: Princeton University Press, 2018.

Mittleman, Alan L. "The Problem of Holiness." *Journal of Analytic Theology* vol. 3 (2015): 161–174.

Moberly, R.W.L. "Isaiah's Vision of God." In *Holiness: Past and Present*, edited by Stephen C. Barton, 47–63. London: T&T Clark, 2003.

Moore, Jonathan D. *English Hypothetical Universalism: John Preston and the Softening of Reformed Theology*. Grand Rapids, MI: Eerdmans Publishing Co., 2007.

Mullins, R.T. "The Difficulty with Demarcating Panentheism." *Sophia* 55 (2016): 325–346.

Murphy, Mark C. *Divine Holiness and Divine Action*. Oxford Studies in Analytic Theology. Oxford: Oxford University Press, 2021.

Murray, C.D. "An interpretive phenomenological analysis of the embodiment of artificial limbs," *Disability and Rehabilitation* 26.16 (2004), 970.

Neufeld, Dietmar. *Reconceiving Texts As Speech Acts: An Analysis of I John*. Leiden: Brill, 1994.

Niehaus, Jeffrey. *God at Sinai: Covenant and Theophany in the Bible and Ancient Near East*. Grand Rapids, MI: Zondervan, 1995.

Oord, Thomas Jay. "Analogies of love between God and creatures: a response to Kevin Vanhoozer." In *Love, Divine and Human: Contemporary Essays in Systematic and Philosophical Theology*, edited by Oliver D. Crisp, James M. Arcadi, and Jordan Wessling, 96–105. London: T&T Clark, 2019.

Otto, Rudolf. *The Idea of the Holy: An Inquiry into the non-rational factor in the idea of the divine and its relation to the rational*. Translated by John W. Harvey. Oxford: Oxford University Press, 1958.

Pawl, Timothy. *In Defense of Conciliar Christology: A Philosophical Essay*. Oxford: Oxford University Press, 2016.

Peacocke, Arthur. *Paths of Science Toward God: The End of All Our Exploring*. Oxford: One World, 2001.

Plumley, J.M. "The Cosmology of Ancient Egypt." In *Ancient Cosmologies*, edited by Carmen Backer and Michael Lowe, 27–49. London: Allen & Unwin, 1975.

Porter, Steven L., and Brandon Rickabaugh. "The Sanctifying Work of the Holy Spirit: Revisiting Alston's Interpersonal Model." *Journal of Analytic Theology* 6 (2018): 112–130.

Proclus. *The Elements of Theology*. Edited by E.R. Dodds. 2nd ed. Oxford: Clarendon, 1963.

Pseudo-Dionysius. *The Celestial Hierarchy*. Accessed May 11, 2023. http://www.ccel.org/ccel/dionysius/celestial.ii.html.

Radner, Ephraim. *Leviticus*. Brazos Theological Commentary on the Bible. Grand Rapids, MI: Brazos Press, 2008.

Raphael, Melissa. *Rudolf Otto and the Concept of Holiness*. Oxford: Clarendon Press, 1997.

Rooker, Mark. *Leviticus*. New American Commentary. Nashville: Broadman & Holman, 2000.

Rorem, Paul. "'Procession and Return' in Thomas Aquinas and His Predecessors." *The Princeton Seminary Bulletin* (1992): 147–163.

Schillebeeckx, Edward. *The Eucharist*. London: Sheed and Ward, 1968.

Schmemann, Alexander. *For the Life of the World*. Crestwood, NY: St. Vladimir's Seminary Press, 1988.

Searle, John. *Speech Acts: An Essay in the Philosophy of Language*. London: Cambridge University Press, 1969.

Stump, Eleonore. *Atonement*. Oxford Studies in Analytic Theology. Oxford: Oxford University Press, 2018.

Stump, Eleonore. *Wandering in Darkness: Narrative and the Problem of Suffering*. Oxford: Clarendon Press, 2010.

Tanner, Kathryn. *Christ the Key*. Cambridge: Cambridge University Press, 2010.

Tanner, Norman. *Decrees of the Ecumenical Councils*: Vol. 1. London: Sheed and Ward, 1990, 411.

Thomas Aquinas. *Summa Theologia* Ia.44.4 resp. Accessed May 11, 2023. http://www.newadvent.org/summa/1044.htm#article4.

Van de Walle, Bernie A. *Rethinking Holiness*. Grand Rapids: Baker Academic, 2017.

Vanderveken, Daniel. *Meaning and Speech Acts*, vol. 1 Principles of Language Use, vol. 2 Formal Semantics of Success and Satisfaction. Cambridge: Cambridge University Press, 1990–1991.

Vanhoozer, Kevin J. "Love without measure? John Webster's unfinished dogmatic account of the love of God, in dialogue with Thomas Jay Oord's interdisciplinary theological account." In *Love, Divine and Human: Contemporary Essays in Systematic and Philosophical Theology*, edited by Oliver D. Crisp, James M. Arcadi, and Jordan Wessling, 77–95. London: T&T Clark, 2019.

Vidu, Adonis. "The Indwelling of the Holy Spirit as Love." In *Love, Divine and Human: Contemporary Essays in Systematic and Philosophical Theology*, edited by Oliver D. Crisp, James M. Arcadi, and Jordan Wessling, 165–186. London: T&T Clark, 2020.

Walton, John H. *Ancient Near Eastern Thought and the Old Testament: Introducing the Conceptual World of the Hebrew Bible*. Grand Rapids, MI: Baker Academic, 2006.

Ward, Rowan. *Words in Action: Speech Act Theory and Biblical Interpretation: Toward a Hermeneutic of Self-Involvement*. Edinburgh: T & T Clark, 2001.

Webster, John. *Holiness*. Grand Rapids: William B. Eerdmans Publishing Co., 2003.

Wessling, Jordan. *Love Divine: A Systematic Account of God's Love for Humanity*. Oxford Studies in Analytic Theology. Oxford: Oxford University Press, 2020.

Williams, Charles. *Descent into Hell: A Novel*. Grand Rapids: William B. Eerdmans Company, 2002.

Wolterstorff, Nicholas. *Acting Liturgically: Philosophical Reflections on Religious Practice*. Oxford University Press, 2018.

Wolterstorff, Nicholas. *Divine Discourse: Philosophical Reflections on the Claim That God Speaks*. Cambridge: Cambridge University Press, 1995.

Wolterstorff, Nicholas. *The God We Worship: An Exploration of Liturgical Theology*. Grand Rapids, MI: William B. Eerdmans Publishing Company, 2015.

Woznicki, Christopher. "Dancing Around the Theological Black Box: The Problem and Metaphysics of Perichoresis." *Philosophia Christi* 22, no. 1 (2020): 103–121.

Woznicki, Christopher. "Peter Martyr Vermigli's Account of Petitionary Prayer: A Reformation Alternative to Contemporary Two-Way Contingency Accounts." *Philosophia Christi* 20, no. 1 (2018): 119–137.

Woznicki, Christopher. "What Are We Doing When We Pray? Rekindling a Reformation Theology of Petitionary Prayer." *Calvin Theological Journal* 53, no. 2 (2018): 319–343.

Woznicki, Christopher. *T. F. Torrance's Christological Anthropology: Discerning Humanity in Christ*. London: Routledge, 2022.

Wright, Elizabeth. "My Prosthetic and I: Identity Representation in Bodily Extension," *Forum: University of Edinburgh Journal of Culture and the Arts* 8 (2009).

# Index

Adams, Marilyn McCord, 50, 150
Alston, William, 91–95, 104–5, 138–41, 149–50, 152
Analytic Theology, 40, 56
Anglicanism, 21, 86, 121–36, 151–53
Anselm, 19–20
Aquinas, 27, 74–75
Arminianism, 126, 134
attributes of God: aseity, 8, 10–11, 26, 81; love, 8, 69, 125; omnipresence, 18, 22–23, 27, 31
Austin, J.L., 91, 166

Baber, Harriett, 112–13
baptism: of infants, 133–34
Batto, Bernard, 76
Briggs, Richard, 91

Calvin, John, 133–34
Christology: abstractist/*additionalist*, 41; Chalcedon, 40, 123, 127; concretist/relational, 41; transformationalist, 40, 41
Classical Theism, 18, 27–29, 33
Cloquet, R.L., 125
creation: *ex nihilo*, 7–8, 14, 26, 76
Crisp, Oliver, 131–34

Dummett, Michael, 111–12

Eastern Orthodoxy, 21, 151, 156
Eucharist (Holy Communion): consubstantiation, 37–38; Corporeal, 38; impanation, 38–39, 46–48; transignification, 109–13; transubstantiation, 37–38, 109–10; Type-H (Hypostatic) Impanation, 46; Type-S (Sacramental) Impanation, 46–47
Evans, Donald, 91

Forrest, Peter, 19–20

Gasser, Georg, 27
Gibson, Edgar, 124–25
Göcke, Benedikt Paul, 26
Goodman, Lenn E., 4, 15
Green, E.T., 123–24
Grice, Paul, 91

Hill, Jonathan, 40
Hus, Jan, 109

illocutionary acts (IA), 91–92; Assertive, 158; Commissive, 99–102, 161–62; Directive, 94–98; Expressive, 154–55
image of God, 72, 76–78

Jenson, Philip, 10, 12

Kroll, Kimberly, 141–42, 147

Litton, E.A., 125–26
Lombard, Peter, 126
Luzzatto, Moshe Hayim, 103
Lycan, William, 91

McDowell, Catherine, 76–77
Mittleman, Alan, 4, 12–13, 65–66, 103
Moberly, Walter, 5
Mullins, R.T., 27
Murphy, Mark C., 9, 18, 57–60, 63, 67

Neufeld, Dietmar, 91

Oord, Thomas, 8
Otto, Rudolf, 57–60

phenomenology, 18, 25, 110
Proclus, 73
Pseudo-Dionysius, 74

Radner, Ephraim, 102
Rooker, Mark, 93

Schillebeeckx, Edward, 108–11
Schmemann, Alexander, 71–72, 78–80, 82, 152, 157–60
Searle, John, 91
Stump, Eleonore, 62–63

Thiselton, Anthony, 91
Thomas, W.H. Griffith, 123, 127
Trisagion, 21–22

Vanderveken, Daniel, 91
Van de Walle, Bernie A., 4, 6, 9, 11–12

Webster, John, 4
Williams, Charles, 58
Wolterstorff, Nicholas, 20–21, 25, 91, 154, 156–57
Wycliffe, John, 109

# About the Author

The Revd Dr. **James M. Arcadi** (PhD, University of Bristol) is the rector of All Souls Anglican Church in Wheaton, IL. He is the author of *An Incarnational Model of the Eucharist* (Cambridge, 2018), co-author of *The Nature and Promise of Analytic Theology* (Brill, 2019), and co-editor of *Analyzing Prayer* (Oxford, 2022), *The T&T Clark Handbook of Analytic Theology* (T&T Clark, 2021), and *Love: Divine and Human* (T&T Clark, 2019). He has taught theology at Gordon College, Fuller Theological Seminary, Trinity Evangelical Divinity School, and currently at Wheaton College Graduate School.